池本幹雄

At the grade school I attended in Uji, Kyoto, there was a faucet that produced tea when turned on.

It had a distinctive aroma, and was delicious.

I recently found out that it was a type of tea called "Kyobancha."

You have to be careful because the tea comes out super-hot.

It's hot enough to sterilize aluminum cups, so you need to mix in some cold water to drink it. Hmm? No, I'm not lying. It's true!

–Mikio Ikemoto, 2018

小太刀右京

Recently, I have had the good fortune to visit the Republic of Kazakhstan. It is a grassland nation in Central Asia.

The wondrous sensation of "The sky is so expansive! And so blue! It goes on forever before getting sucked into the horizon at all points of the compass!" was quite lovely.

Well, I hope that in similar fashion, Boruto and his friends' adventures will continue to be loved all over the world. Period.

–Ukyo Kodachi, 2018

BORUTO
-NARUTO NEXT GENERATIONS-

VOLUME 6

SHONEN JUMP MANGA EDITION

Creator/Supervisor MASASHI KISHIMOTO
Art by MIKIO IKEMOTO
Script by UKYO KODACHI

Translation: Mari Morimoto
Touch-up Art & Lettering: Snir Aharon
Design: Alice Lewis
Editor: Alexis Kirsch

Printed in the U.S.A.

Published by VIZ Media, LLC
P.O. Box 77010
San Francisco, CA 94107

10 9 8 7 6 5 4 3 2 1
First printing, June 2019

VIZ MEDIA
viz.com

SHONEN JUMP
shonenjump.com

ratings.viz.com
RATED T TEEN

PARENTAL ADVISORY
BORUTO is rated T for Teen and is recommended for ages 13 and up. This volume contains fantasy violence.

BORUTO
‑NARUTO NEXT GENERATIONS‑

VOLUME 6

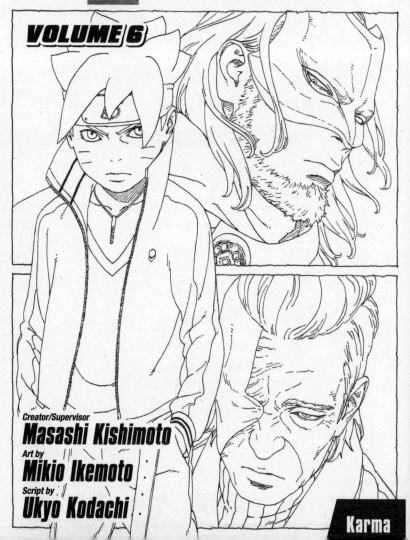

Creator/Supervisor
Masashi Kishimoto

Art by
Mikio Ikemoto

Script by
Ukyo Kodachi

Karma

BORUTO -NARUTO NEXT GENERATIONS- CHARACTERS

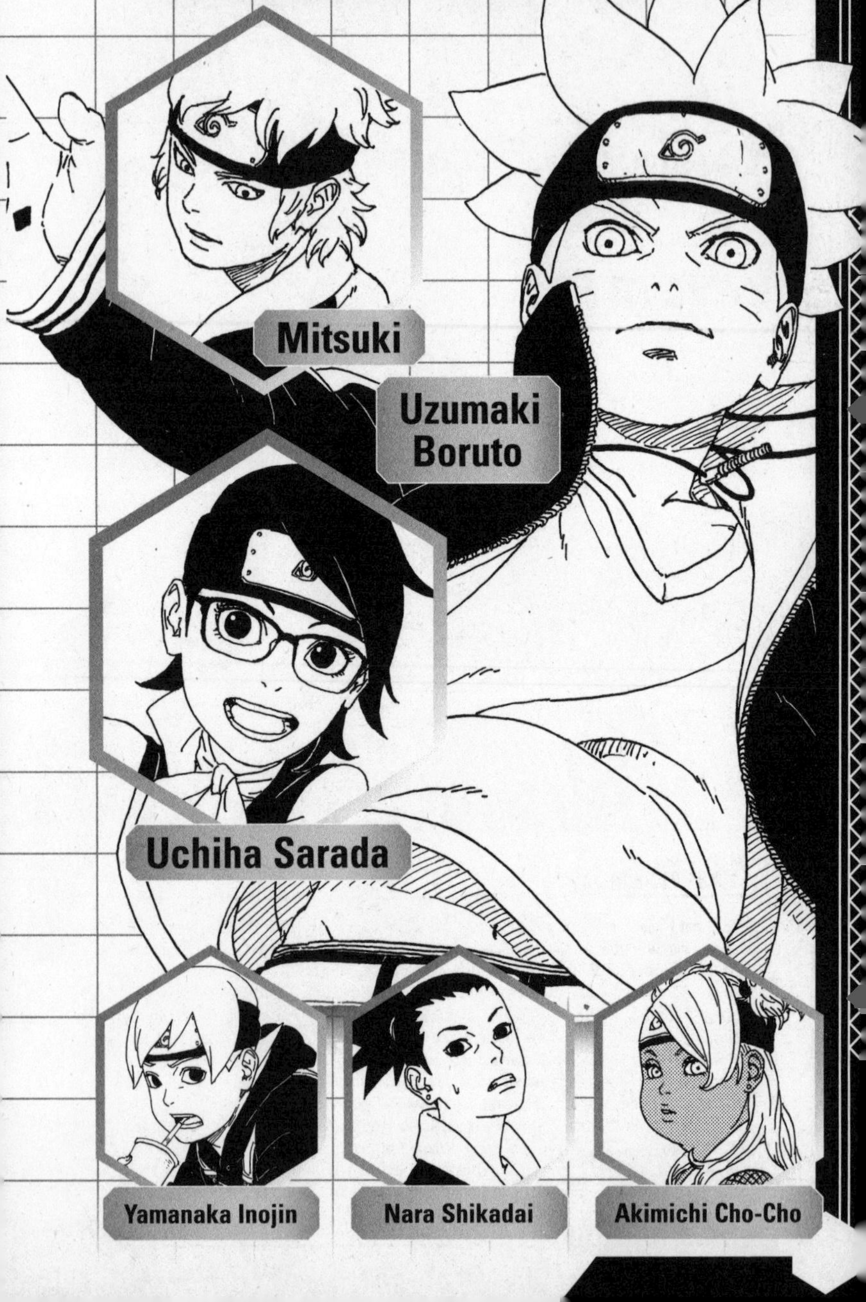
Mitsuki
Uzumaki Boruto
Uchiha Sarada
Yamanaka Inojin
Nara Shikadai
Akimichi Cho-Cho

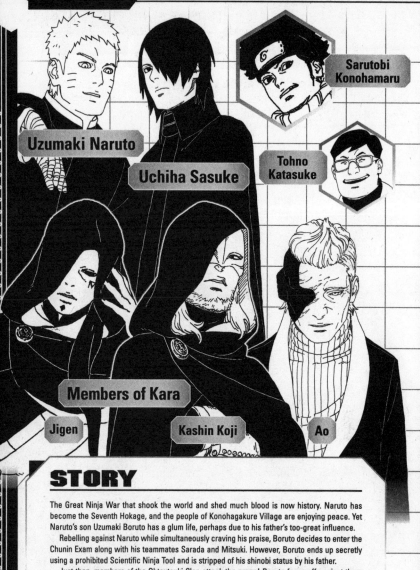

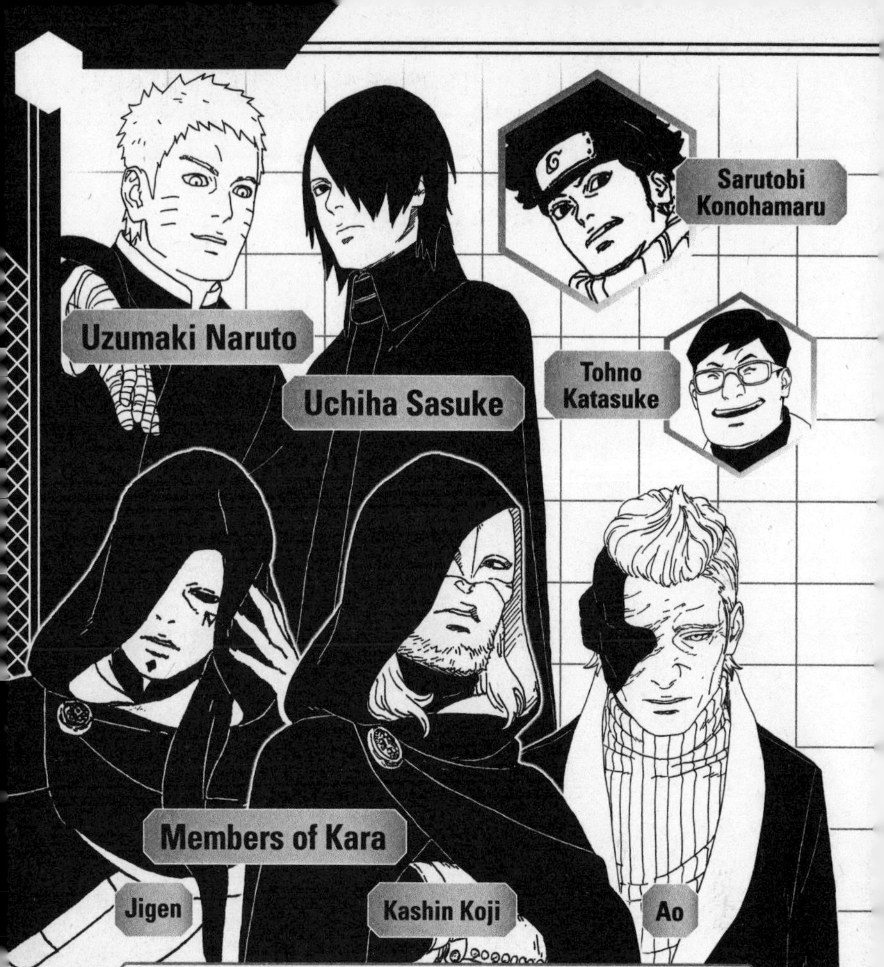
Sarutobi Konohamaru
Uzumaki Naruto
Tohno Katasuke
Uchiha Sasuke
Members of Kara
Jigen
Kashin Koji
Ao

STORY

The Great Ninja War that shook the world and shed much blood is now history. Naruto has become the Seventh Hokage, and the people of Konohagakure Village are enjoying peace. Yet Naruto's son Uzumaki Boruto has a glum life, perhaps due to his father's too-great influence.

Rebelling against Naruto while simultaneously craving his praise, Boruto decides to enter the Chunin Exam along with his teammates Sarada and Mitsuki. However, Boruto ends up secretly using a prohibited Scientific Ninja Tool and is stripped of his shinobi status by his father.

Just then, members of the Ohtsutsuki Clan attack the arena! Boruto faces off against them alongside Naruto, Sasuke, and others, and they achieve victory with a Rasengan that father and son weave together. However, a strange mark appears on Boruto's right palm…

Later, with a new resolve to become a ninja, Boruto is tasked with searching for Konohamaru, who had gone missing during a mission. When they arrive at the airship crash site that Konohamaru had been investigating, Boruto and his team are attacked by Scientific Ninja Tool-powered puppets. Saved by Katasuke's quick wits, Boruto manages to rendezvous with Konohamaru, but then the former Mist Ninja Ao shows up and aims a gun at them…

BORUTO

-NARUTO NEXT GENERATIONS-

VOLUME 6
KARMA

CONTENTS

▌▌▌▌ Number 20: Scientific Ninja Tools

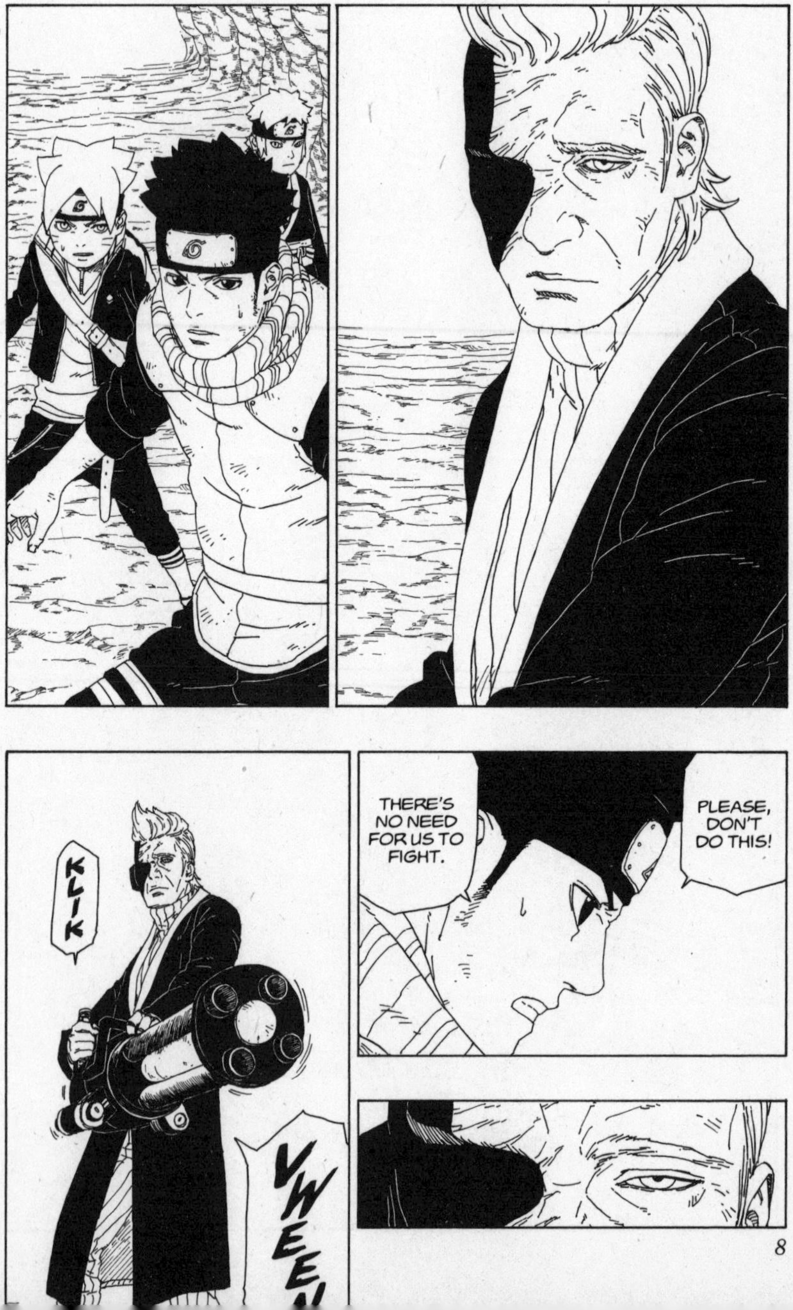
PLEASE, DON'T DO THIS!
THERE'S NO NEED FOR US TO FIGHT.
KLIK
VWEEN

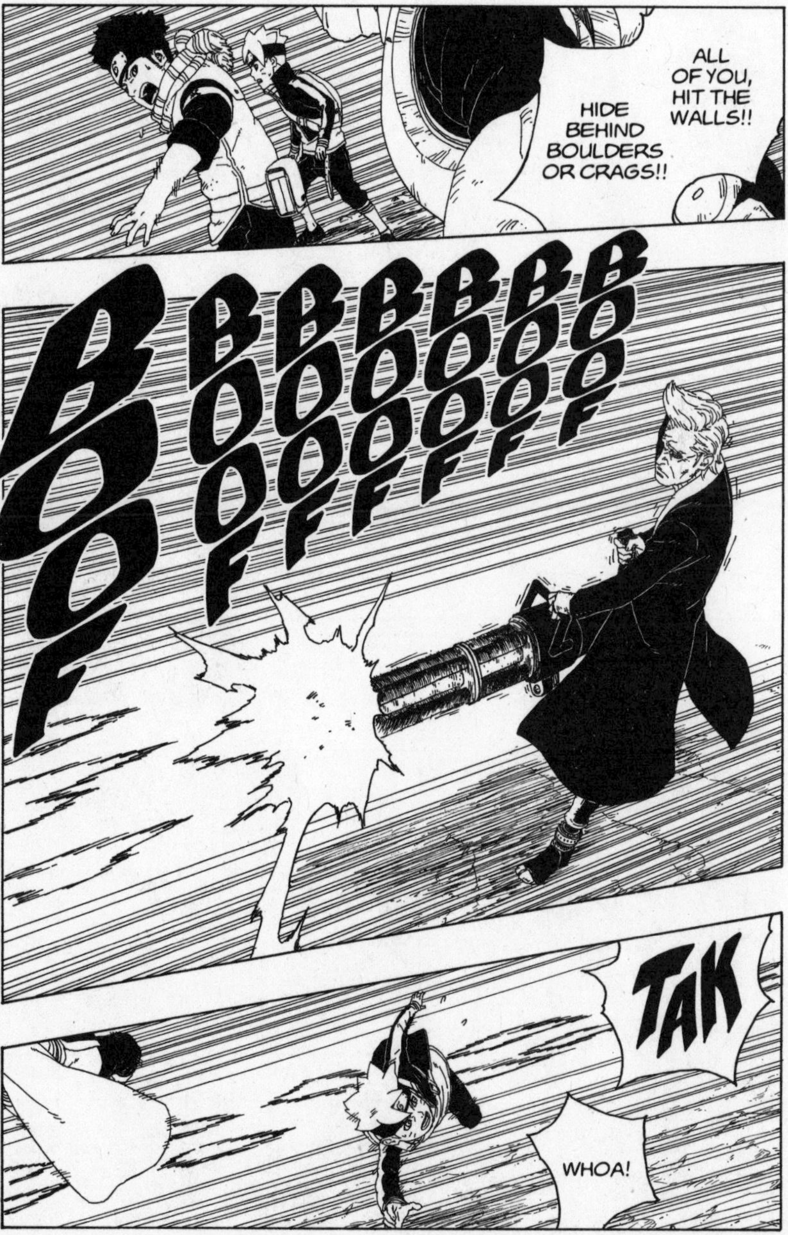
ALL OF YOU, HIT THE WALLS!!
HIDE BEHIND BOULDERS OR CRAGS!!
BOOF BOOF BOOF BOOF BOOF BOOF BOOF BOOF
TAK
WHOA!

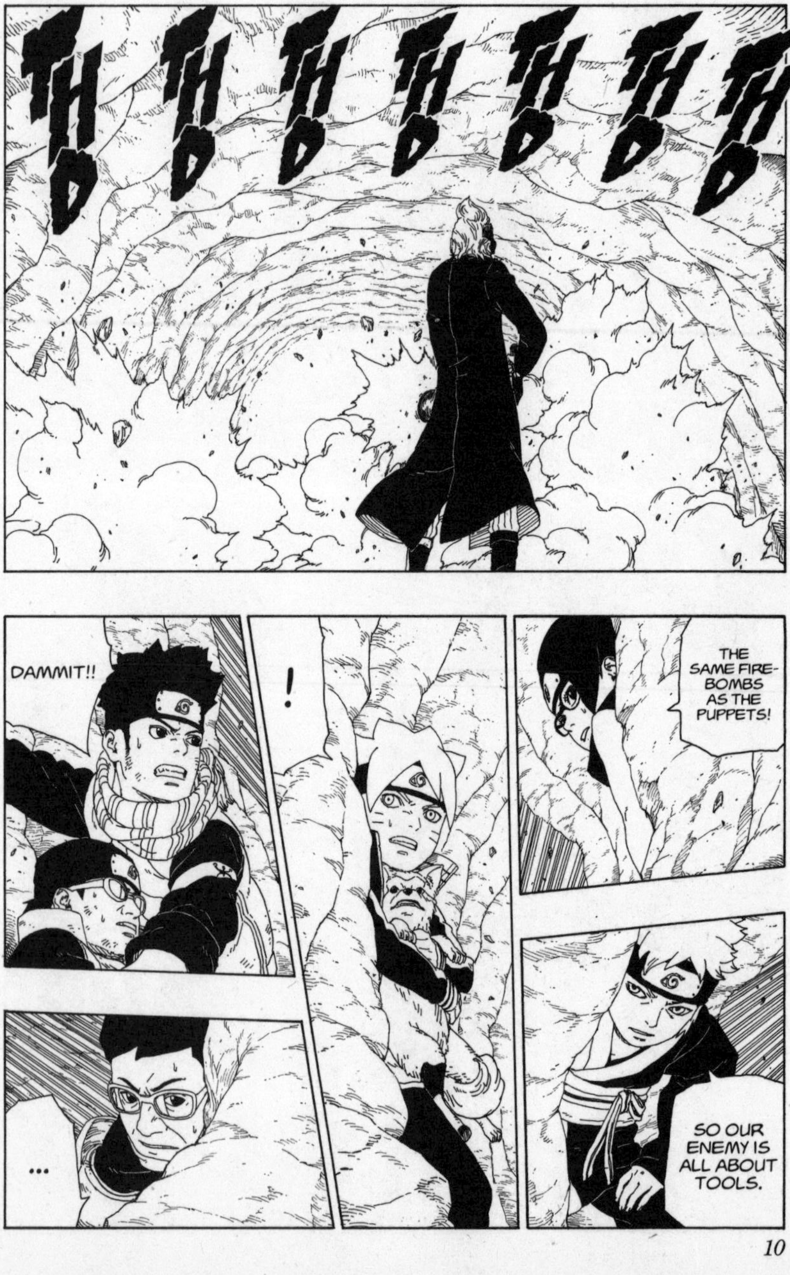
THD THD THD THD THD THD THD
THE SAME FIRE-BOMBS AS THE PUPPETS!
SO OUR ENEMY IS ALL ABOUT TOOLS.
!
DAMMIT!!
...

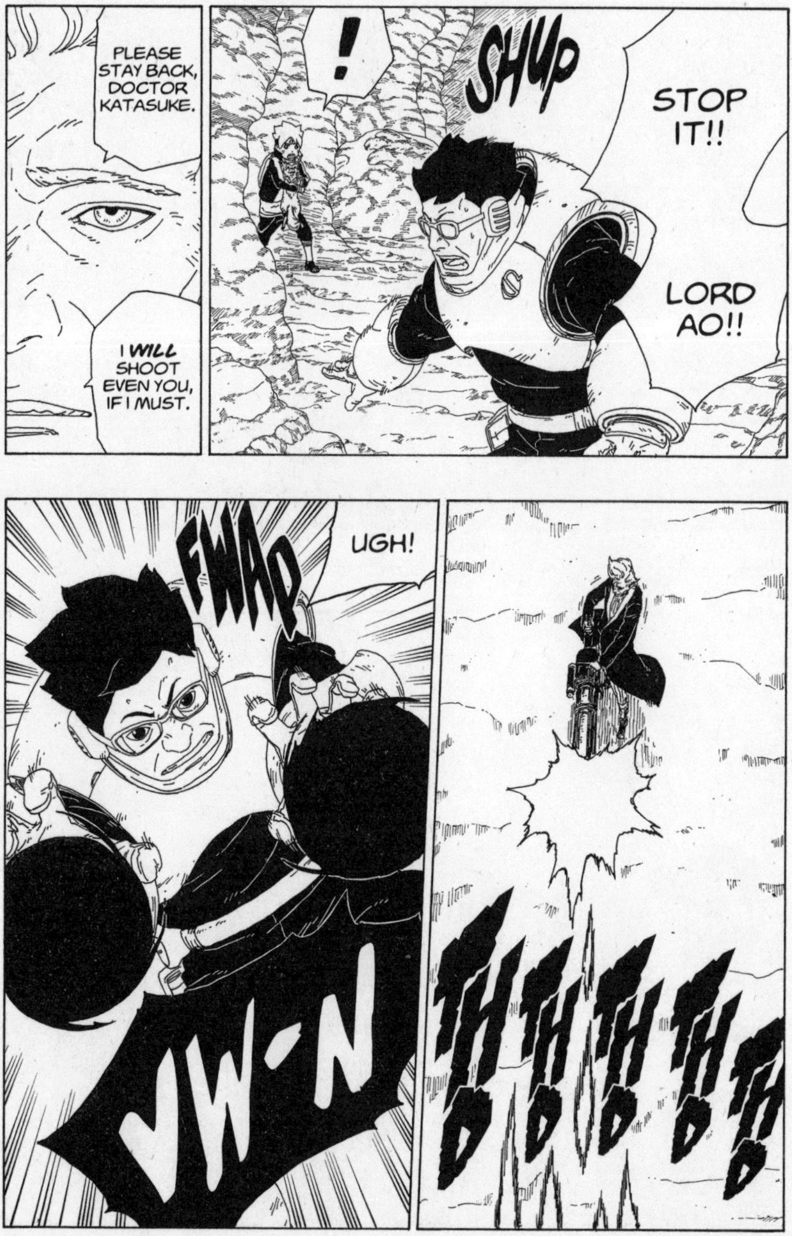
STOP IT!!
LORD AO!!
SHUP
!
PLEASE STAY BACK, DOCTOR KATASUKE.
I WILL SHOOT EVEN YOU, IF I MUST.
UGH!
FWAP
VW-N

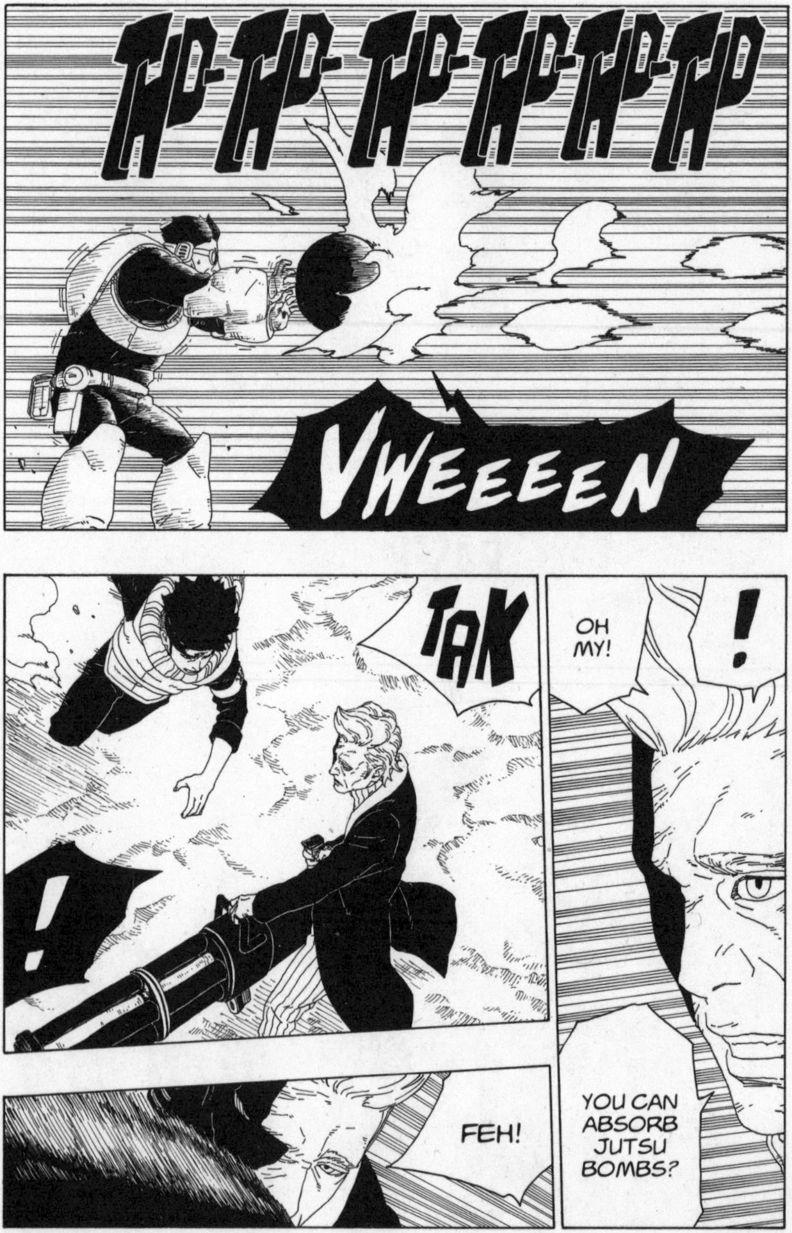
TAP-TAP-TAP-TAP-TAP-TAP-TAP
VWEEEEN
!
OH MY!
YOU CAN ABSORB JUTSU BOMBS?
TAK
!
FEH!

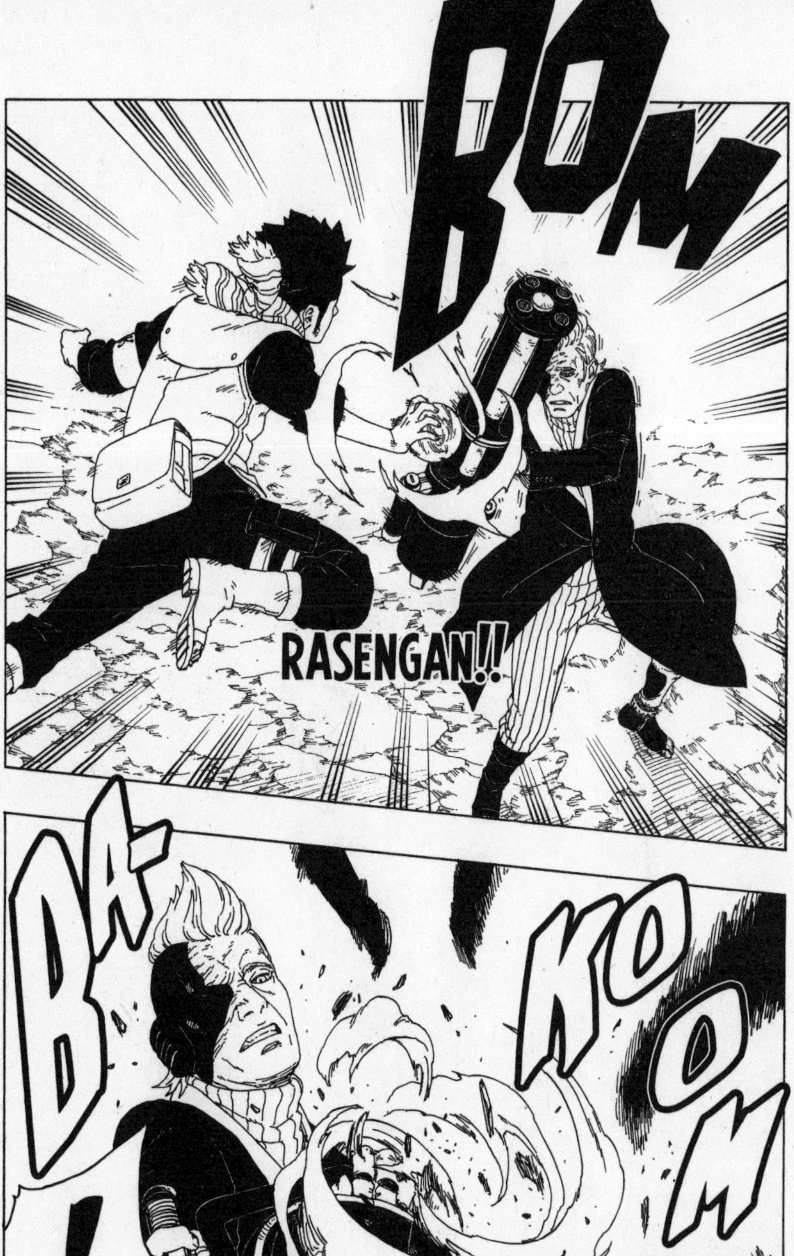
BOOM
RASENGAN!!
KOOM
BA-
!

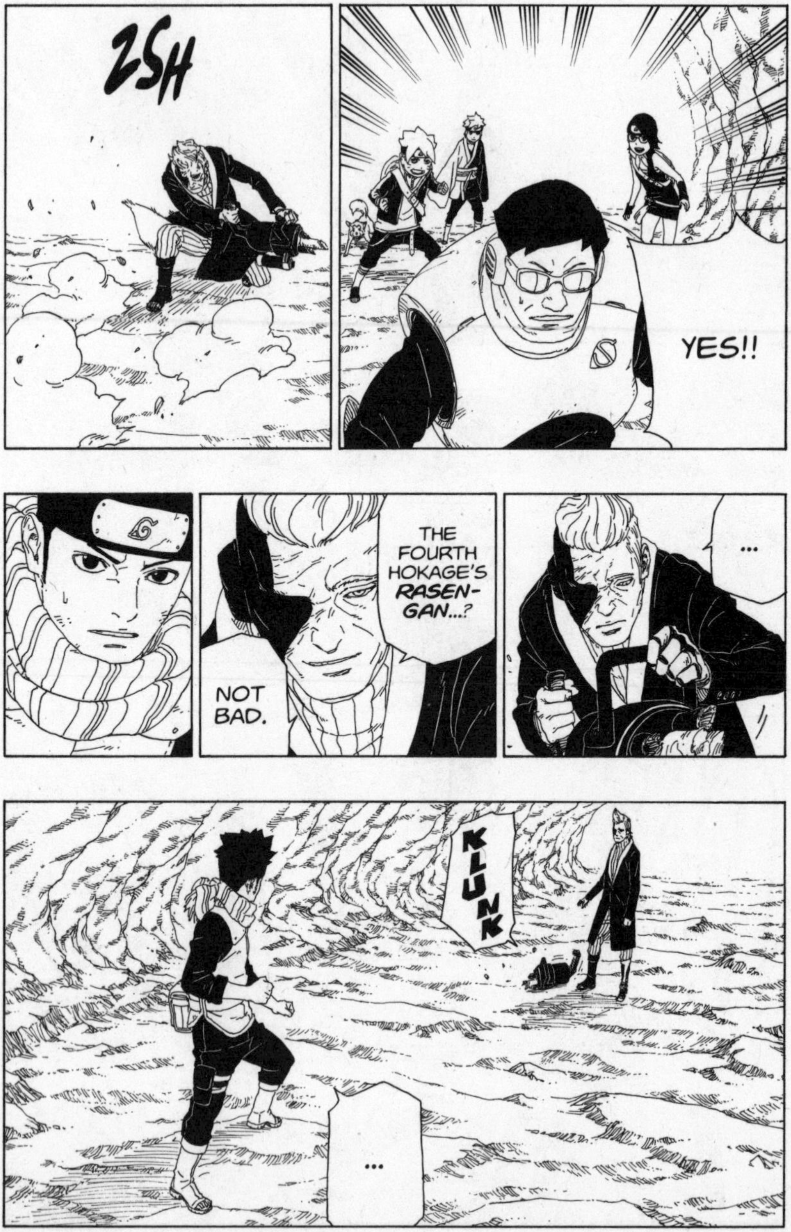
YES!!
ZSH
...
THE FOURTH HOKAGE'S RASEN-GAN...?
NOT BAD.
KLUNK
...

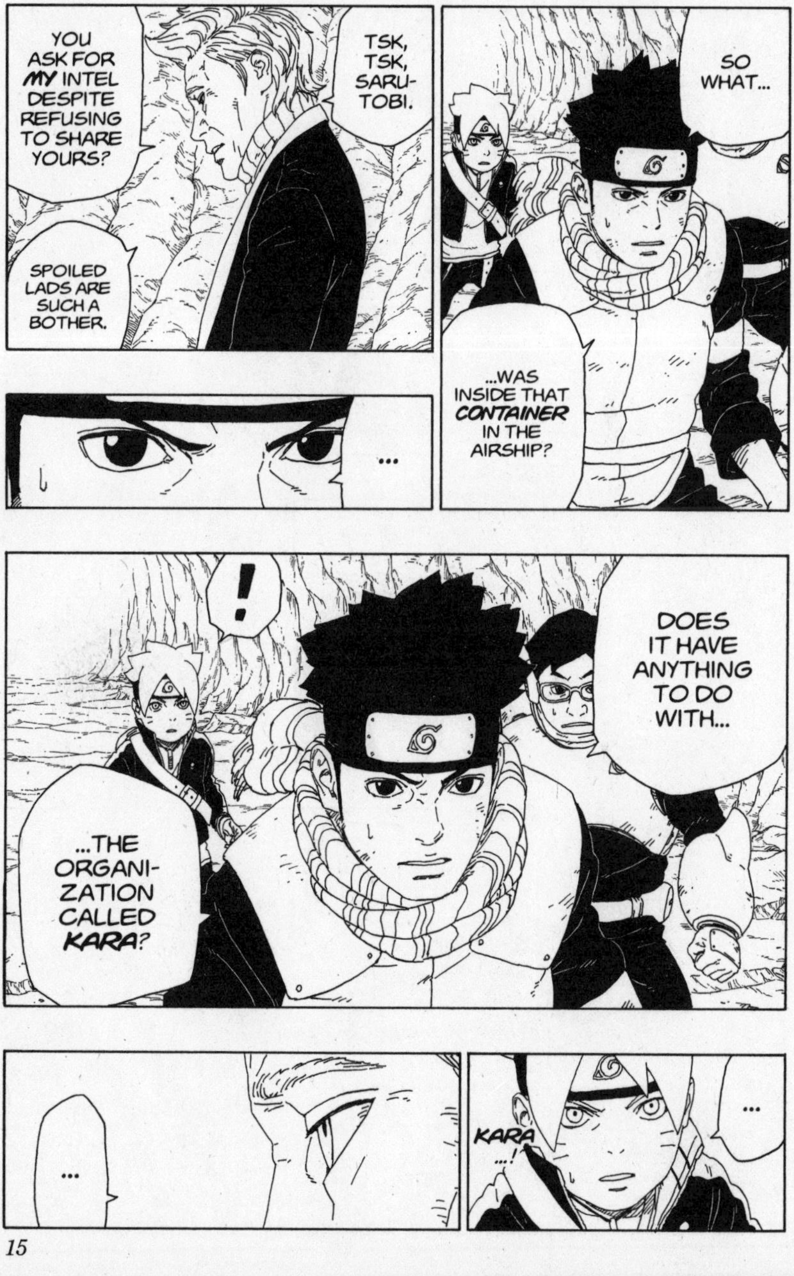
SO WHAT...
...WAS INSIDE THAT CONTAINER IN THE AIRSHIP?
TSK, TSK, SARU-TOBI.
YOU ASK FOR MY INTEL DESPITE REFUSING TO SHARE YOURS?
SPOILED LADS ARE SUCH A BOTHER.
...
DOES IT HAVE ANYTHING TO DO WITH...
!
...THE ORGANI-ZATION CALLED KARA?
...
KARA ...!
...

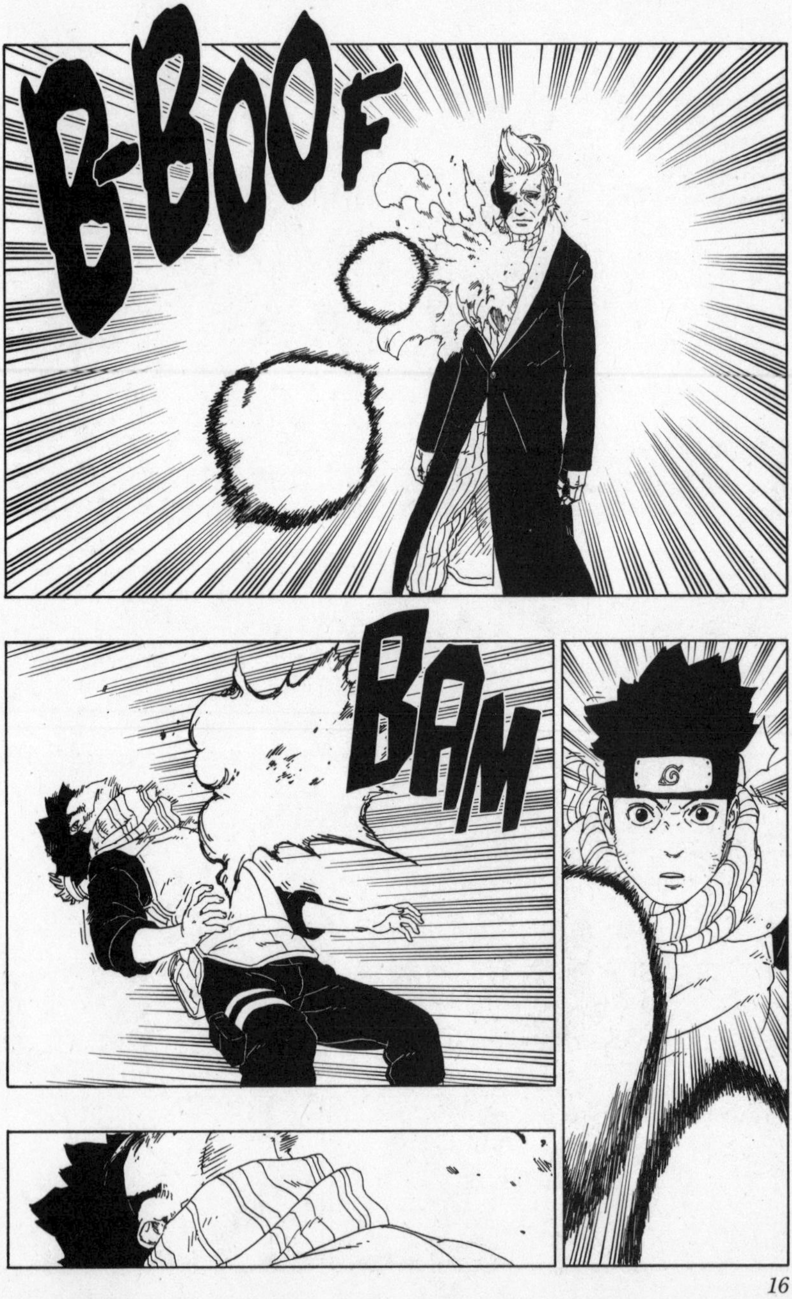
B-BOOF
BAM

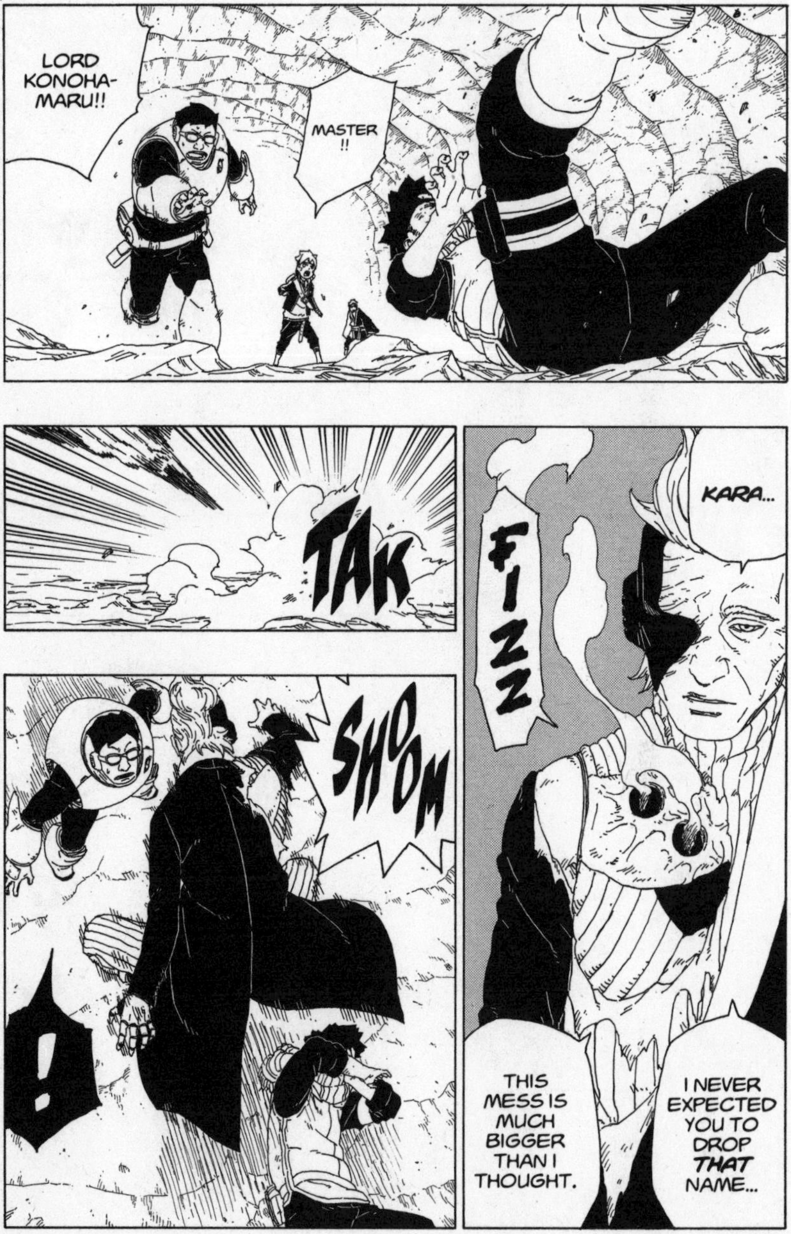
MASTER !!
LORD KONOHA-MARU!!
KARA...
FIZZ
I NEVER EXPECTED YOU TO DROP *THAT* NAME...
THIS MESS IS MUCH BIGGER THAN I THOUGHT.
TAK
SHOOM
!

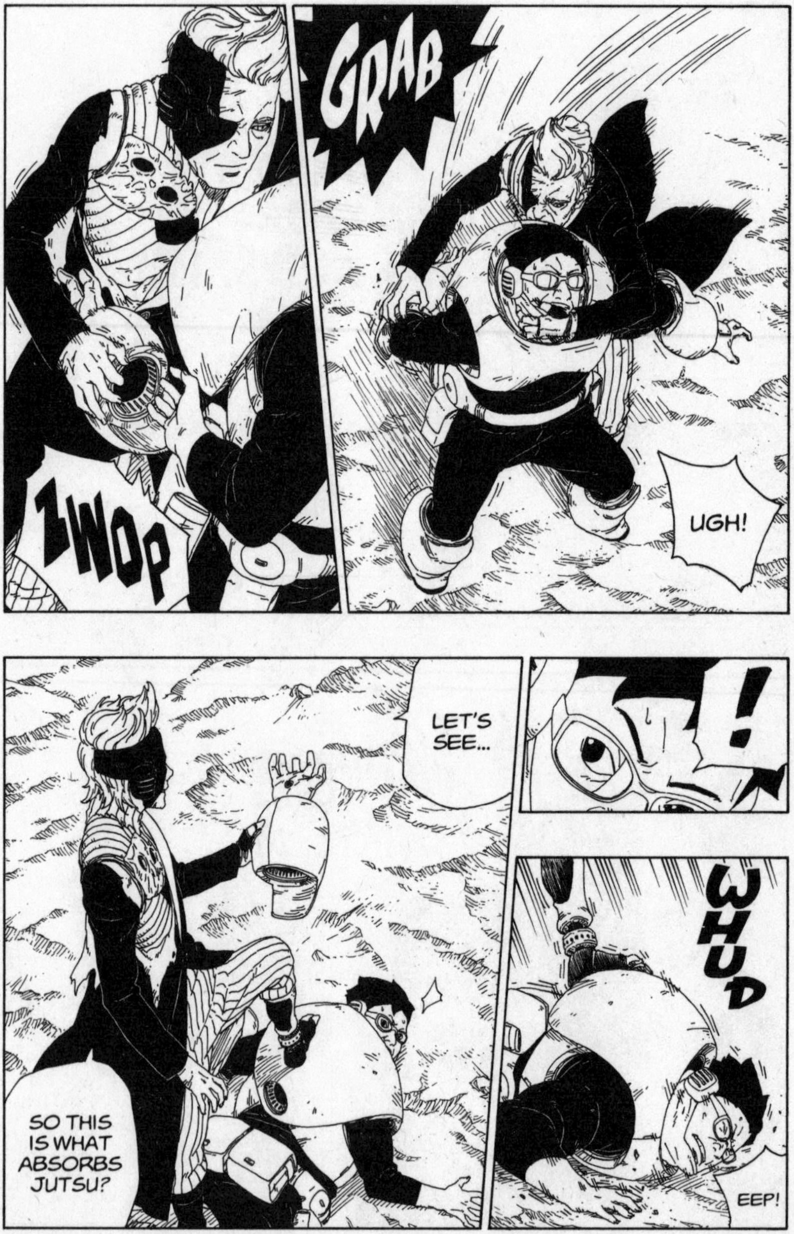
GRAB
UGH!
ZWOP
!
WHUD
EEP!
LET'S SEE...
SO THIS IS WHAT ABSORBS JUTSU?

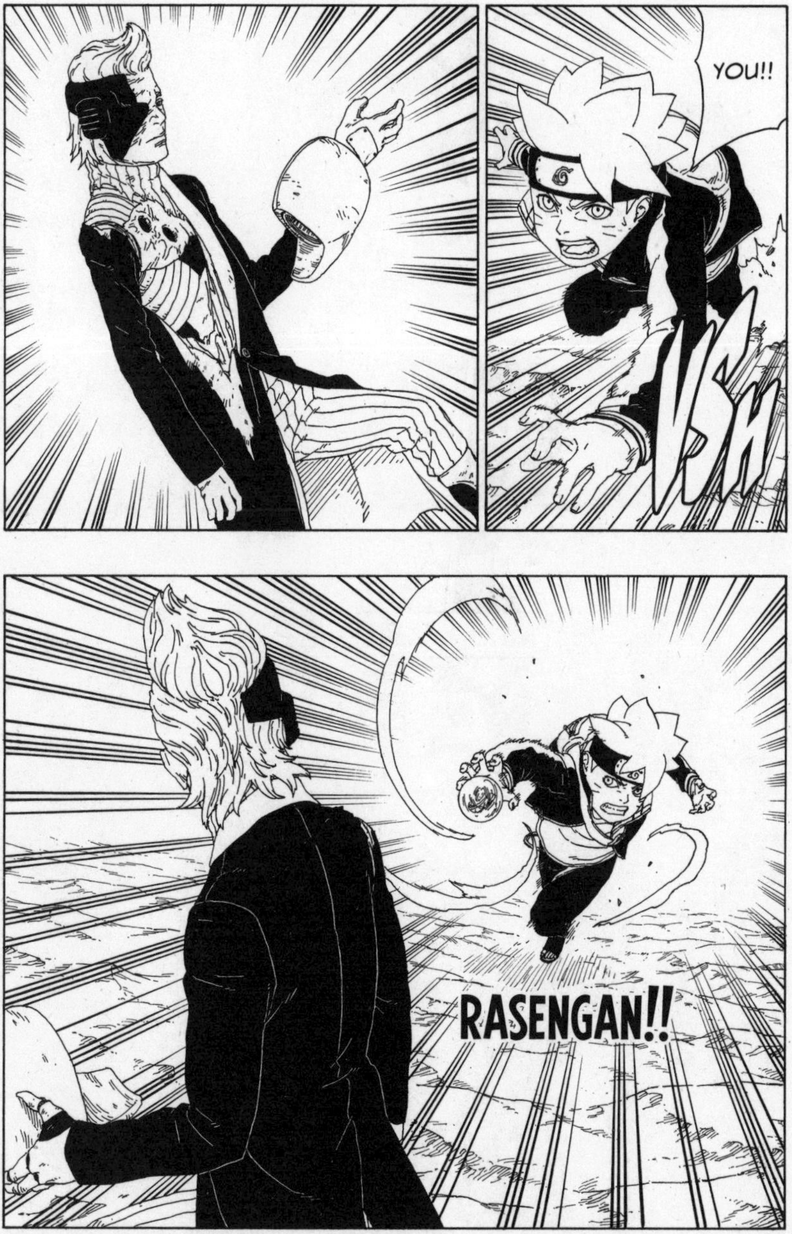
YOU!!
VSH
RASENGAN!!

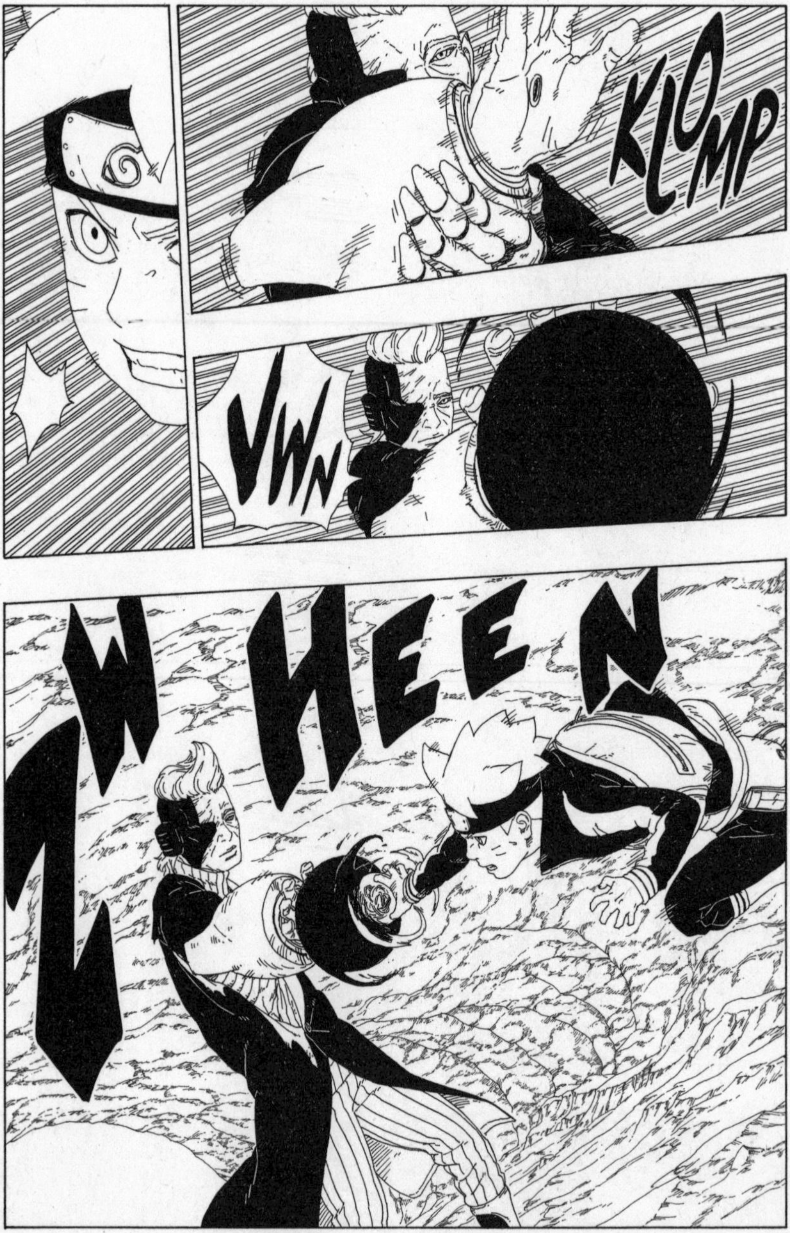
KLOMP
VWN
ZWHEEN

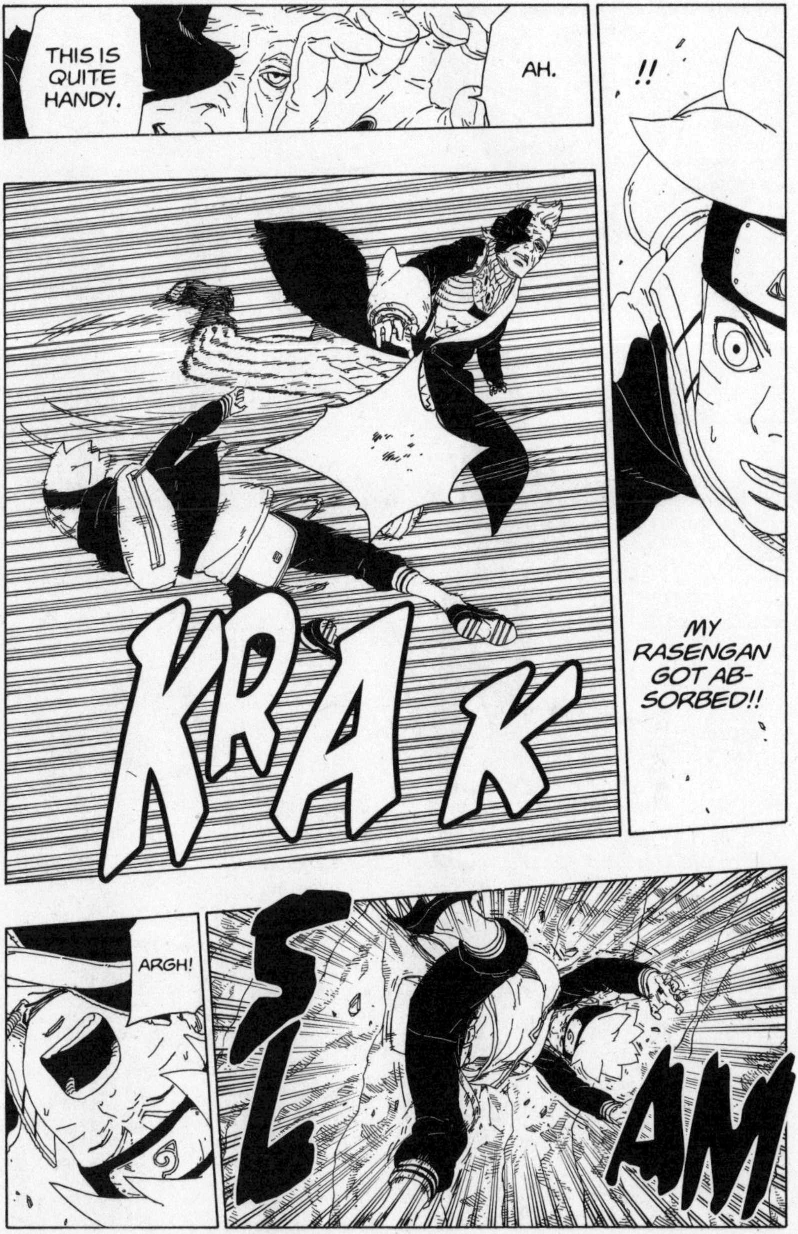
!!
MY RASENGAN GOT ABSORBED!!
AH.
THIS IS QUITE HANDY.
KRAK
SLAM
ARGH!

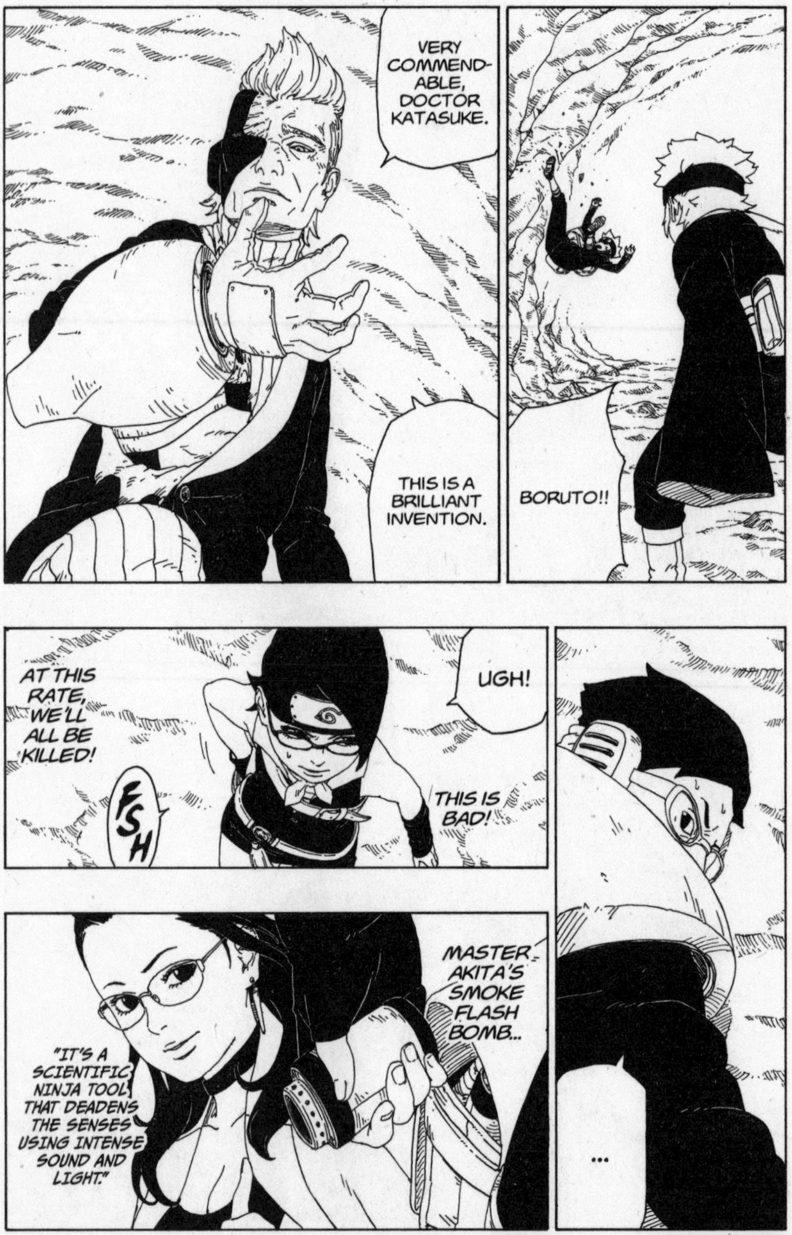
BORUTO!!
VERY COMMENDABLE, DOCTOR KATASUKE.
THIS IS A BRILLIANT INVENTION.
...
UGH!
THIS IS BAD!
AT THIS RATE, WE'LL ALL BE KILLED!
FSH
MASTER AKITA'S SMOKE FLASH BOMB...
"IT'S A SCIENTIFIC NINJA TOOL THAT DEADENS THE SENSES USING INTENSE SOUND AND LIGHT."

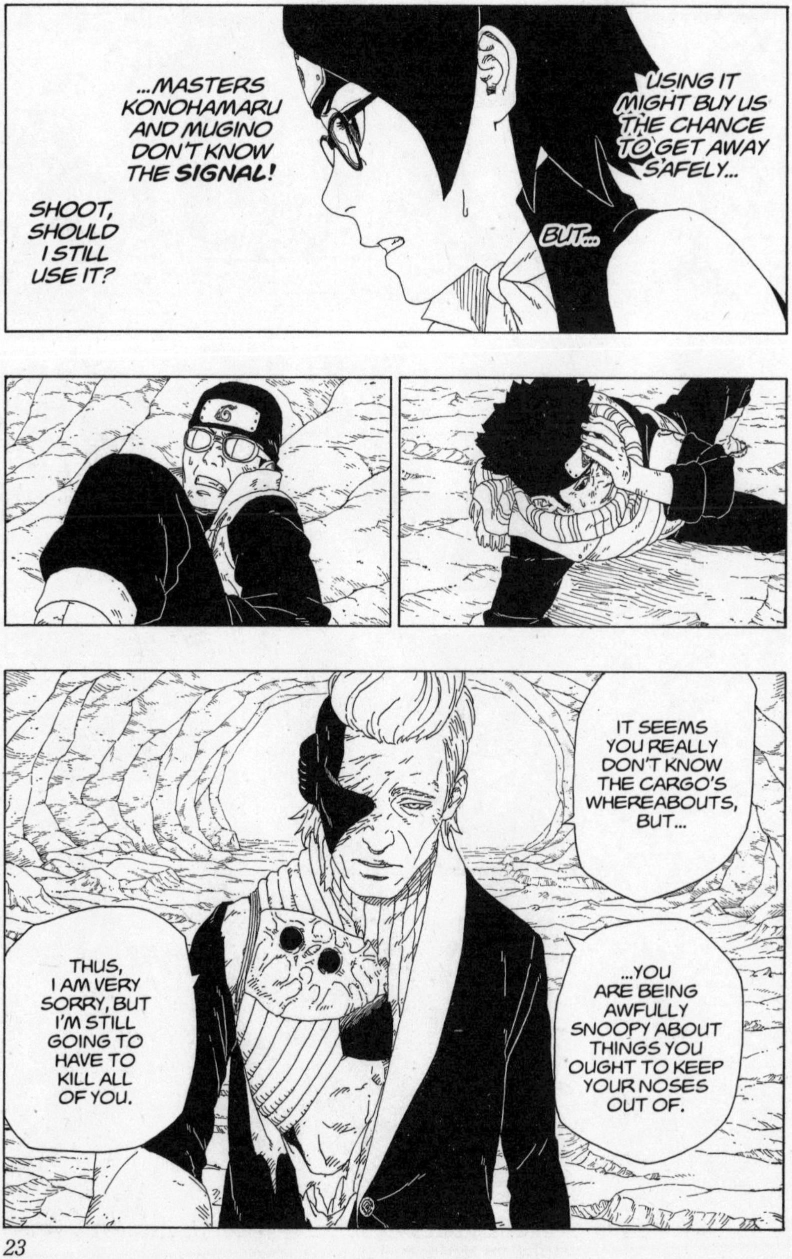
USING IT MIGHT BUY US THE CHANCE TO GET AWAY SAFELY...
BUT...
...MASTERS KONOHAMARU AND MUGINO DON'T KNOW THE **SIGNAL**!
SHOOT, SHOULD I STILL USE IT?
IT SEEMS YOU REALLY DON'T KNOW THE CARGO'S WHEREABOUTS, BUT...
...YOU ARE BEING AWFULLY SNOOPY ABOUT THINGS YOU OUGHT TO KEEP YOUR NOSES OUT OF.
THUS, I AM VERY SORRY, BUT I'M STILL GOING TO HAVE TO KILL ALL OF YOU.

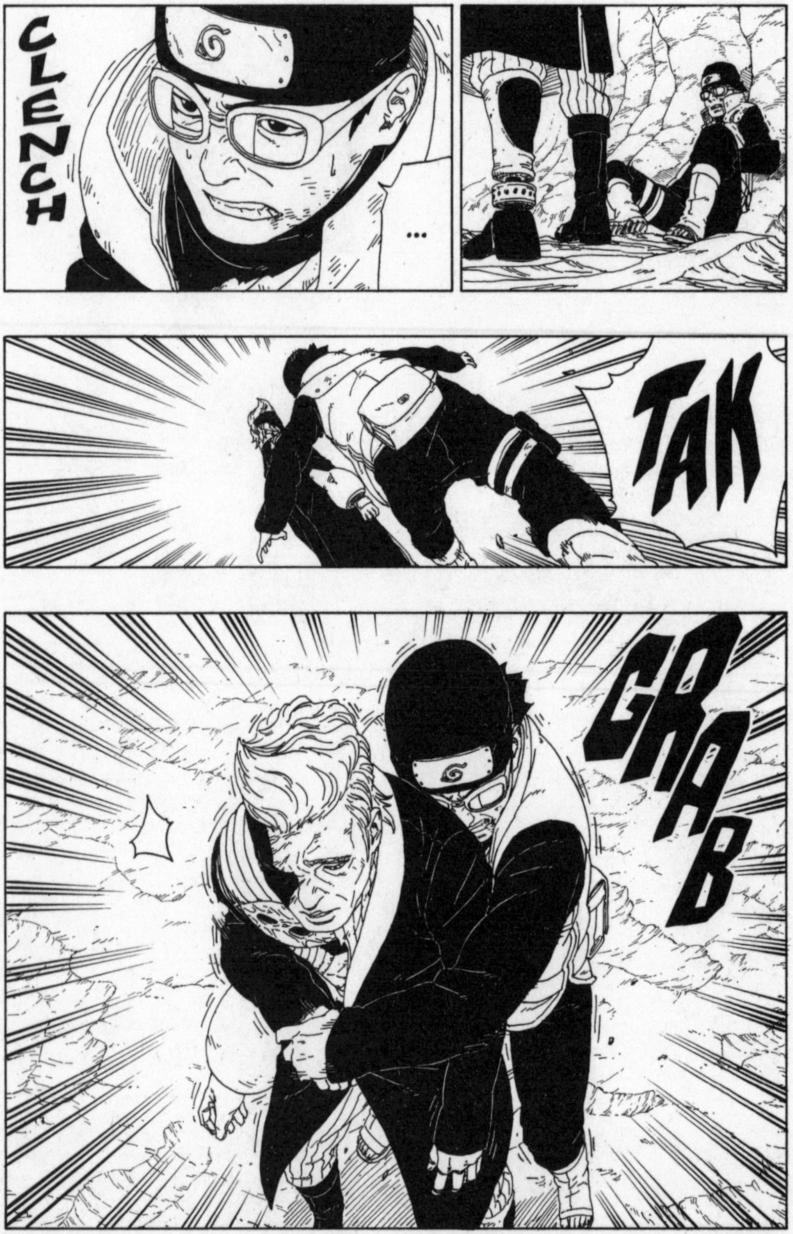
CLENCH
...
TAK
GRAB

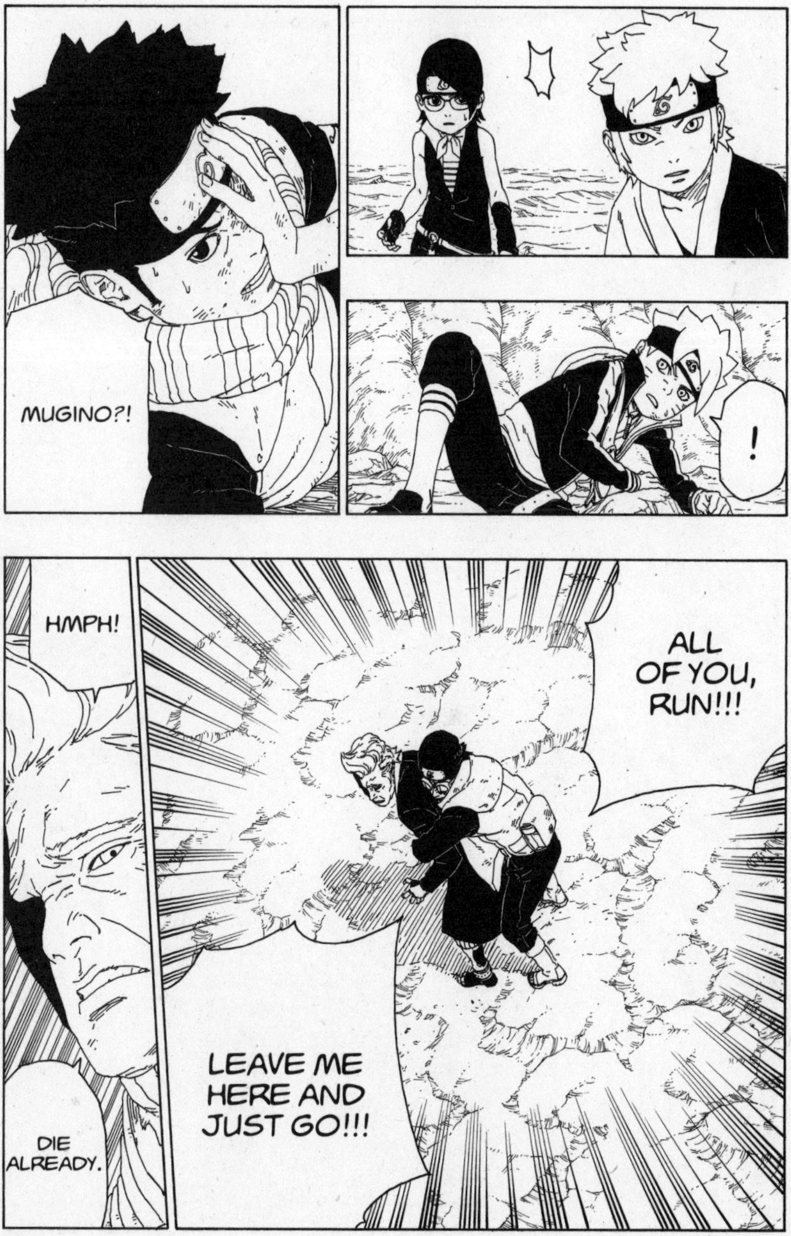
!
MUGINO?!
ALL OF YOU, RUN!!!
LEAVE ME HERE AND JUST GO!!!
HMPH!
DIE ALREADY.

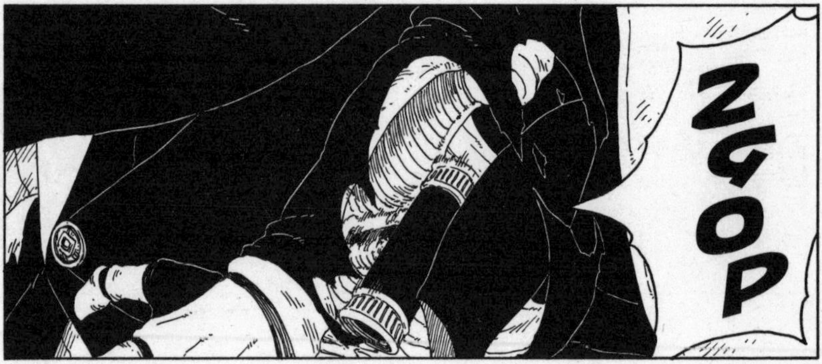
ZGOP

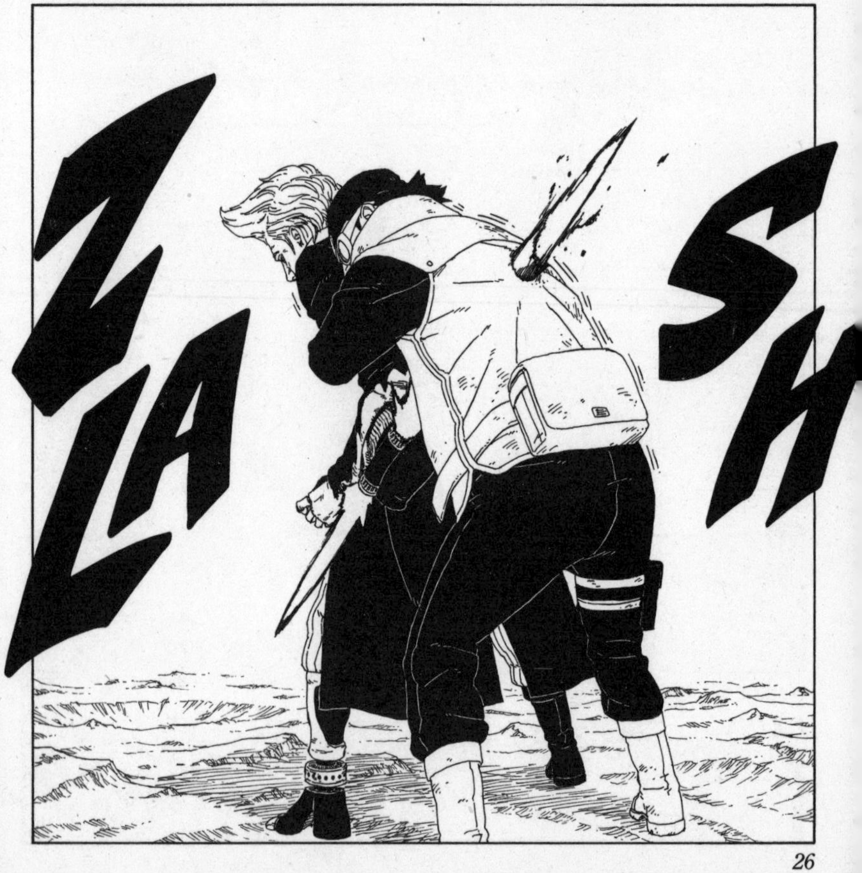
ZZA
SH

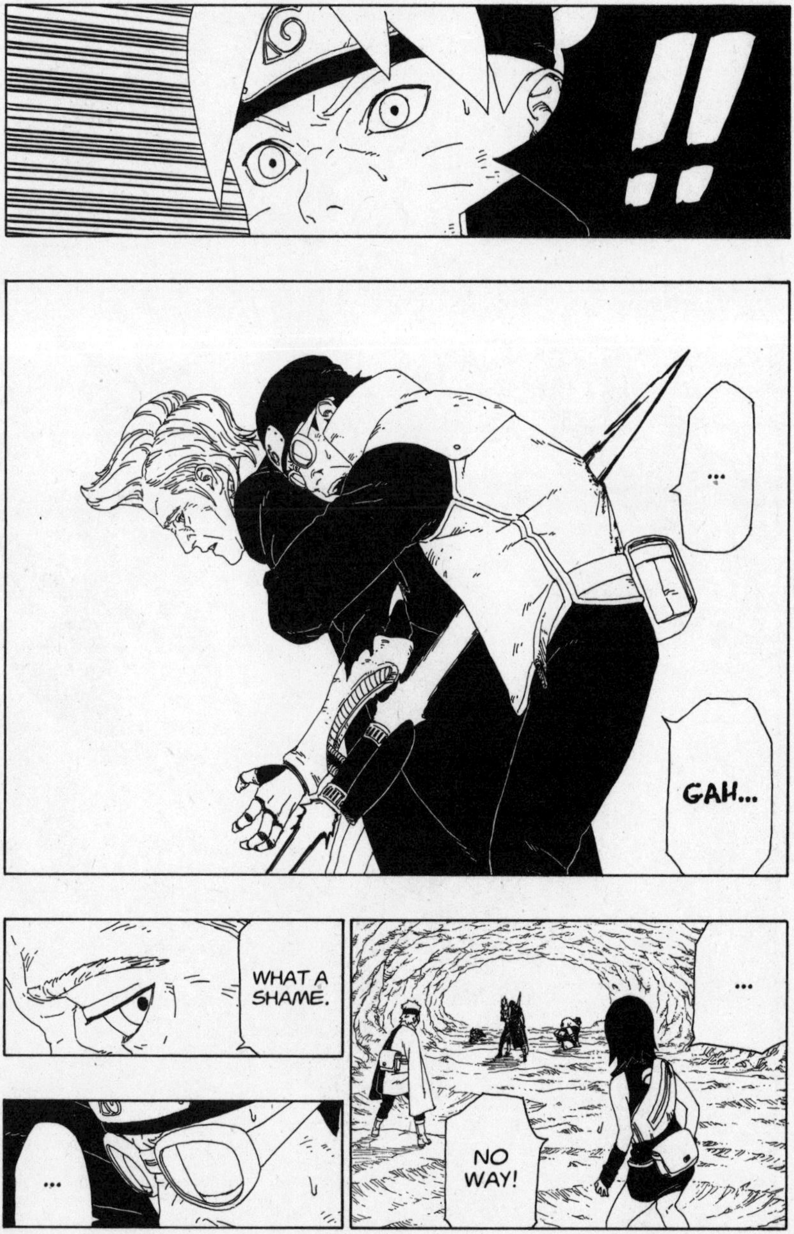
!!
...
GAH...
...
NO WAY!
WHAT A SHAME.
...

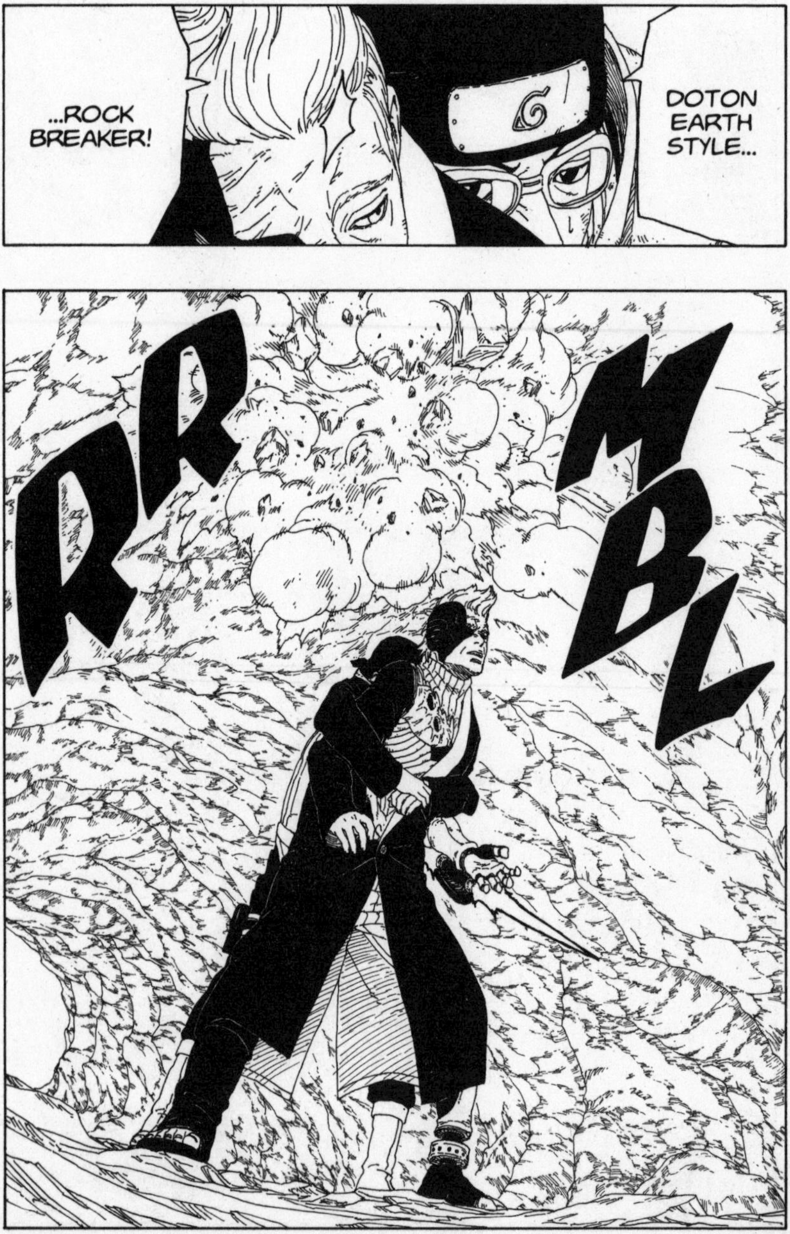
DOTON EARTH STYLE...
...ROCK BREAKER!
RR MBL

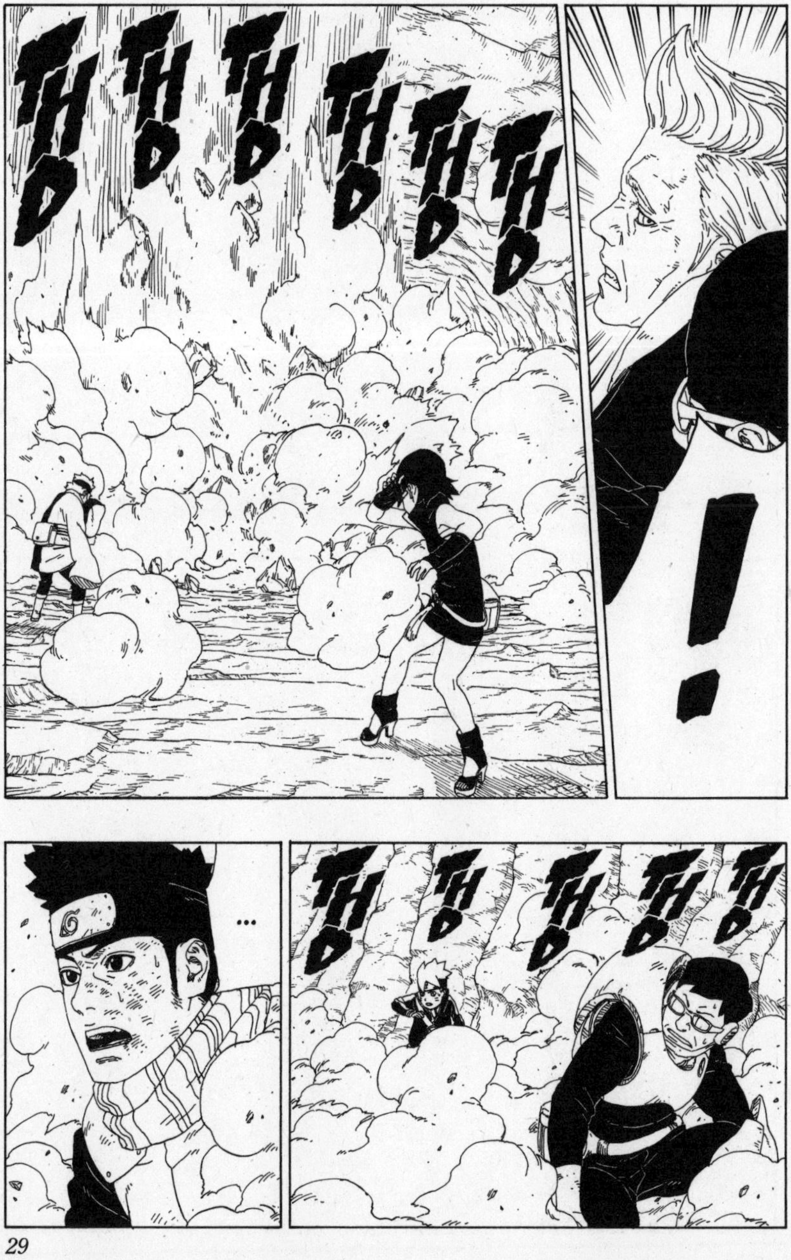
!
THUD
THUD
THUD
THUD
THUD
THUD
THUD
THUD
THUD
THUD
THUD
THUD
...

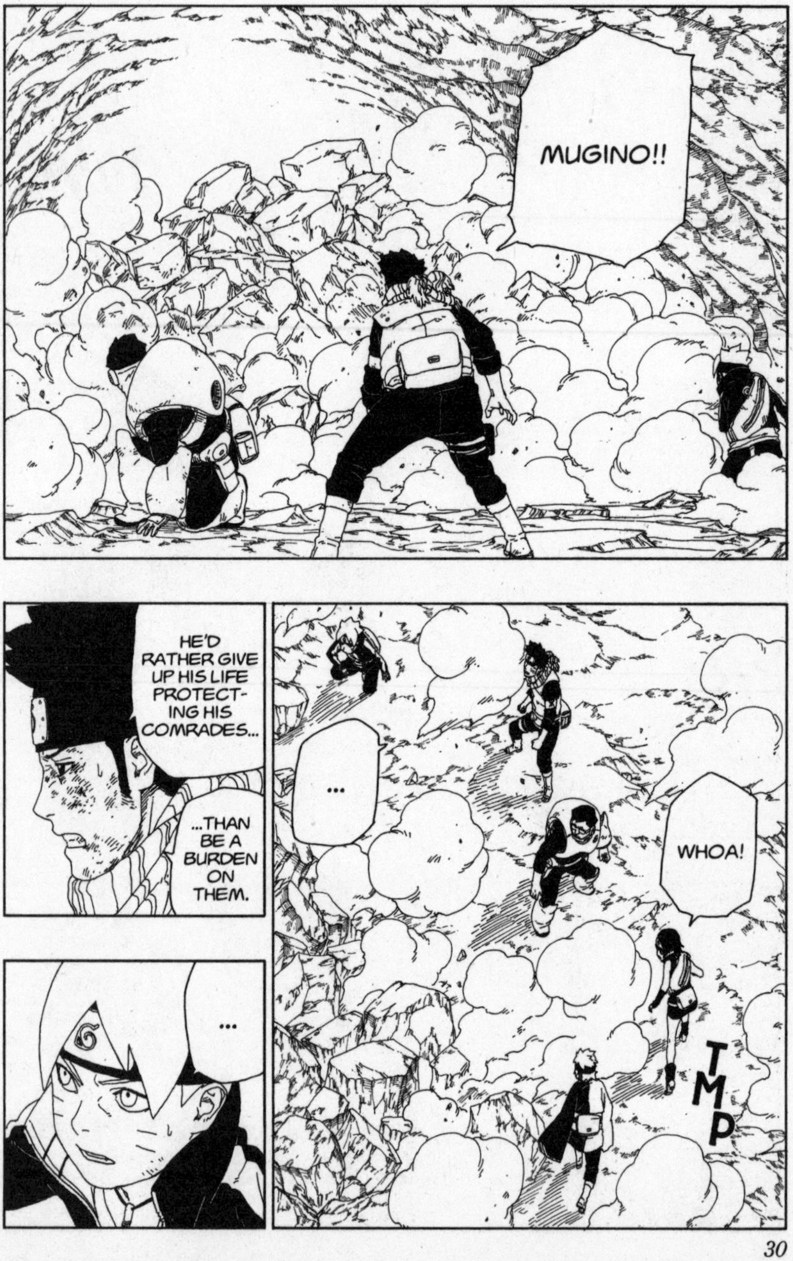
MUGINO!!
WHOA!
...
TMP
HE'D RATHER GIVE UP HIS LIFE PROTECTING HIS COMRADES...
...THAN BE A BURDEN ON THEM.
...

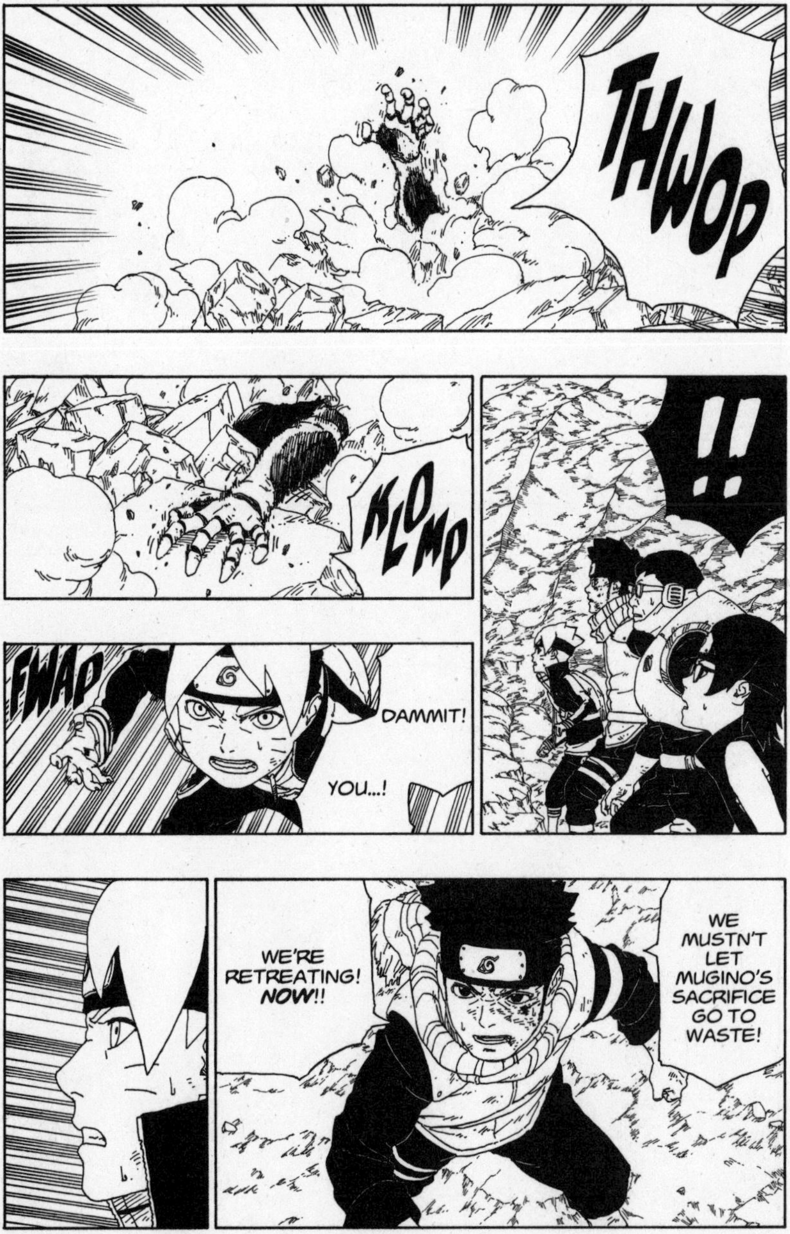
THWOP
!!
KLOMP
DAMMIT!
YOU...!
FWAP
WE MUSTN'T LET MUGINO'S SACRIFICE GO TO WASTE!
WE'RE RETREATING! NOW!!

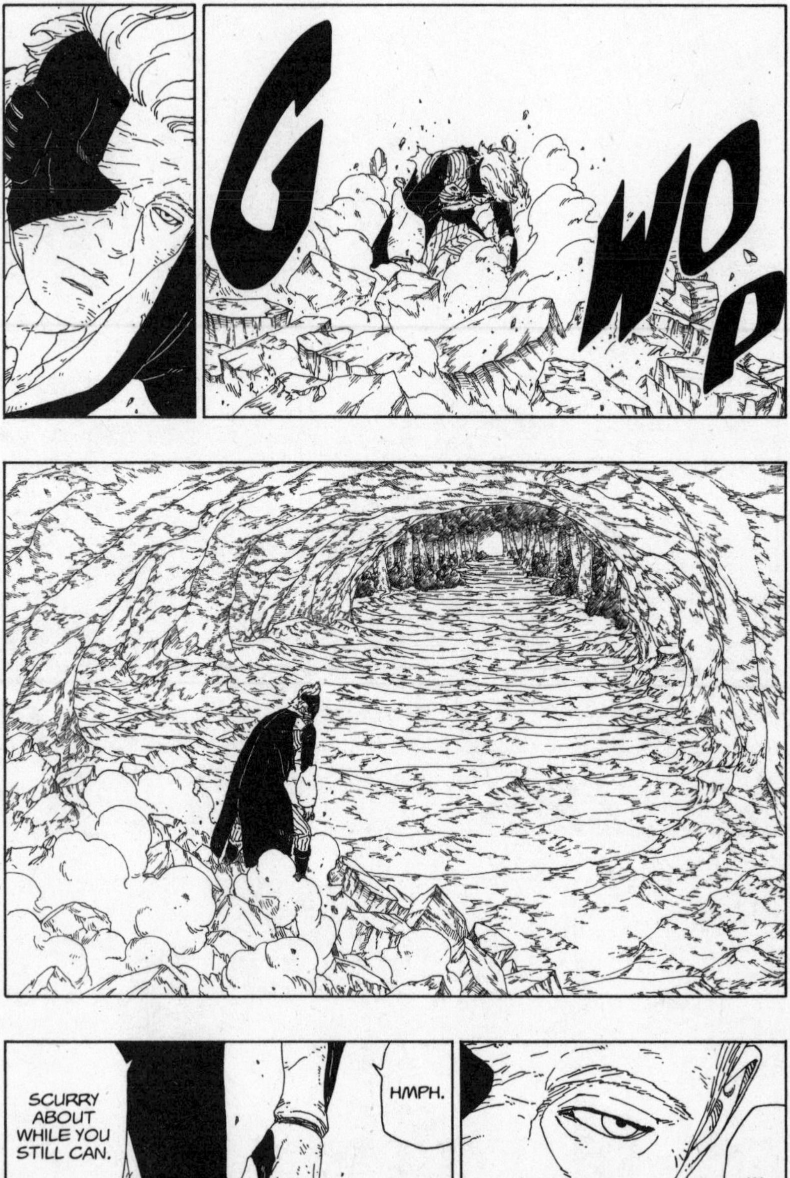
GWOP
...
HMPH.
SCURRY ABOUT WHILE YOU STILL CAN.

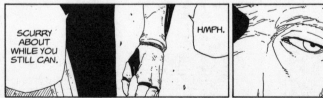

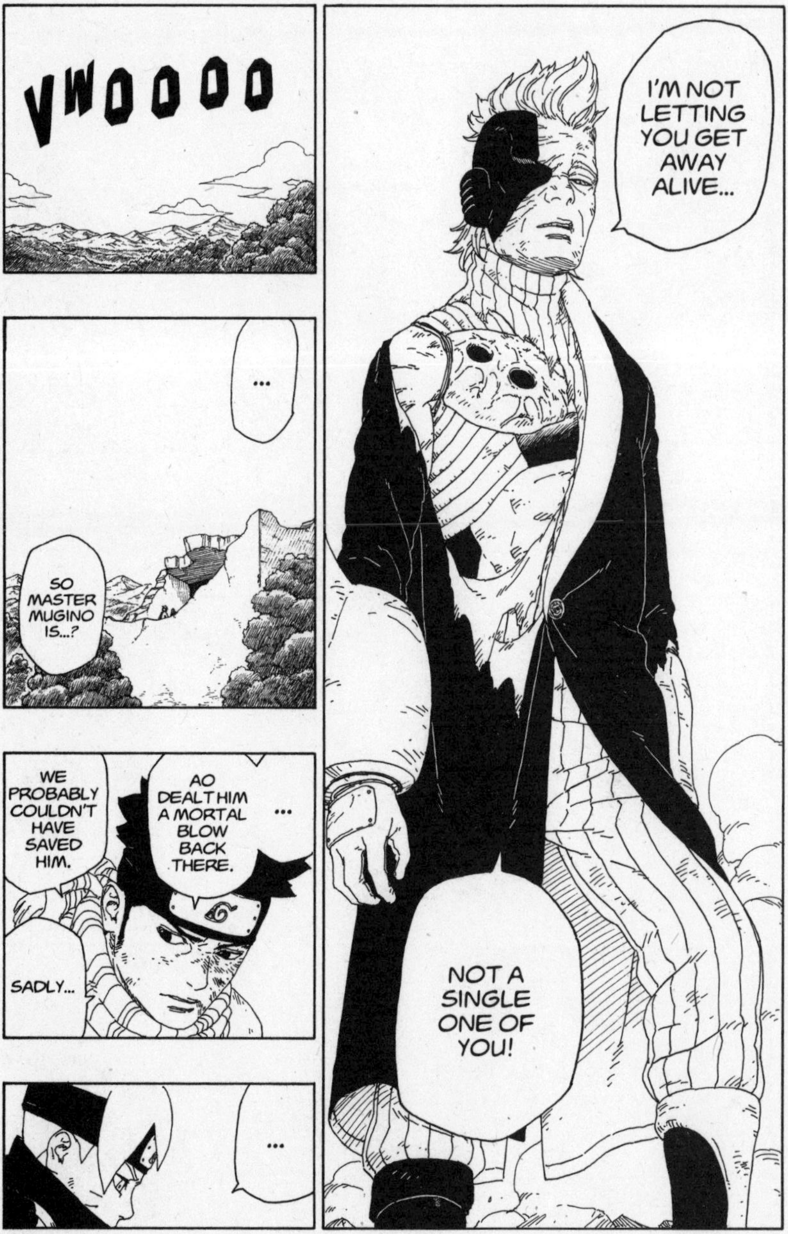

I'M NOT LETTING YOU GET AWAY ALIVE...
NOT A SINGLE ONE OF YOU!
VWOOOO
...
SO MASTER MUGINO IS...?
...
AO DEALT HIM A MORTAL BLOW BACK THERE.
WE PROBABLY COULDN'T HAVE SAVED HIM.
SADLY...
...

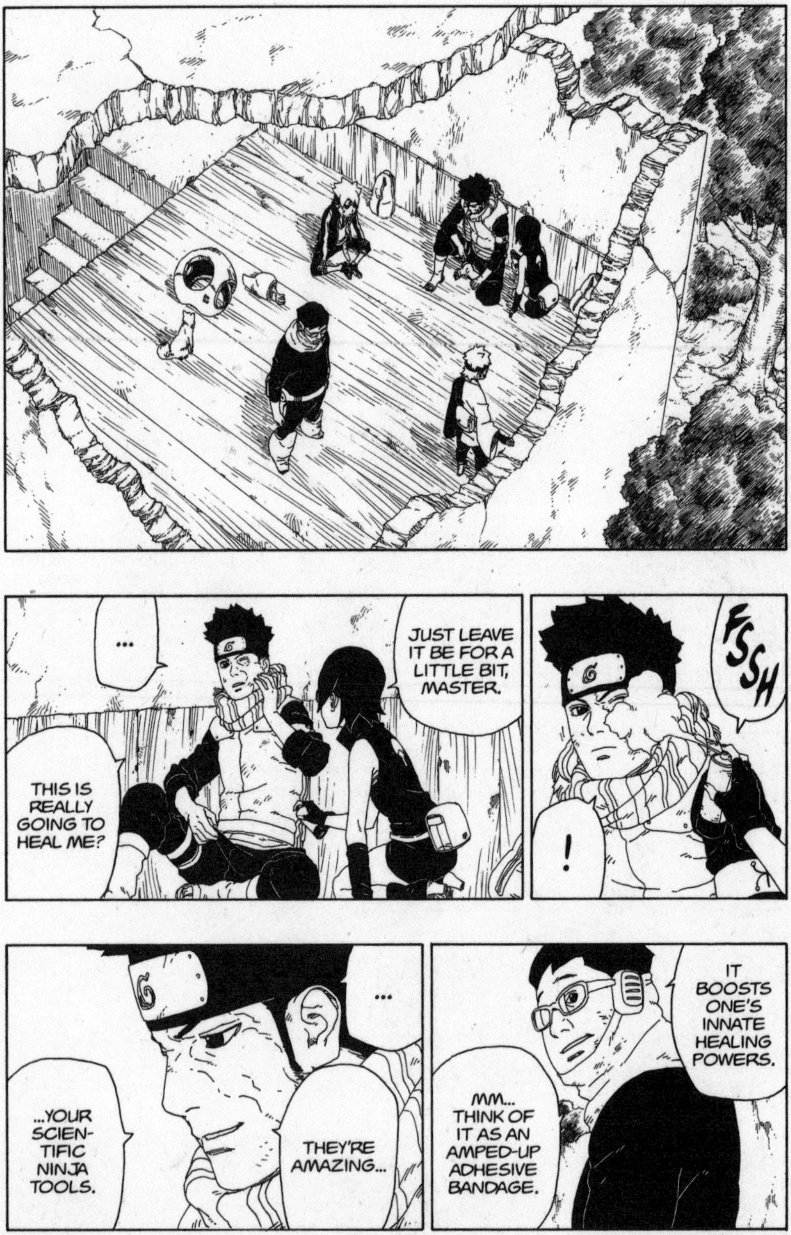
FSSH
!
JUST LEAVE IT BE FOR A LITTLE BIT, MASTER.
...
THIS IS REALLY GOING TO HEAL ME?
IT BOOSTS ONE'S INNATE HEALING POWERS.
MM... THINK OF IT AS AN AMPED-UP ADHESIVE BANDAGE.
...
THEY'RE AMAZING...
...YOUR SCIENTIFIC NINJA TOOLS.

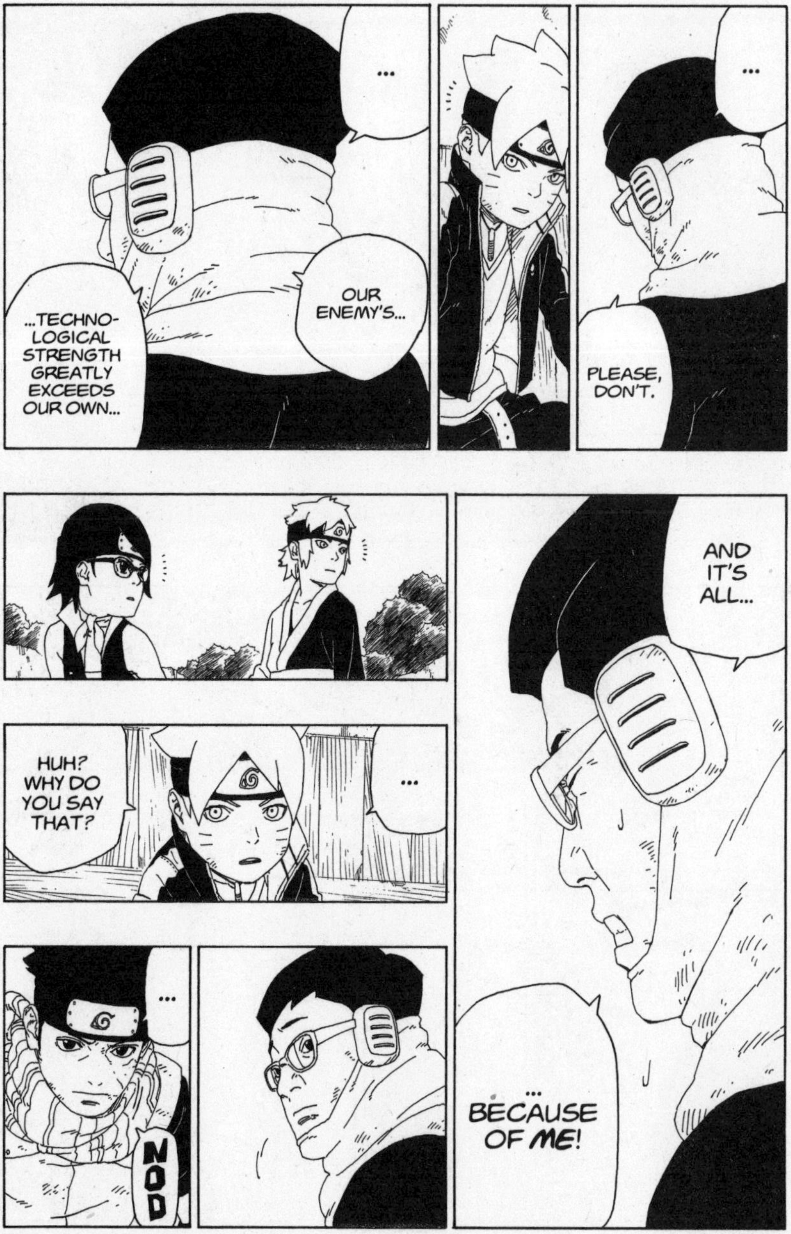
...
PLEASE, DON'T.
...
OUR ENEMY'S...
...TECHNO-LOGICAL STRENGTH GREATLY EXCEEDS OUR OWN...
AND IT'S ALL...
... BECAUSE OF ME!
...
HUH? WHY DO YOU SAY THAT?
...
NOD

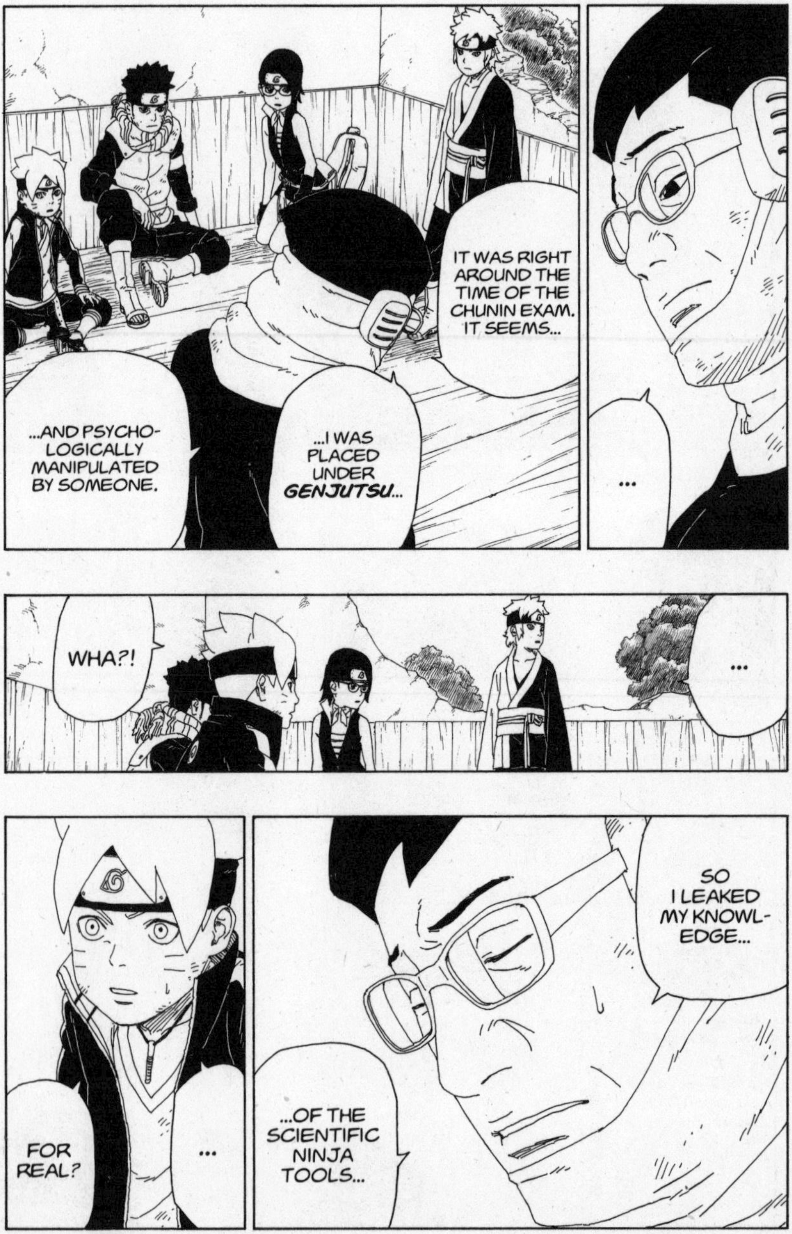
...
IT WAS RIGHT AROUND THE TIME OF THE CHUNIN EXAM. IT SEEMS...
...I WAS PLACED UNDER **GENJUTSU**...
...AND PSYCHO-LOGICALLY MANIPULATED BY SOMEONE.
...
WHA?!
SO I LEAKED MY KNOWL-EDGE...
...OF THE SCIENTIFIC NINJA TOOLS...
...
FOR REAL?

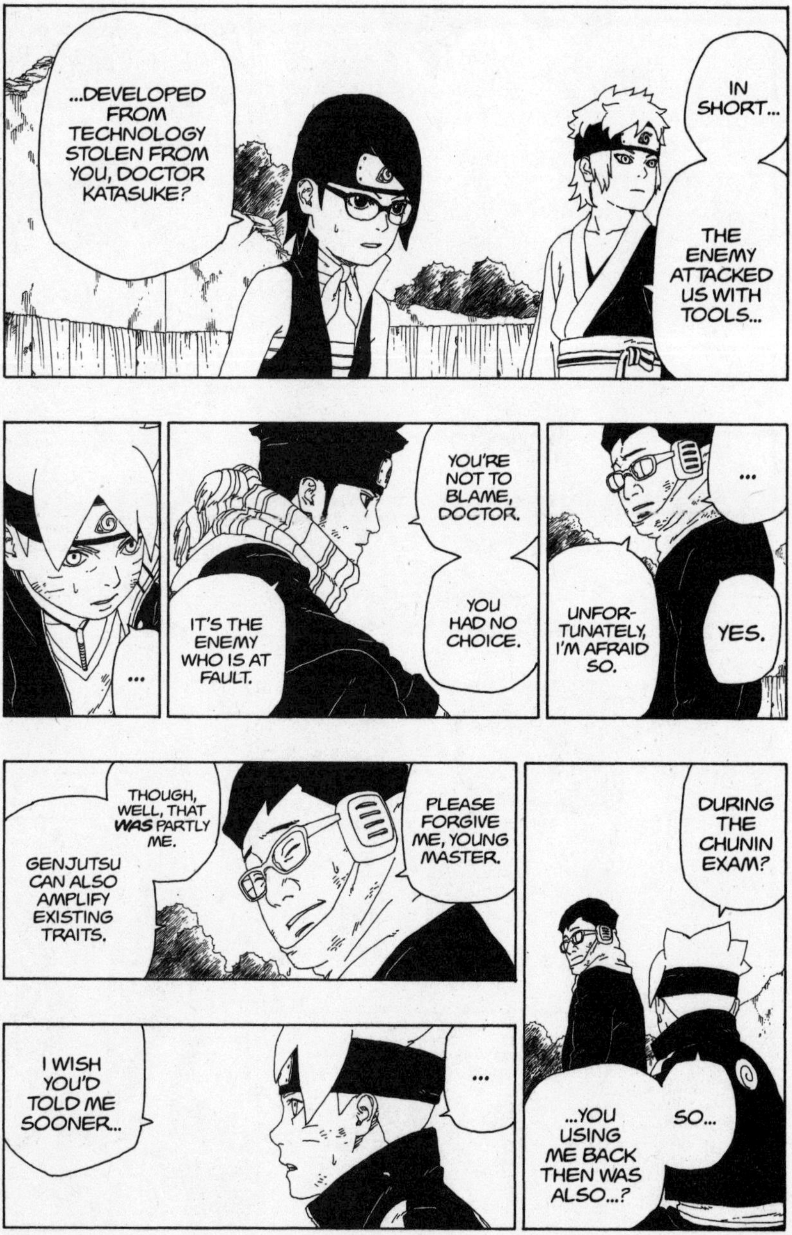
IN SHORT...
THE ENEMY ATTACKED US WITH TOOLS...
...DEVELOPED FROM TECHNOLOGY STOLEN FROM YOU, DOCTOR KATASUKE?
...
YES.
UNFORTUNATELY, I'M AFRAID SO.
YOU'RE NOT TO BLAME, DOCTOR.
YOU HAD NO CHOICE.
IT'S THE ENEMY WHO IS AT FAULT.
...
DURING THE CHUNIN EXAM?
SO...
...YOU USING ME BACK THEN WAS ALSO...?
PLEASE FORGIVE ME, YOUNG MASTER.
THOUGH, WELL, THAT **WAS** PARTLY ME.
GENJUTSU CAN ALSO AMPLIFY EXISTING TRAITS.
...
I WISH YOU'D TOLD ME SOONER...

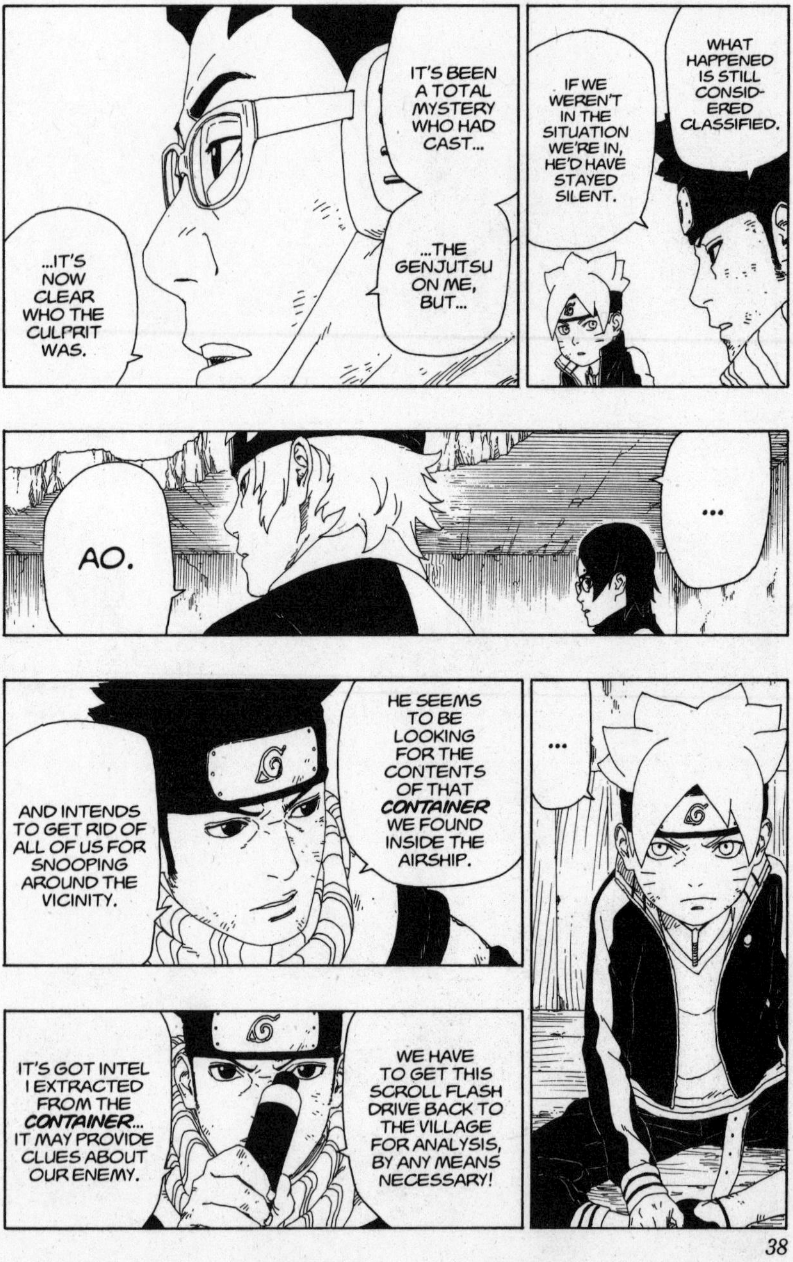
WHAT HAPPENED IS STILL CONSIDERED CLASSIFIED.
IF WE WEREN'T IN THE SITUATION WE'RE IN, HE'D HAVE STAYED SILENT.
IT'S BEEN A TOTAL MYSTERY WHO HAD CAST...
...THE GENJUTSU ON ME, BUT...
...IT'S NOW CLEAR WHO THE CULPRIT WAS.
...
AO.
...
HE SEEMS TO BE LOOKING FOR THE CONTENTS OF THAT *CONTAINER* WE FOUND INSIDE THE AIRSHIP.
AND INTENDS TO GET RID OF ALL OF US FOR SNOOPING AROUND THE VICINITY.
WE HAVE TO GET THIS SCROLL FLASH DRIVE BACK TO THE VILLAGE FOR ANALYSIS, BY ANY MEANS NECESSARY!
IT'S GOT INTEL I EXTRACTED FROM THE *CONTAINER*... IT MAY PROVIDE CLUES ABOUT OUR ENEMY.

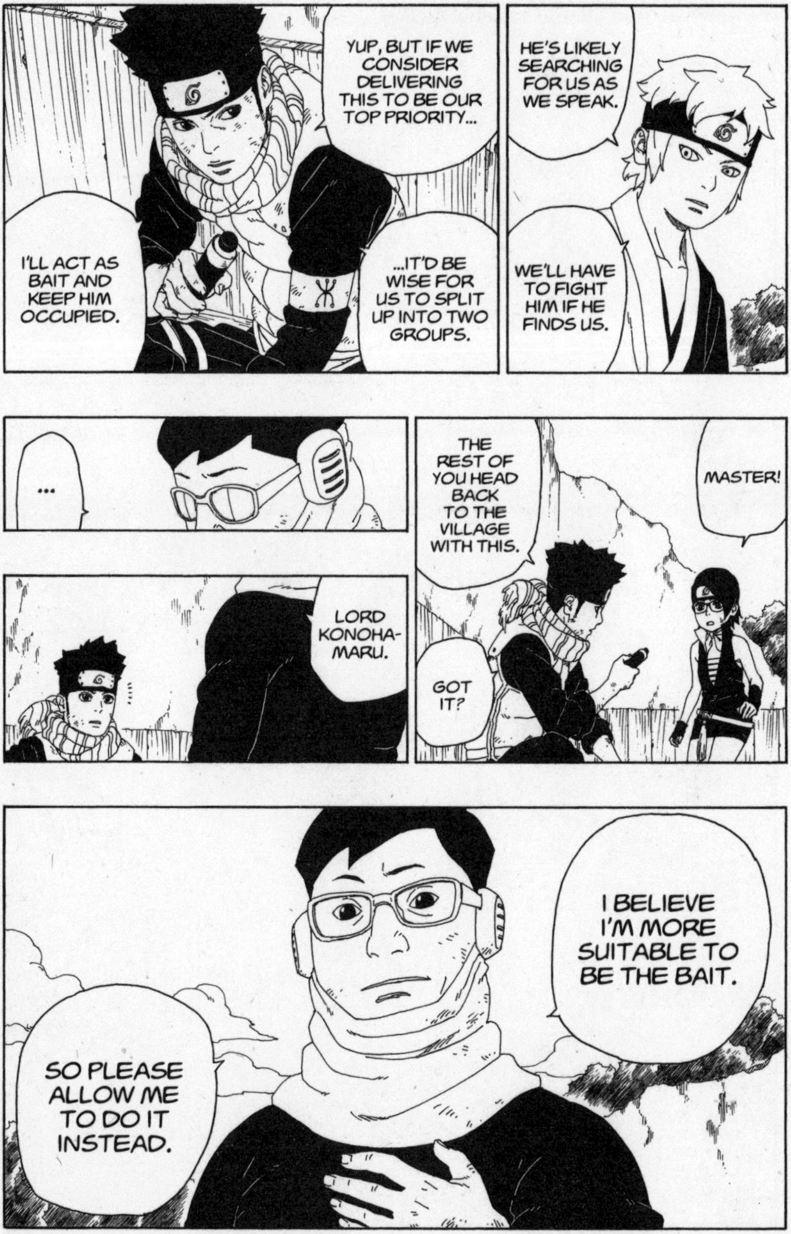
HE'S LIKELY SEARCHING FOR US AS WE SPEAK.
WE'LL HAVE TO FIGHT HIM IF HE FINDS US.
YUP, BUT IF WE CONSIDER DELIVERING THIS TO BE OUR TOP PRIORITY...
...IT'D BE WISE FOR US TO SPLIT UP INTO TWO GROUPS.
I'LL ACT AS BAIT AND KEEP HIM OCCUPIED.
MASTER!
THE REST OF YOU HEAD BACK TO THE VILLAGE WITH THIS.
GOT IT?
...
LORD KONOHA-MARU.
I BELIEVE I'M MORE SUITABLE TO BE THE BAIT.
SO PLEASE ALLOW ME TO DO IT INSTEAD.

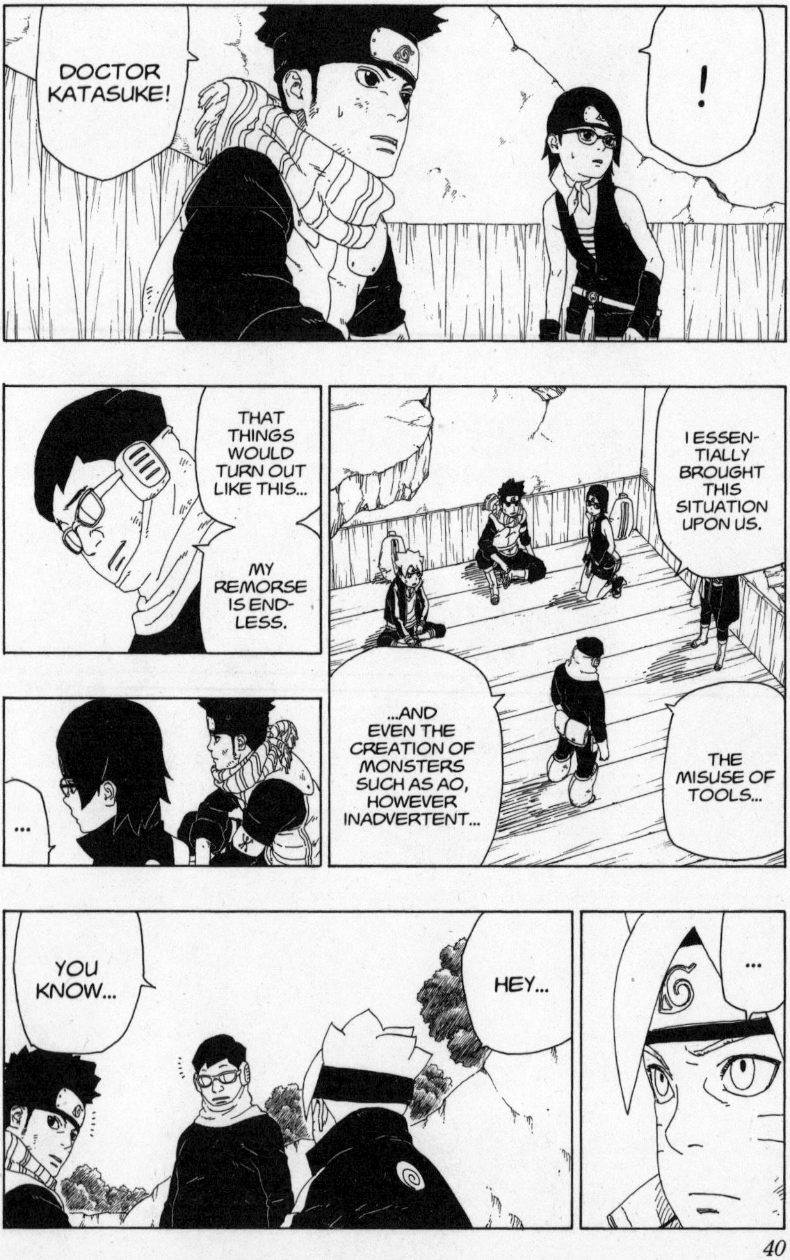
!
DOCTOR KATASUKE!
I ESSEN-TIALLY BROUGHT THIS SITUATION UPON US.
THE MISUSE OF TOOLS...
...AND EVEN THE CREATION OF MONSTERS SUCH AS AO, HOWEVER INADVERTENT...
THAT THINGS WOULD TURN OUT LIKE THIS...
MY REMORSE IS END-LESS.
...
...
HEY...
YOU KNOW...

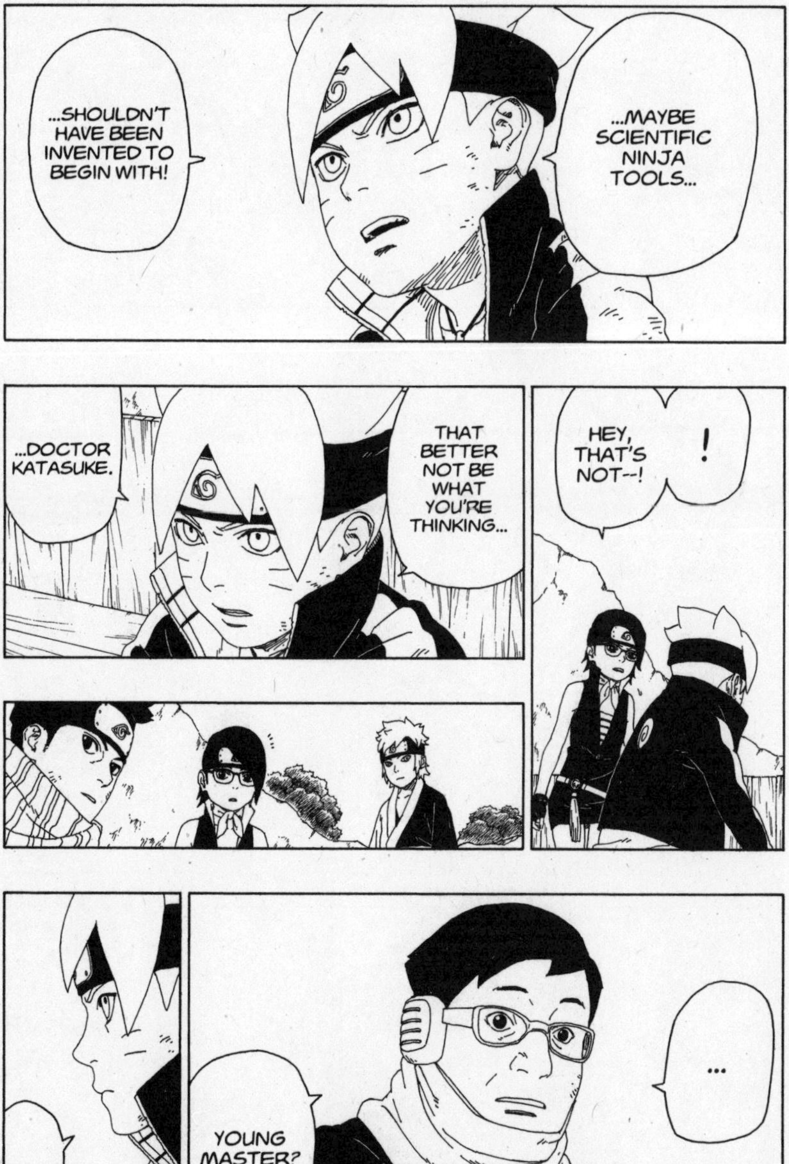
...MAYBE SCIENTIFIC NINJA TOOLS...
...SHOULDN'T HAVE BEEN INVENTED TO BEGIN WITH!
!
HEY, THAT'S NOT--!
THAT BETTER NOT BE WHAT YOU'RE THINKING...
...DOCTOR KATASUKE.
...
YOUNG MASTER?
...

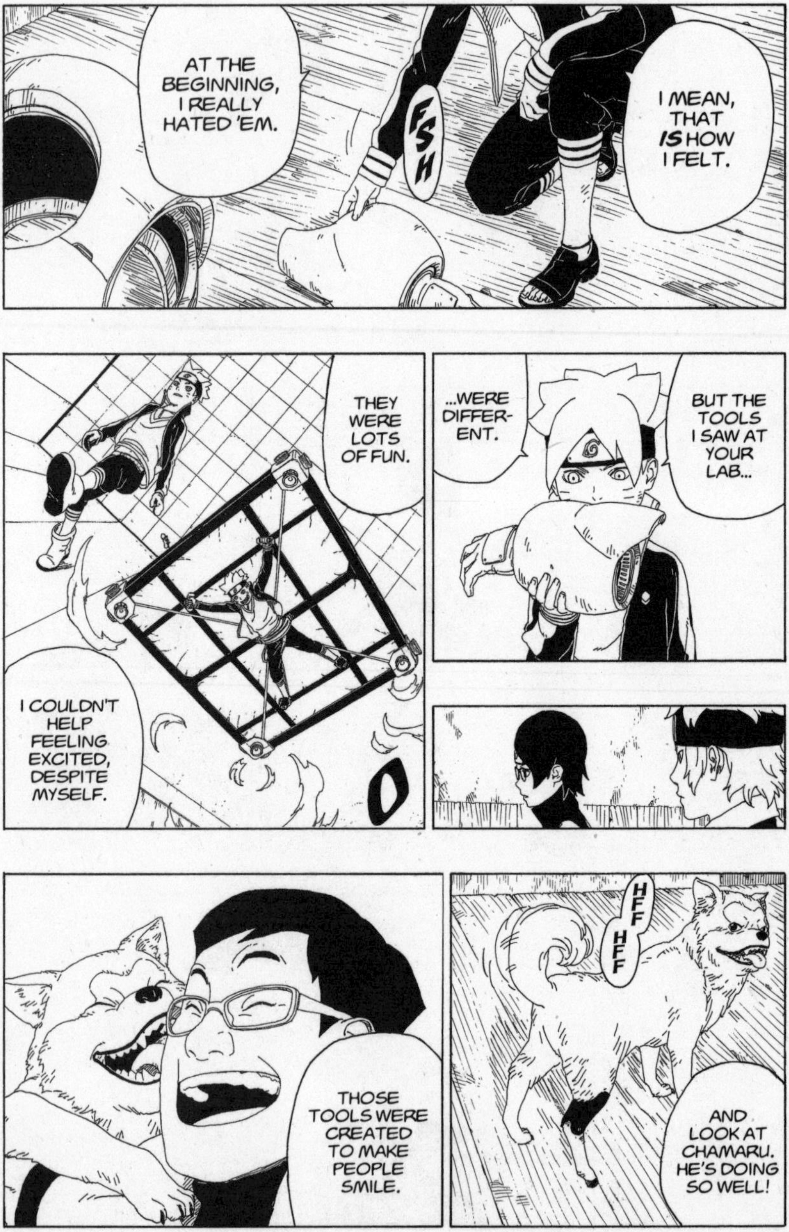
AT THE BEGINNING, I REALLY HATED 'EM.
I MEAN, THAT *IS* HOW I FELT.
FSH
BUT THE TOOLS I SAW AT YOUR LAB...
...WERE DIFFERENT.
THEY WERE LOTS OF FUN.
I COULDN'T HELP FEELING EXCITED, DESPITE MYSELF.
HFF HFF
AND LOOK AT CHAMARU. HE'S DOING SO WELL!
THOSE TOOLS WERE CREATED TO MAKE PEOPLE SMILE.

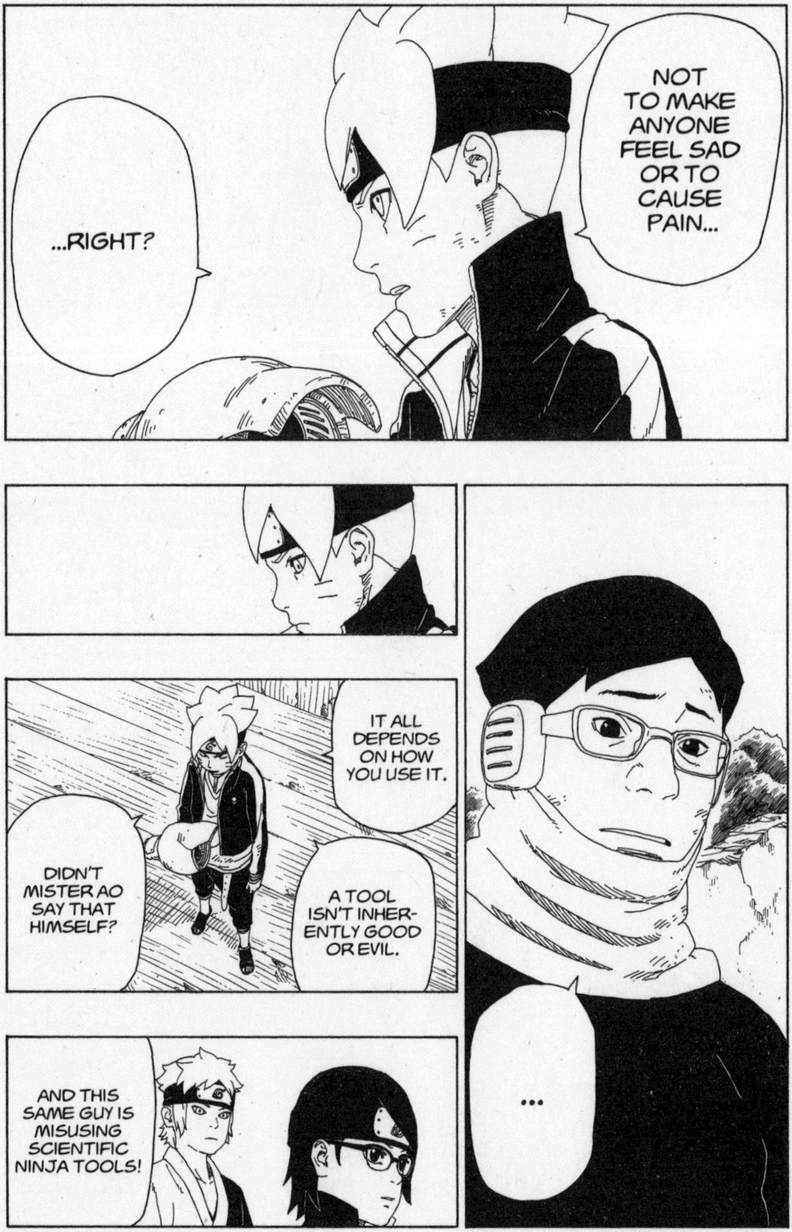
NOT TO MAKE ANYONE FEEL SAD OR TO CAUSE PAIN...
...RIGHT?
...
IT ALL DEPENDS ON HOW YOU USE IT.
A TOOL ISN'T INHERENTLY GOOD OR EVIL.
DIDN'T MISTER AO SAY THAT HIMSELF?
AND THIS SAME GUY IS MISUSING SCIENTIFIC NINJA TOOLS!

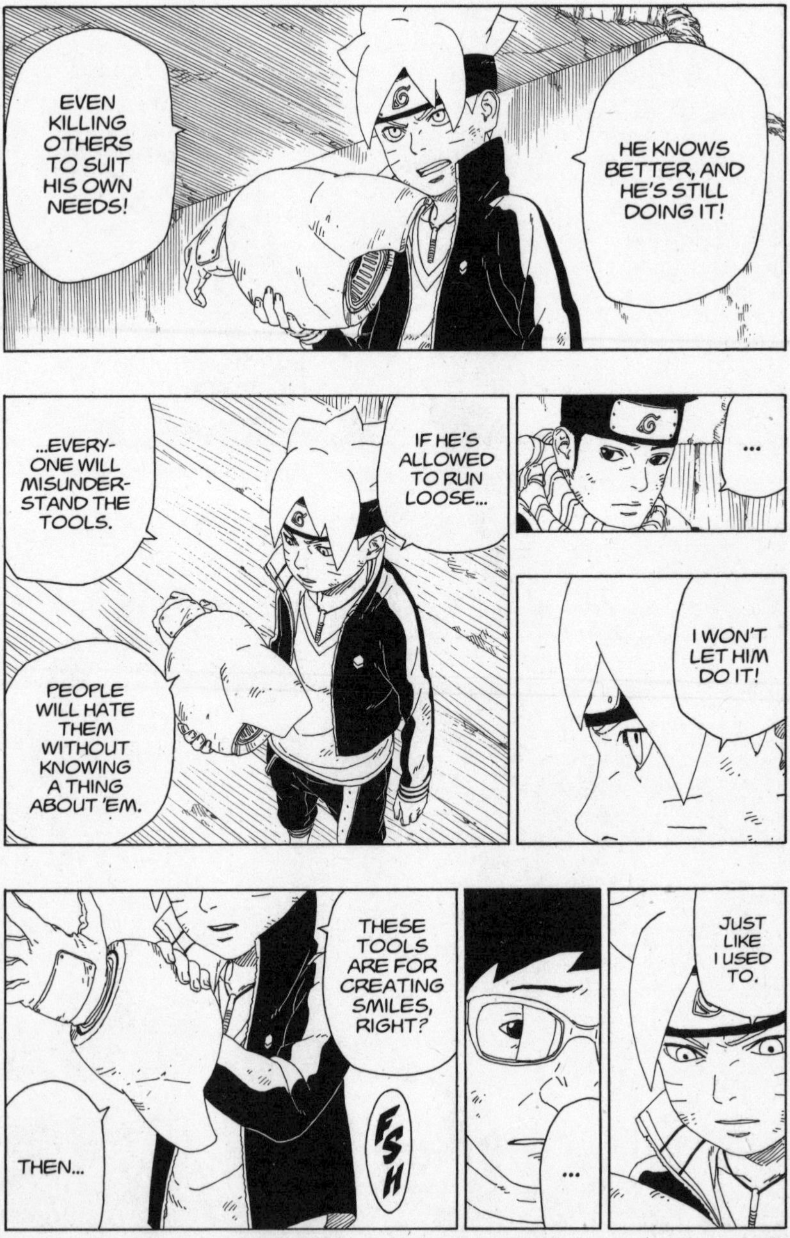
HE KNOWS BETTER, AND HE'S STILL DOING IT!
EVEN KILLING OTHERS TO SUIT HIS OWN NEEDS!
...
I WON'T LET HIM DO IT!
IF HE'S ALLOWED TO RUN LOOSE...
...EVERY-ONE WILL MISUNDER-STAND THE TOOLS.
PEOPLE WILL HATE THEM WITHOUT KNOWING A THING ABOUT 'EM.
JUST LIKE I USED TO.
...
THESE TOOLS ARE FOR CREATING SMILES, RIGHT?
FSH
THEN...

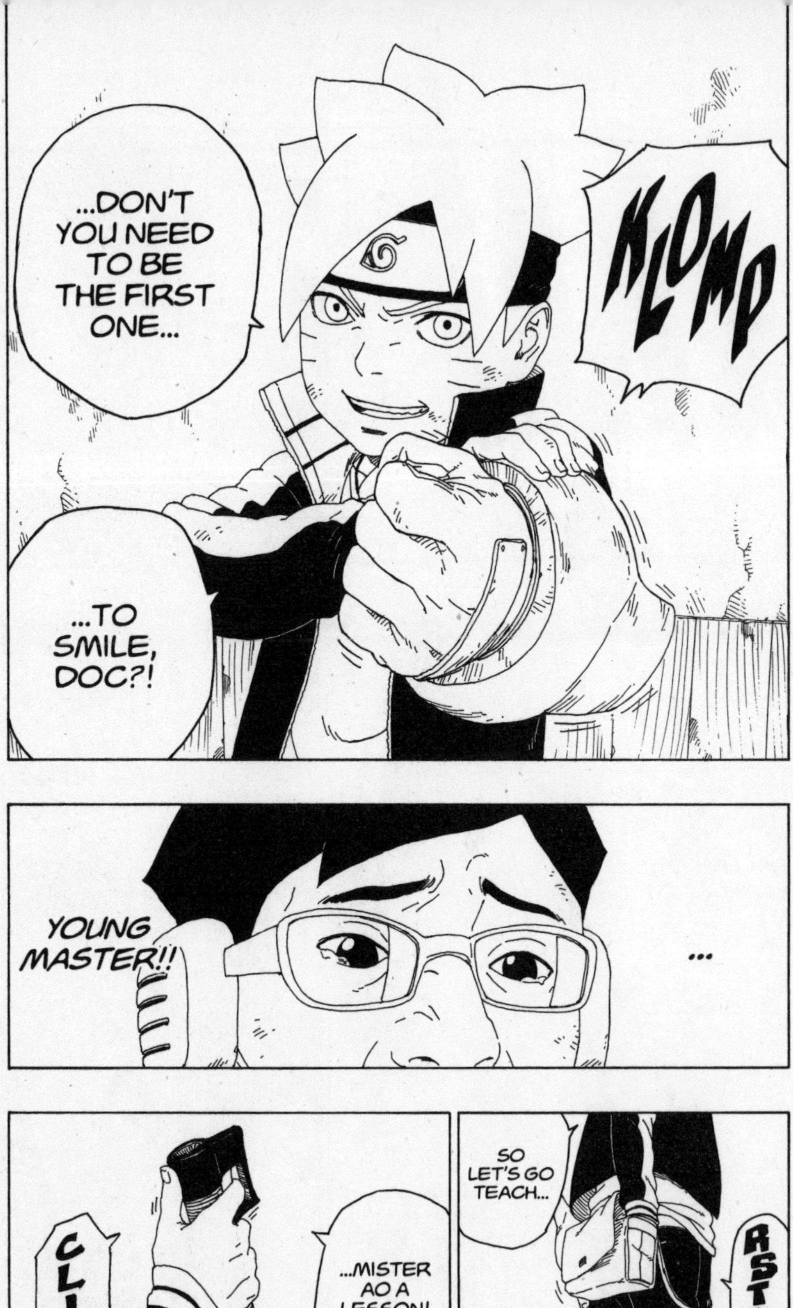
KLOMP
...DON'T YOU NEED TO BE THE FIRST ONE...
...TO SMILE, DOC?!
...
YOUNG MASTER!!
SO LET'S GO TEACH...
RSTL
...MISTER AO A LESSON!
CLIK

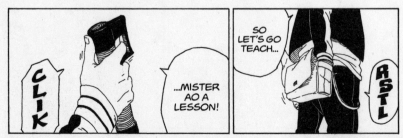

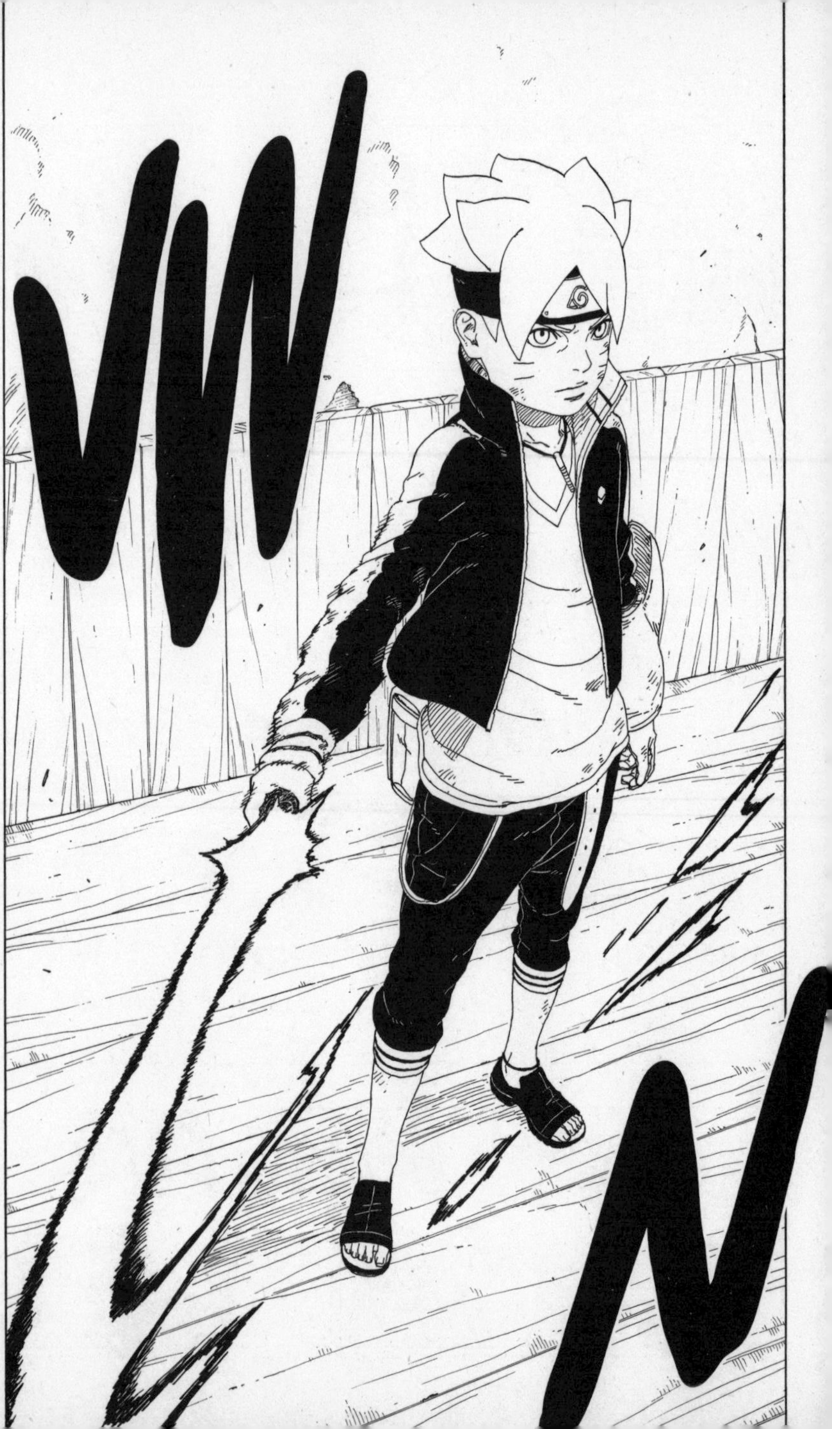

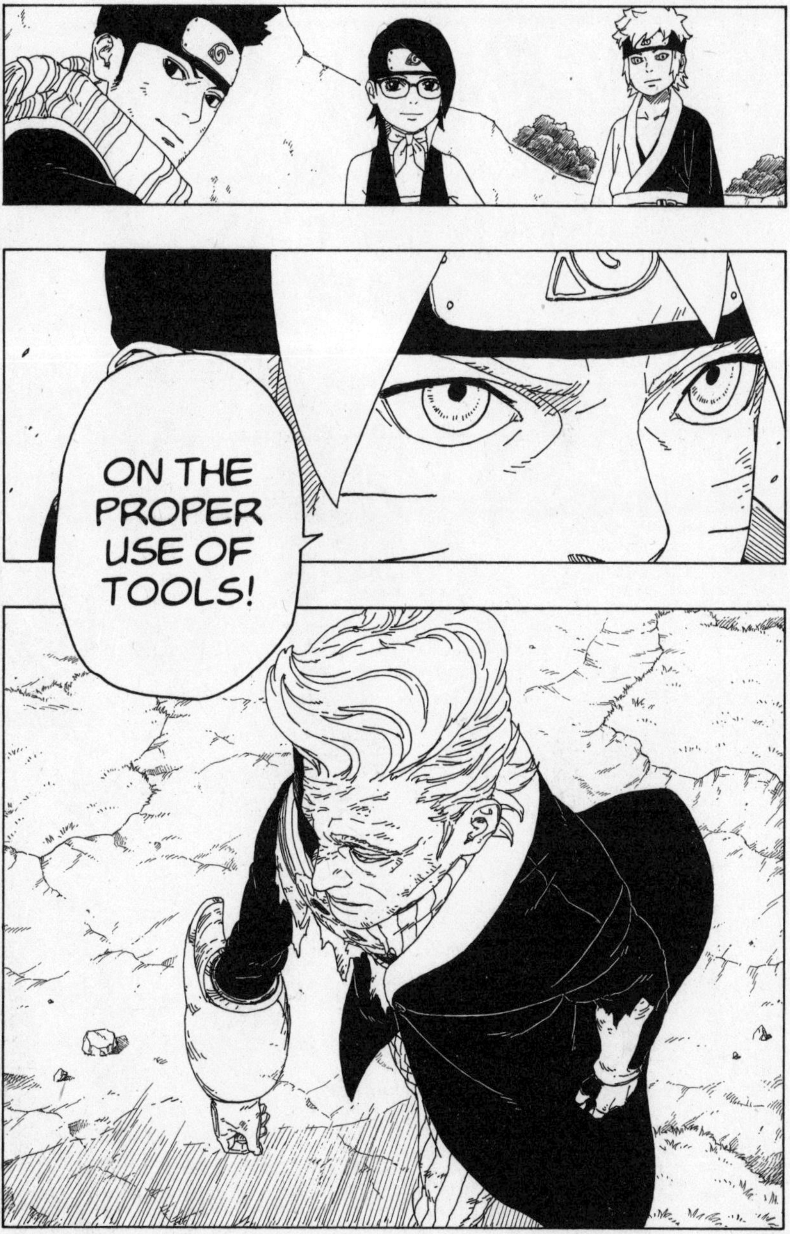
ON THE PROPER USE OF TOOLS!

NINJA ENCYCLOPEDIA · ENTRY 16

YAMANAKA SAI

"What's most important is not giving up."

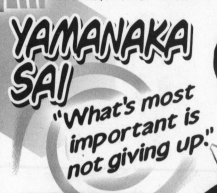

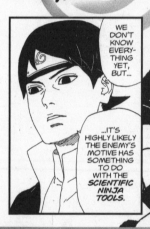

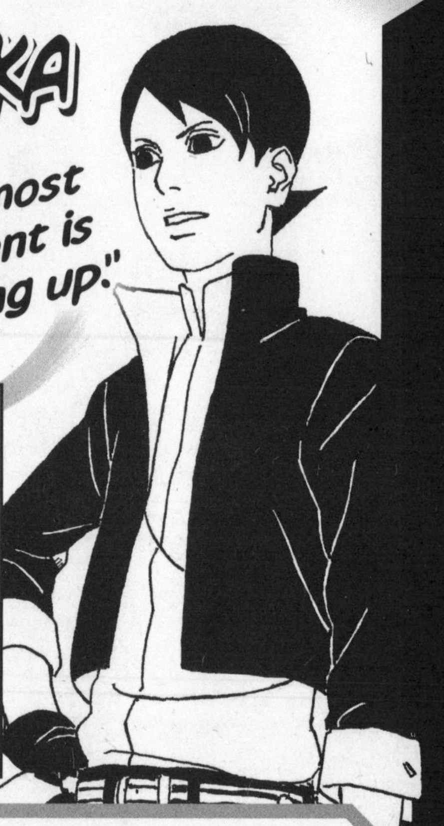

WE DON'T KNOW EVERYTHING YET, BUT...
...IT'S HIGHLY LIKELY THE ENEMY'S MOTIVE HAS SOMETHING TO DO WITH THE SCIENTIFIC NINJA TOOLS.

● Attributes

Strength	140	Dexterity	160
Intelligence	144	Chakra	150
Perception	155	Negotiation	120

● Skills

Art (Painting) ☆☆☆☆☆ Intel crafting ☆☆☆☆

● Ninja Arts

Art of Cartoon Beast Mimicry, Sealing Jutsu: Crouched Tiger Bullet, Ink Doppelganger Jutsu, etc.

*Average attribute value is 60 for ordinary people and 90 for genin. Skill values range from 1 to 5☆ with 5☆ signifying super top-notch.

Number 21: How You Use It

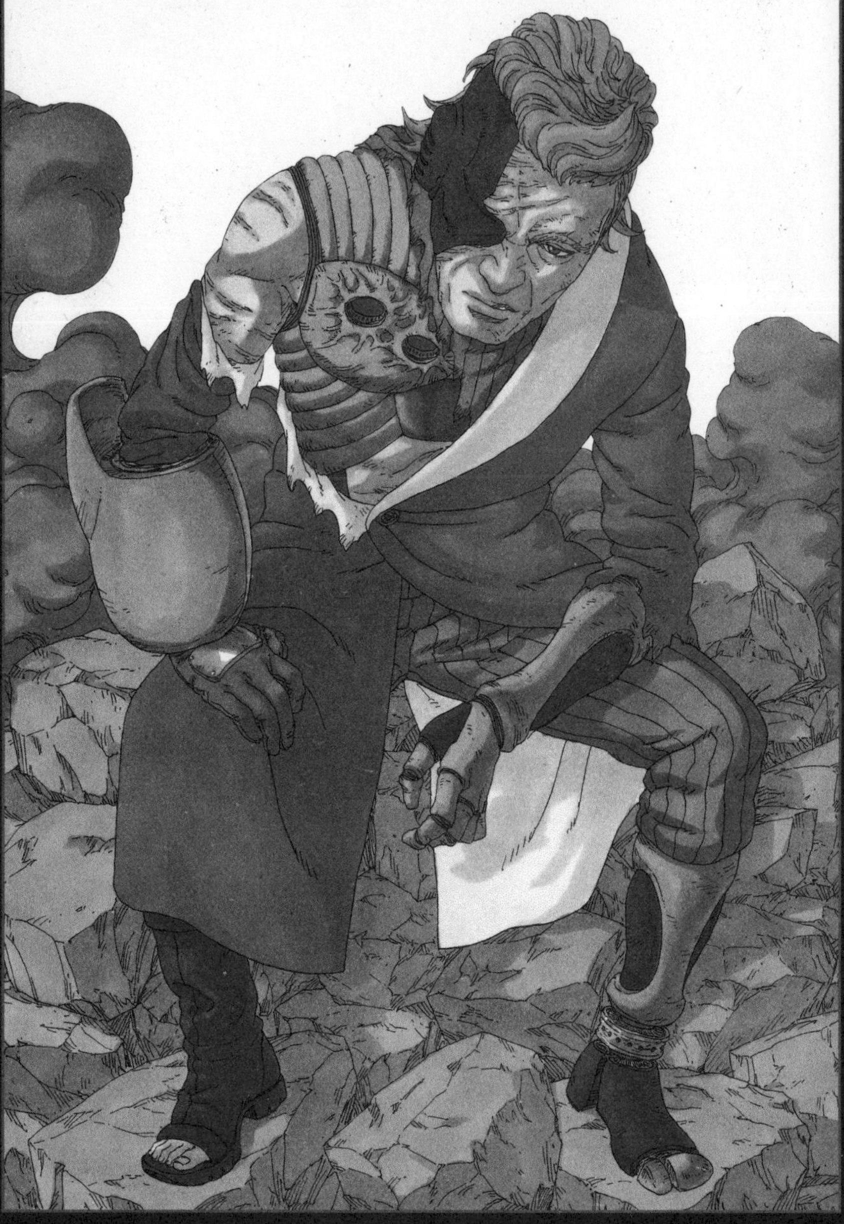

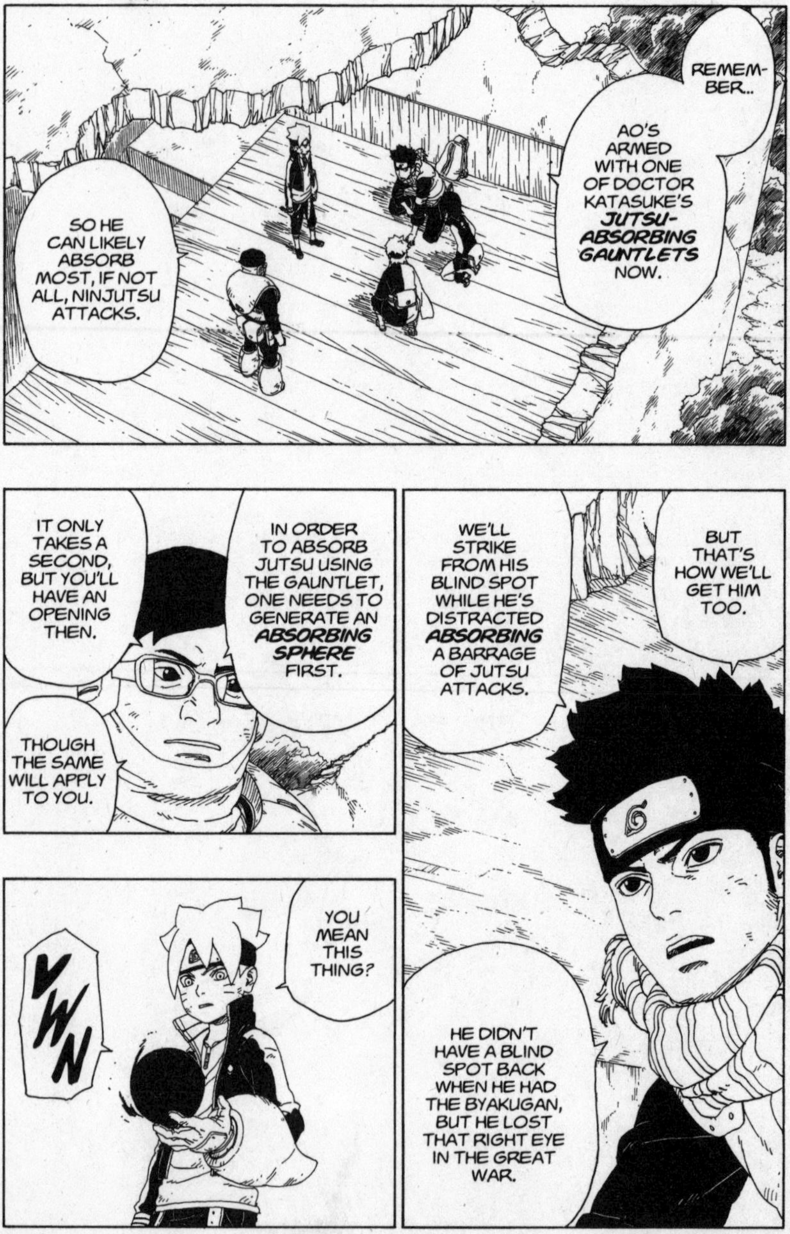
REMEMBER...
AO'S ARMED WITH ONE OF DOCTOR KATASUKE'S ***JUTSU-ABSORBING GAUNTLETS*** NOW.
SO HE CAN LIKELY ABSORB MOST, IF NOT ALL, NINJUTSU ATTACKS.
BUT THAT'S HOW WE'LL GET HIM TOO.
WE'LL STRIKE FROM HIS BLIND SPOT WHILE HE'S DISTRACTED ***ABSORBING*** A BARRAGE OF JUTSU ATTACKS.
HE DIDN'T HAVE A BLIND SPOT BACK WHEN HE HAD THE BYAKUGAN, BUT HE LOST THAT RIGHT EYE IN THE GREAT WAR.
IN ORDER TO ABSORB JUTSU USING THE GAUNTLET, ONE NEEDS TO GENERATE AN ***ABSORBING SPHERE*** FIRST.
IT ONLY TAKES A SECOND, BUT YOU'LL HAVE AN OPENING THEN.
THOUGH THE SAME WILL APPLY TO YOU.
YOU MEAN THIS THING?
VWN

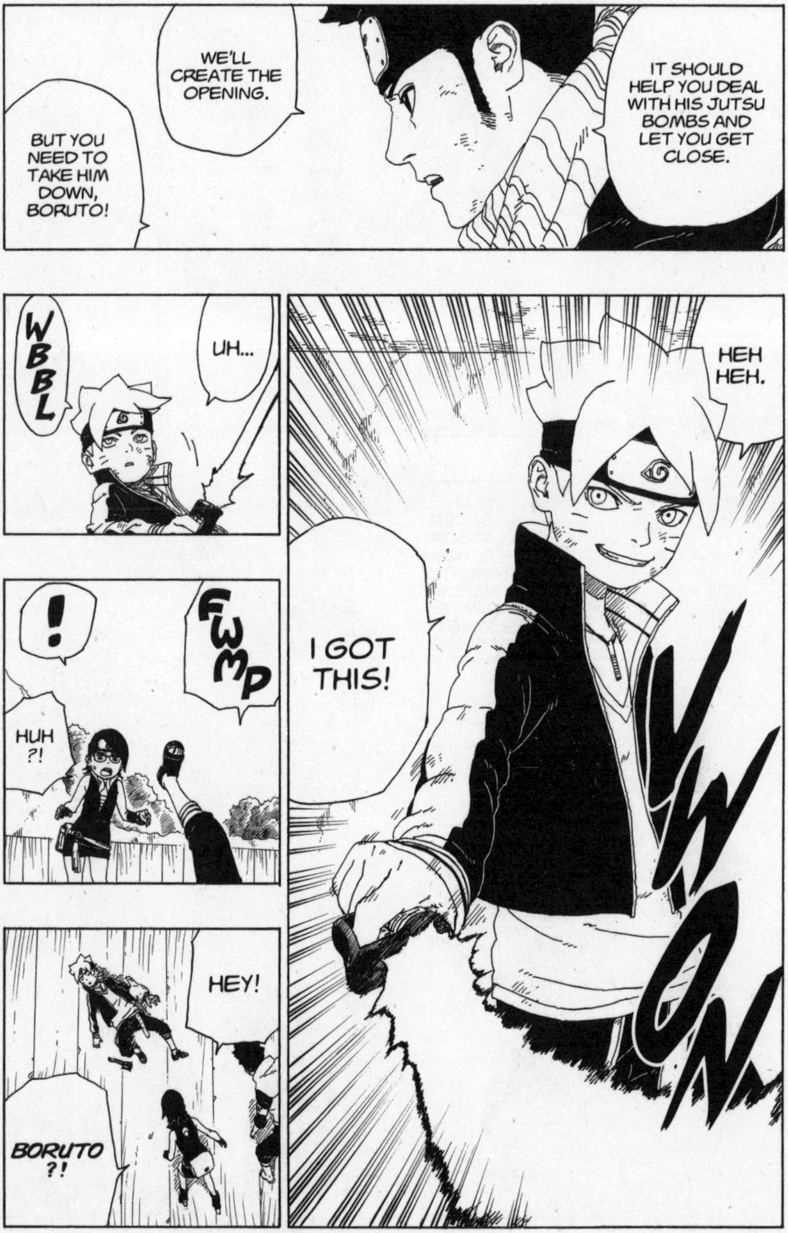
IT SHOULD HELP YOU DEAL WITH HIS JUTSU BOMBS AND LET YOU GET CLOSE.
WE'LL CREATE THE OPENING.
BUT YOU NEED TO TAKE HIM DOWN, BORUTO!
HEH HEH.
I GOT THIS!
VWON
UH...
WBBL
FWMP
!
HUH ?!
HEY!
BORUTO ?!

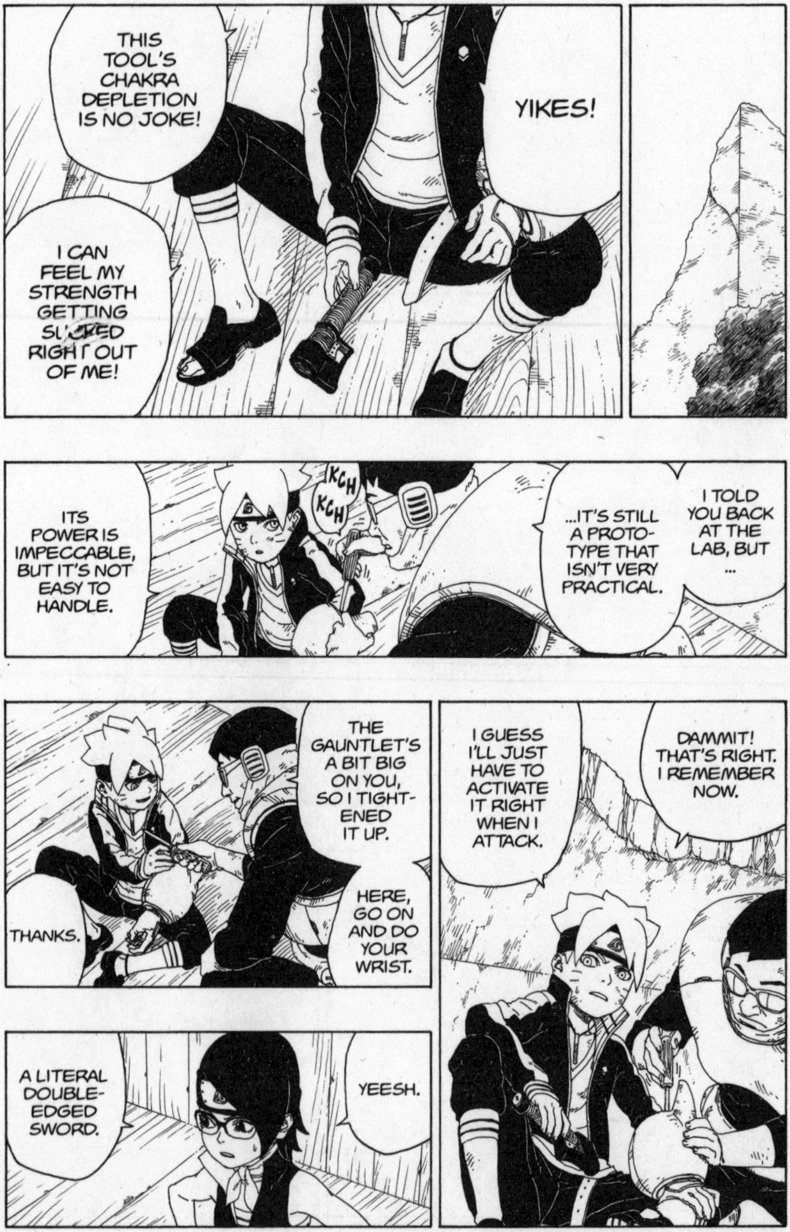
YIKES!
THIS TOOL'S CHAKRA DEPLETION IS NO JOKE!
I CAN FEEL MY STRENGTH GETTING SUCKED RIGHT OUT OF ME!
I TOLD YOU BACK AT THE LAB, BUT ...
...IT'S STILL A PROTO-TYPE THAT ISN'T VERY PRACTICAL.
KCH
KCH
ITS POWER IS IMPECCABLE, BUT IT'S NOT EASY TO HANDLE.
DAMMIT! THAT'S RIGHT. I REMEMBER NOW.
I GUESS I'LL JUST HAVE TO ACTIVATE IT RIGHT WHEN I ATTACK.
THE GAUNTLET'S A BIT BIG ON YOU, SO I TIGHT-ENED IT UP.
HERE, GO ON AND DO YOUR WRIST.
THANKS.
YEESH.
A LITERAL DOUBLE-EDGED SWORD.

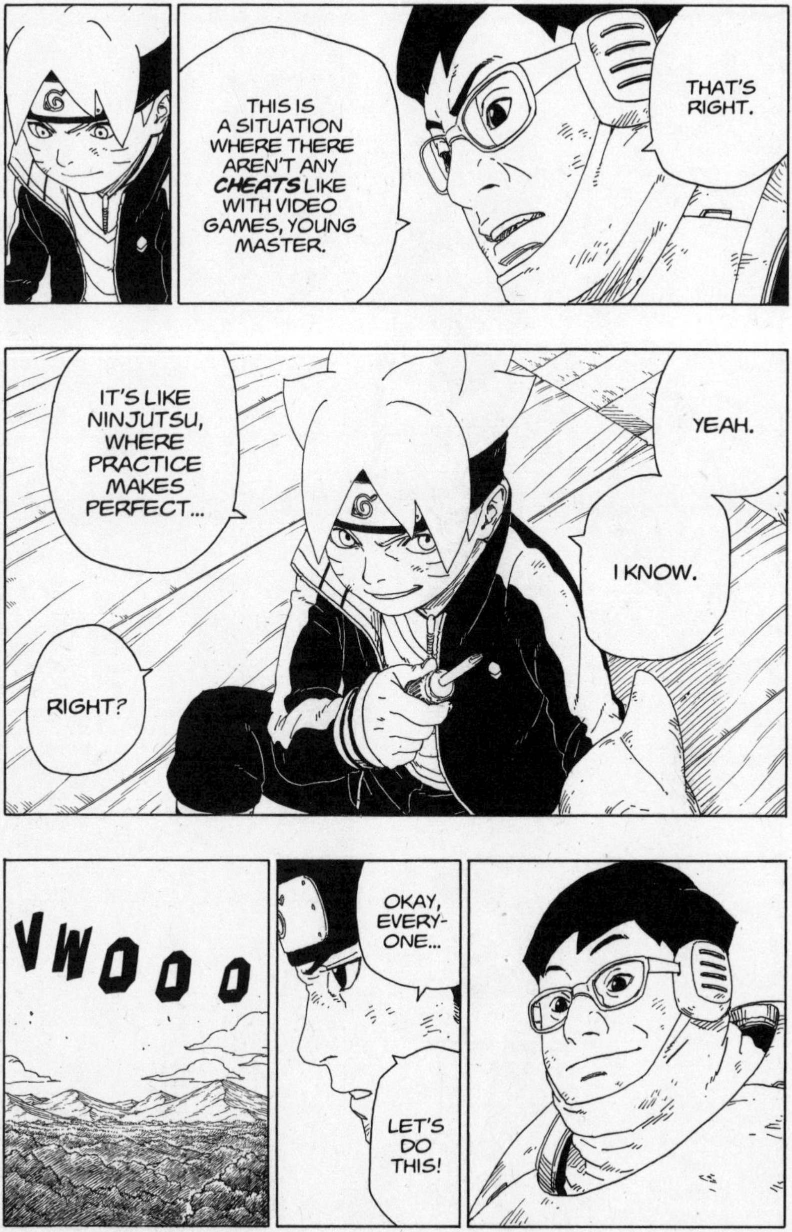
THAT'S RIGHT.
THIS IS A SITUATION WHERE THERE AREN'T ANY *CHEATS* LIKE WITH VIDEO GAMES, YOUNG MASTER.
IT'S LIKE NINJUTSU, WHERE PRACTICE MAKES PERFECT...
RIGHT?
YEAH.
I KNOW.
OKAY, EVERY-ONE...
LET'S DO THIS!
VWOOO

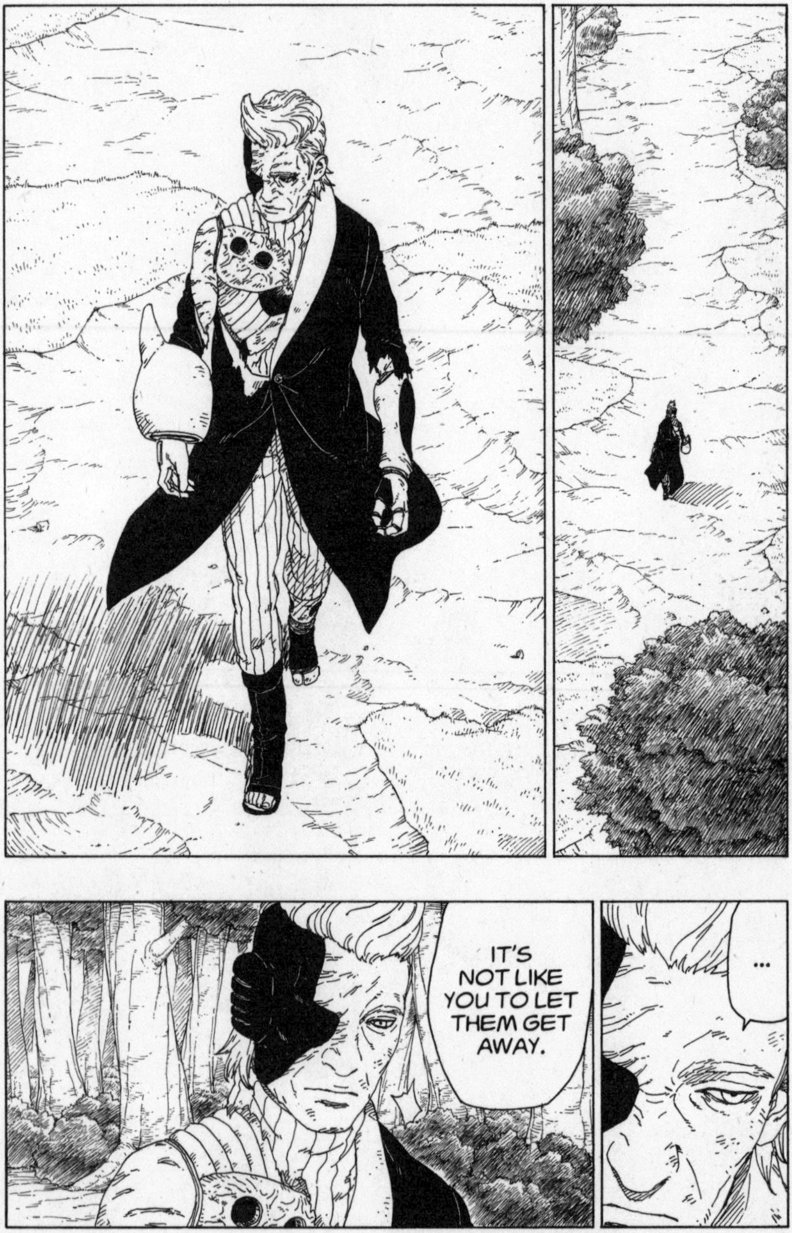
...
IT'S NOT LIKE YOU TO LET THEM GET AWAY.

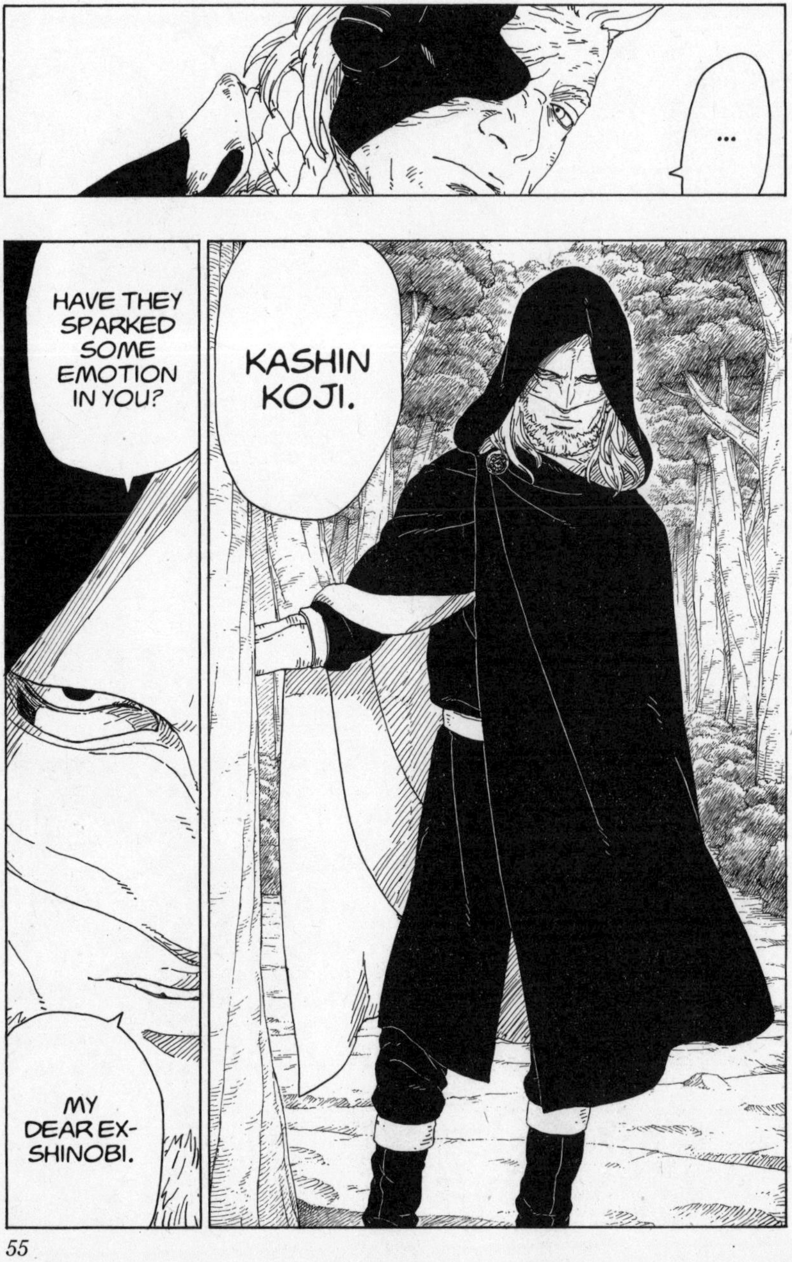
...
KASHIN KOJI.
HAVE THEY SPARKED SOME EMOTION IN YOU?
MY DEAR EX-SHINOBI.

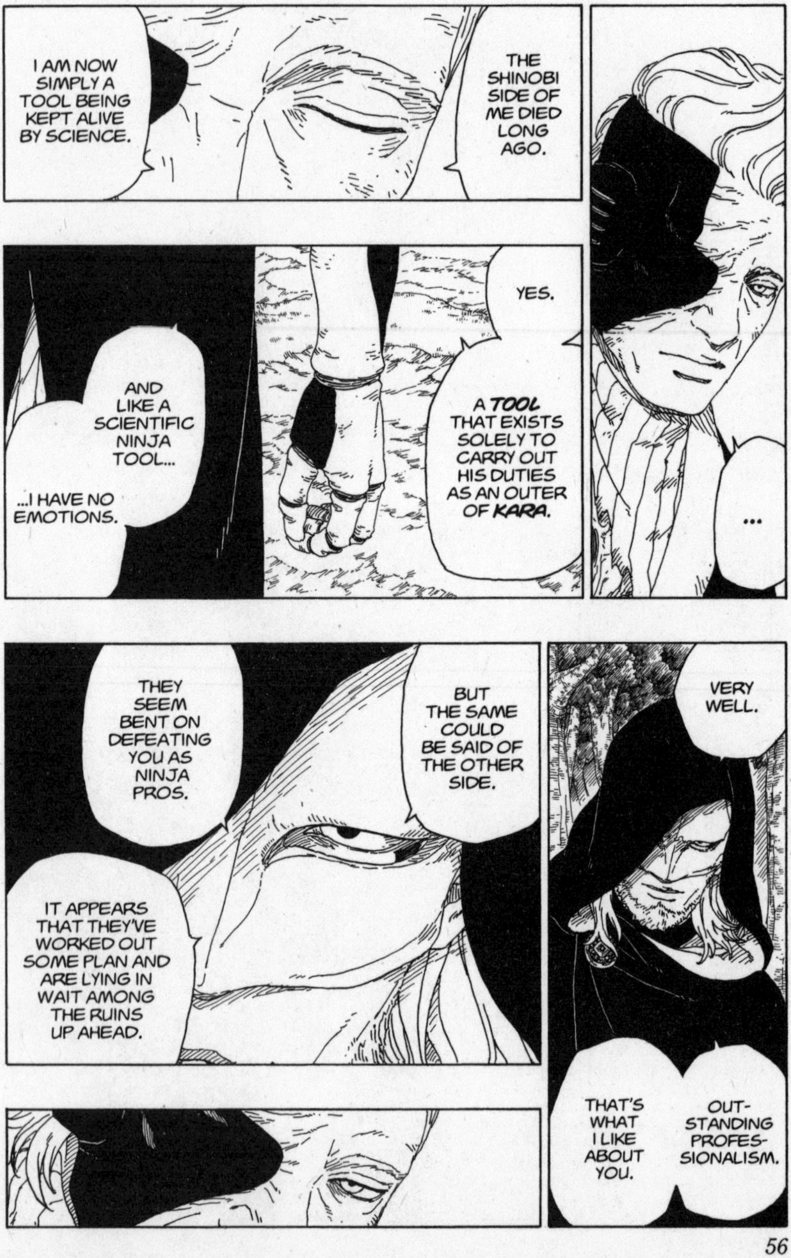
...
THE SHINOBI SIDE OF ME DIED LONG AGO.
I AM NOW SIMPLY A TOOL BEING KEPT ALIVE BY SCIENCE.
YES.
A ***TOOL*** THAT EXISTS SOLELY TO CARRY OUT HIS DUTIES AS AN OUTER OF ***KARA***.
AND LIKE A SCIENTIFIC NINJA TOOL...
...I HAVE NO EMOTIONS.
VERY WELL.
OUT-STANDING PROFES-SIONALISM.
THAT'S WHAT I LIKE ABOUT YOU.
BUT THE SAME COULD BE SAID OF THE OTHER SIDE.
THEY SEEM BENT ON DEFEATING YOU AS NINJA PROS.
IT APPEARS THAT THEY'VE WORKED OUT SOME PLAN AND ARE LYING IN WAIT AMONG THE RUINS UP AHEAD.

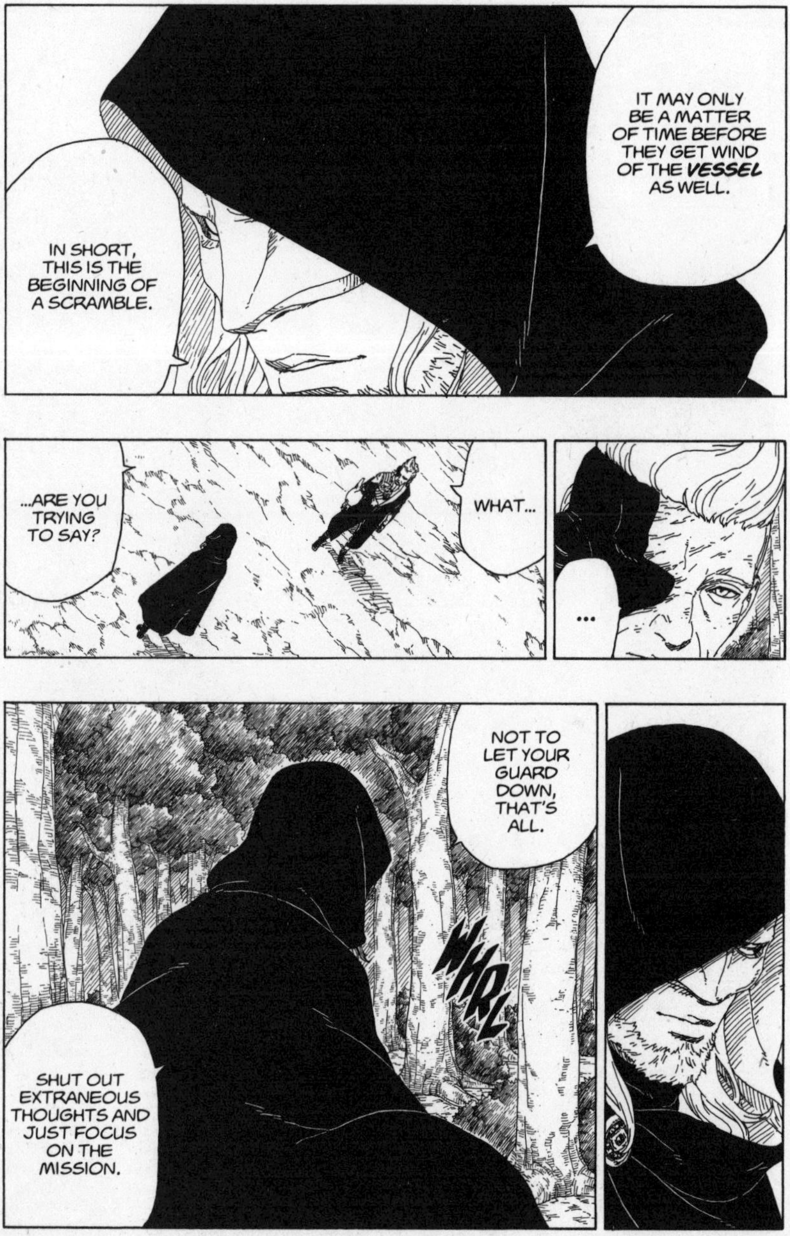
IT MAY ONLY BE A MATTER OF TIME BEFORE THEY GET WIND OF THE **VESSEL** AS WELL.
IN SHORT, THIS IS THE BEGINNING OF A SCRAMBLE.
...
WHAT...
...ARE YOU TRYING TO SAY?
NOT TO LET YOUR GUARD DOWN, THAT'S ALL.
WHRL
SHUT OUT EXTRANEOUS THOUGHTS AND JUST FOCUS ON THE MISSION.

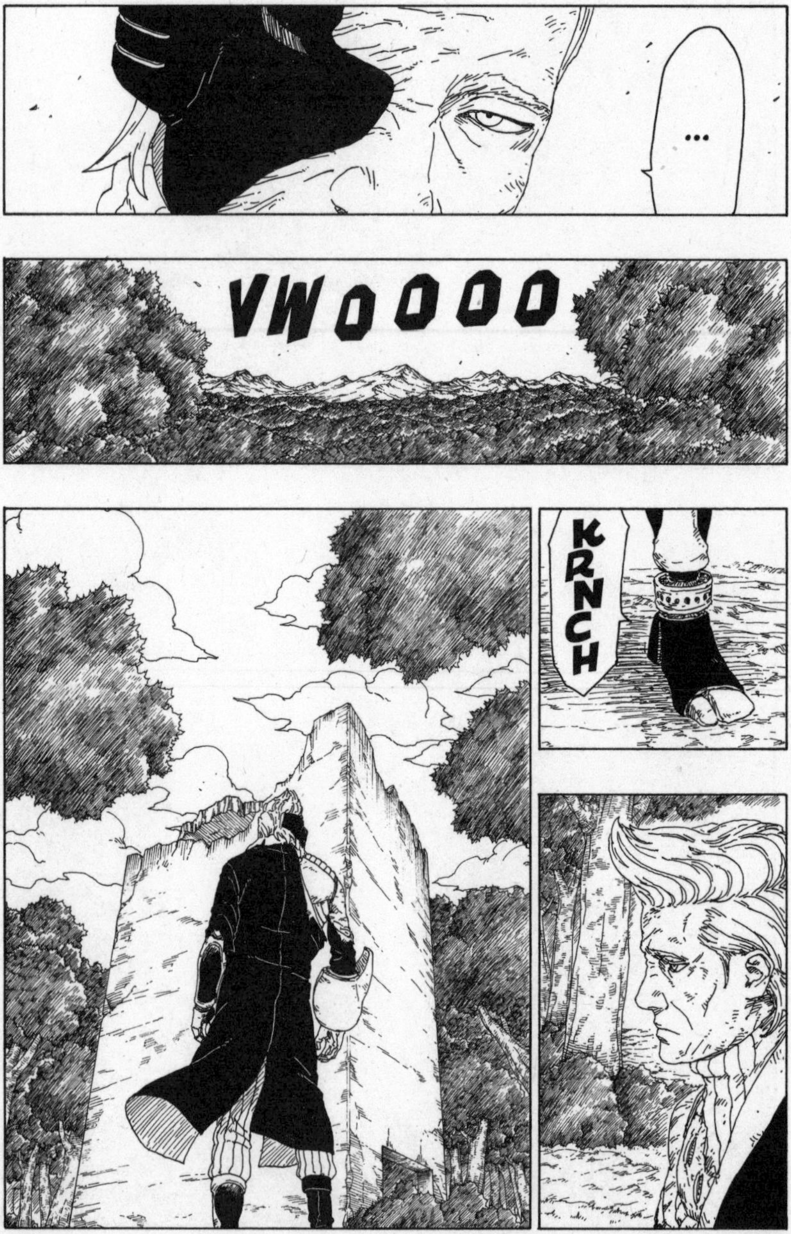
...
VWOOOO
KRNCH

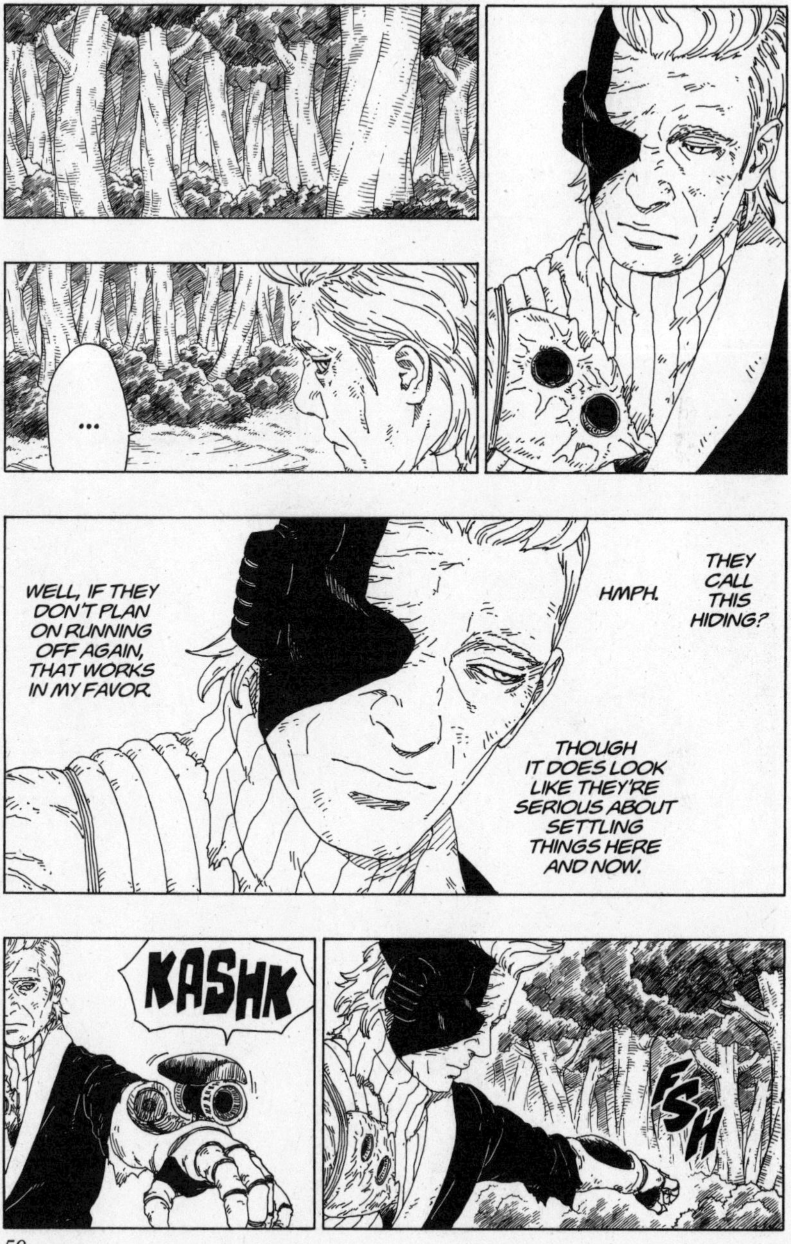
...
THEY CALL THIS HIDING?
HMPH.
THOUGH IT DOES LOOK LIKE THEY'RE SERIOUS ABOUT SETTLING THINGS HERE AND NOW.
WELL, IF THEY DON'T PLAN ON RUNNING OFF AGAIN, THAT WORKS IN MY FAVOR.
FSH
KASHK

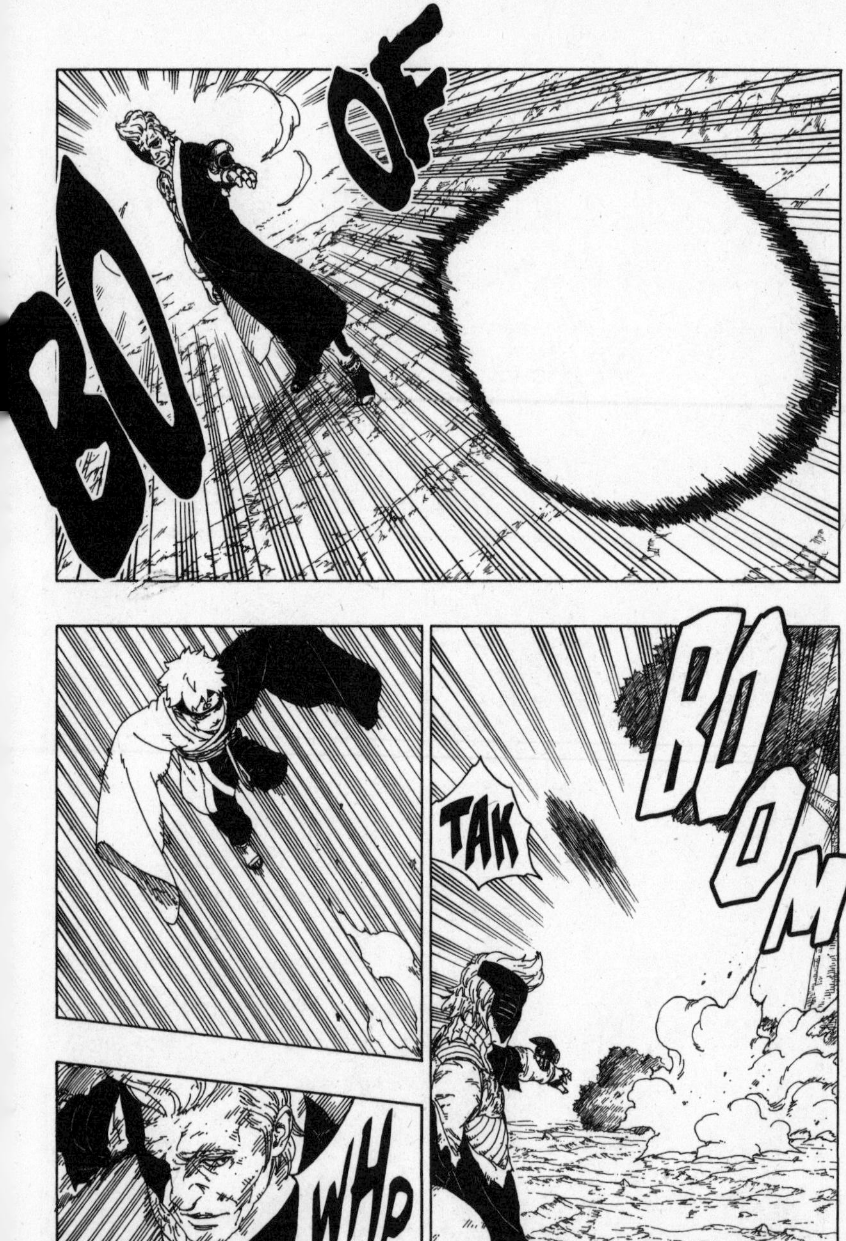
BOOF
BOOM
TAK
WHP

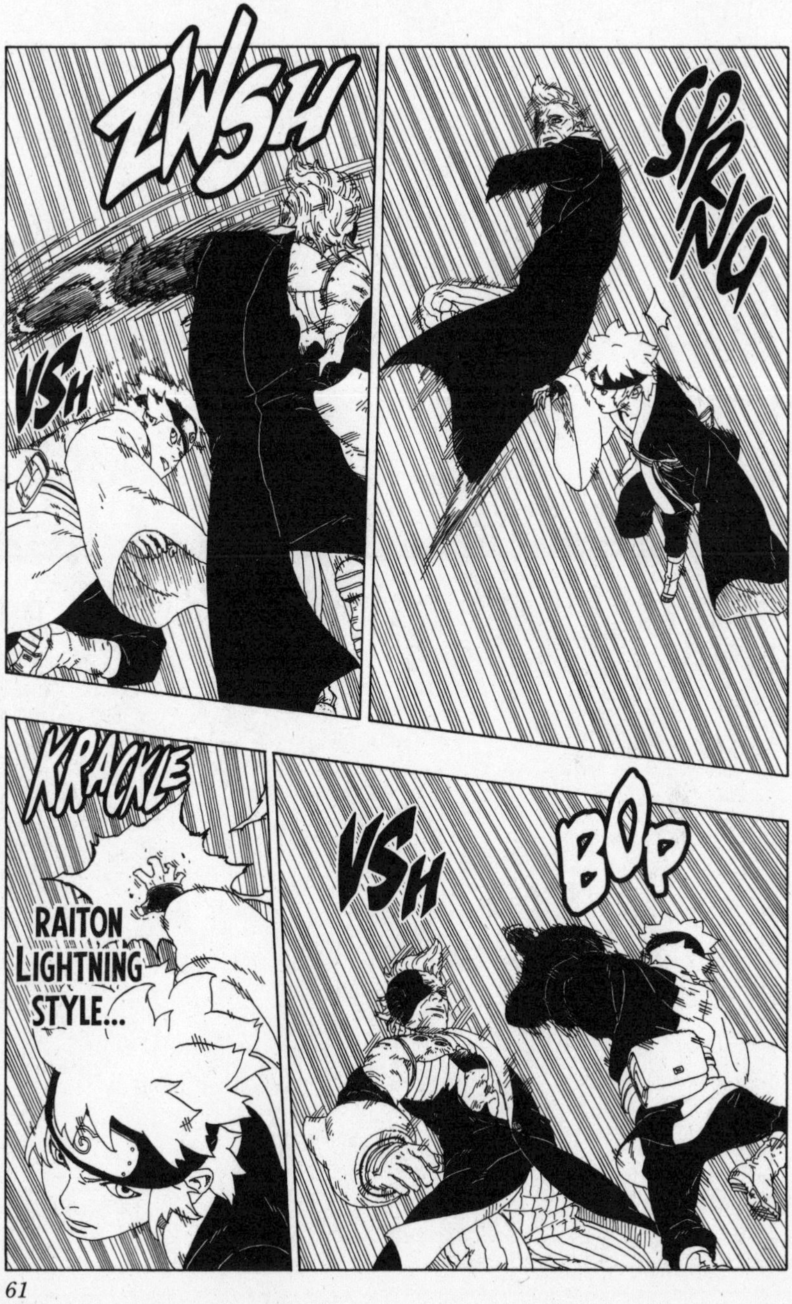
SPRNG
ZWSH
VSH
BOP
VSH
KRACKLE
RAITON
LIGHTNING
STYLE...

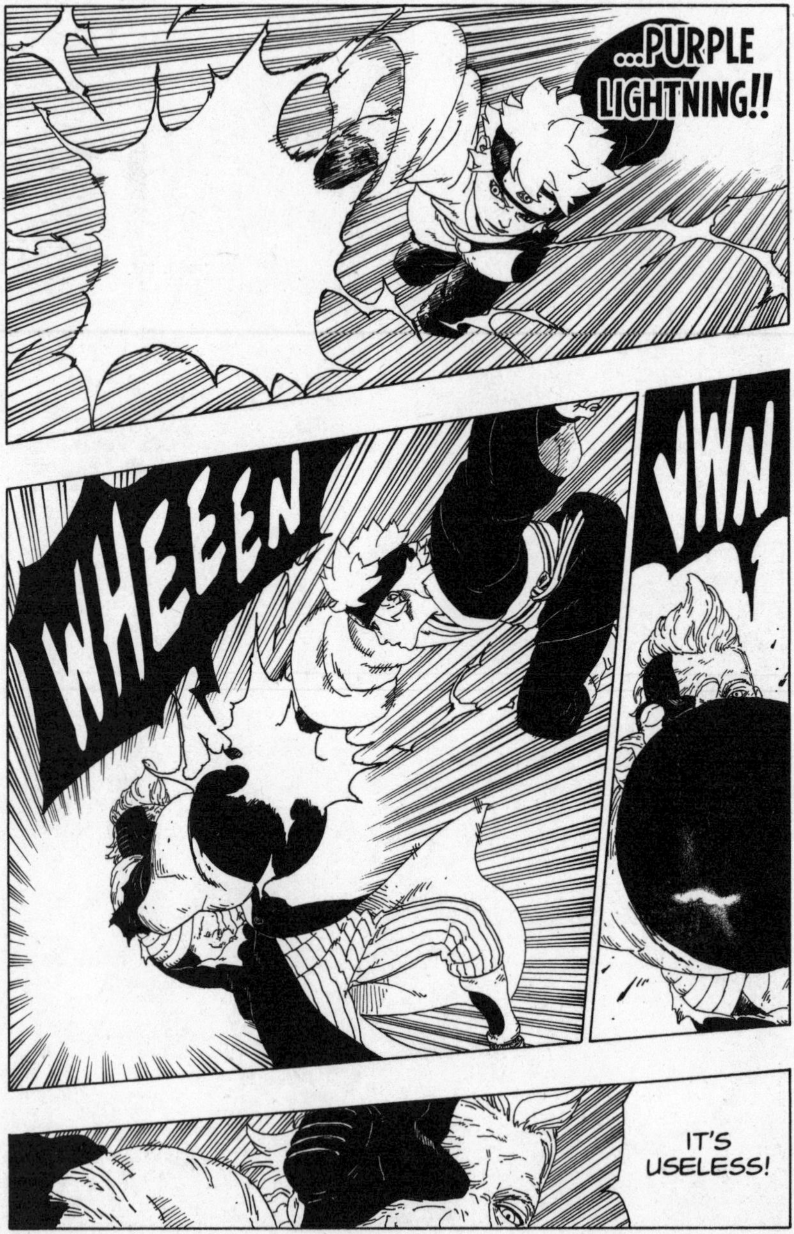
...PURPLE LIGHTNING!!
VWN
WHEEEN
IT'S USELESS!

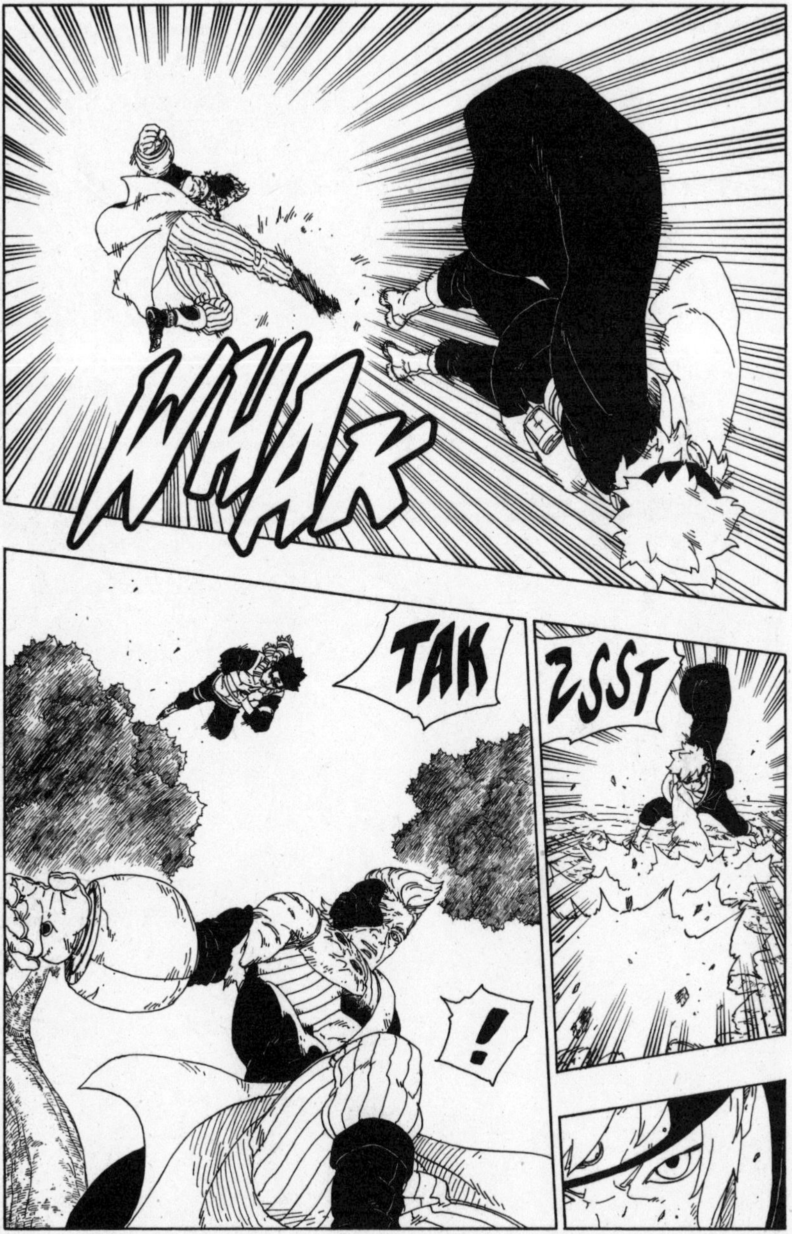
WHAK
ZSST
TAK
!

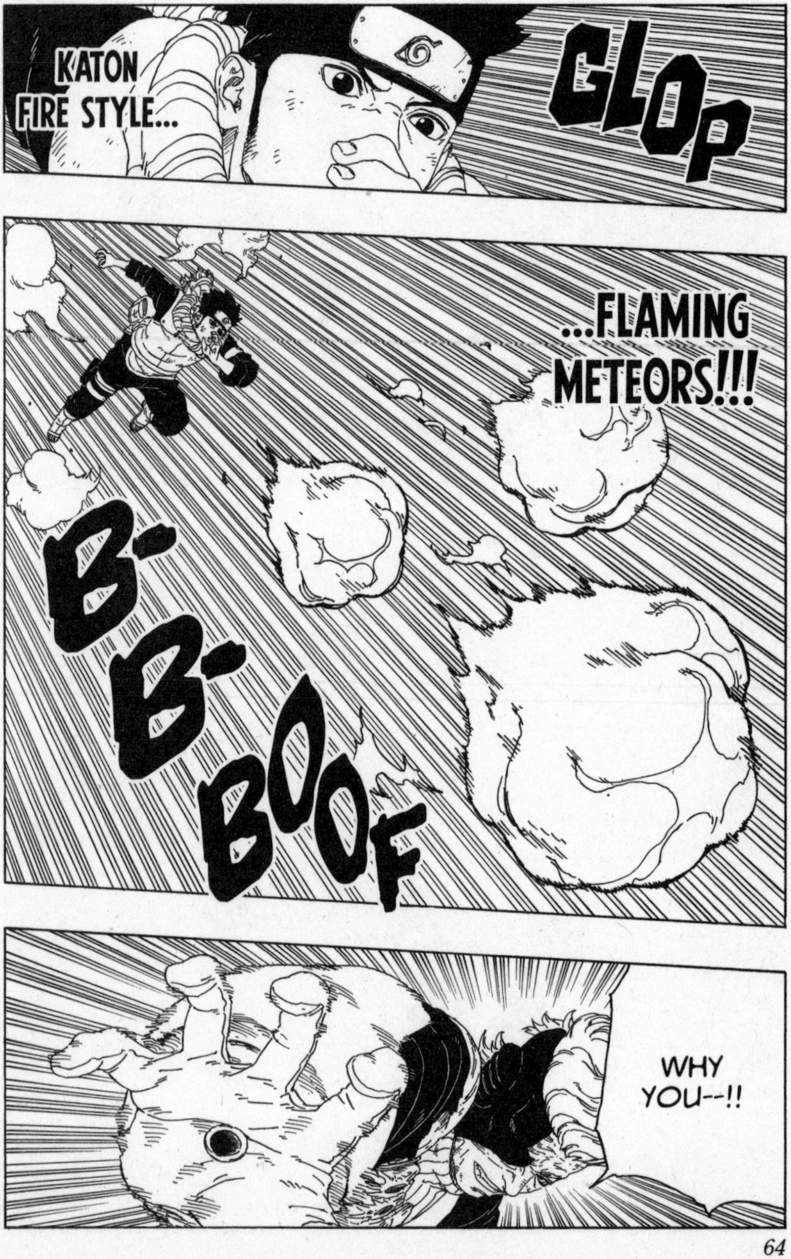
GLOP
KATON FIRE STYLE...
...FLAMING METEORS!!!
B-B-BOOF
WHY YOU--!!

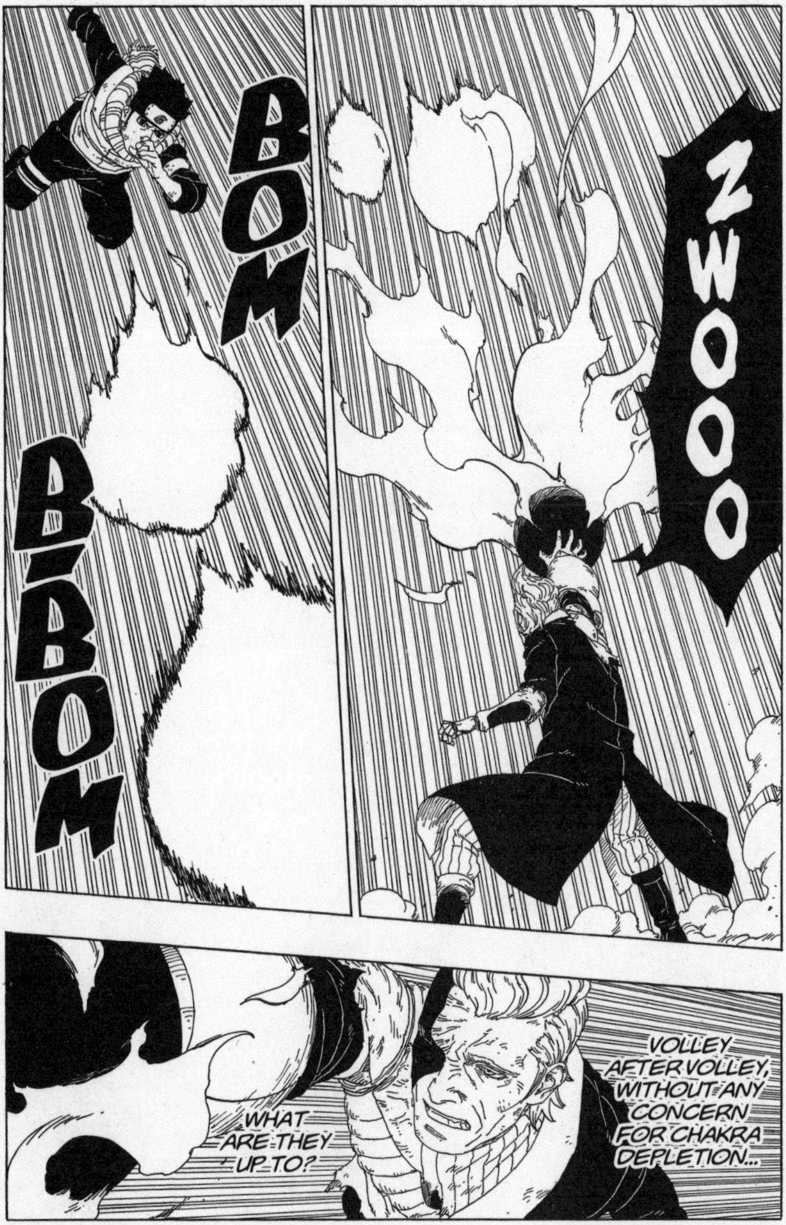
ZWOOO
BOM
BABOM
VOLLEY AFTER VOLLEY, WITHOUT ANY CONCERN FOR CHAKRA DEPLETION...
WHAT ARE THEY UP TO?

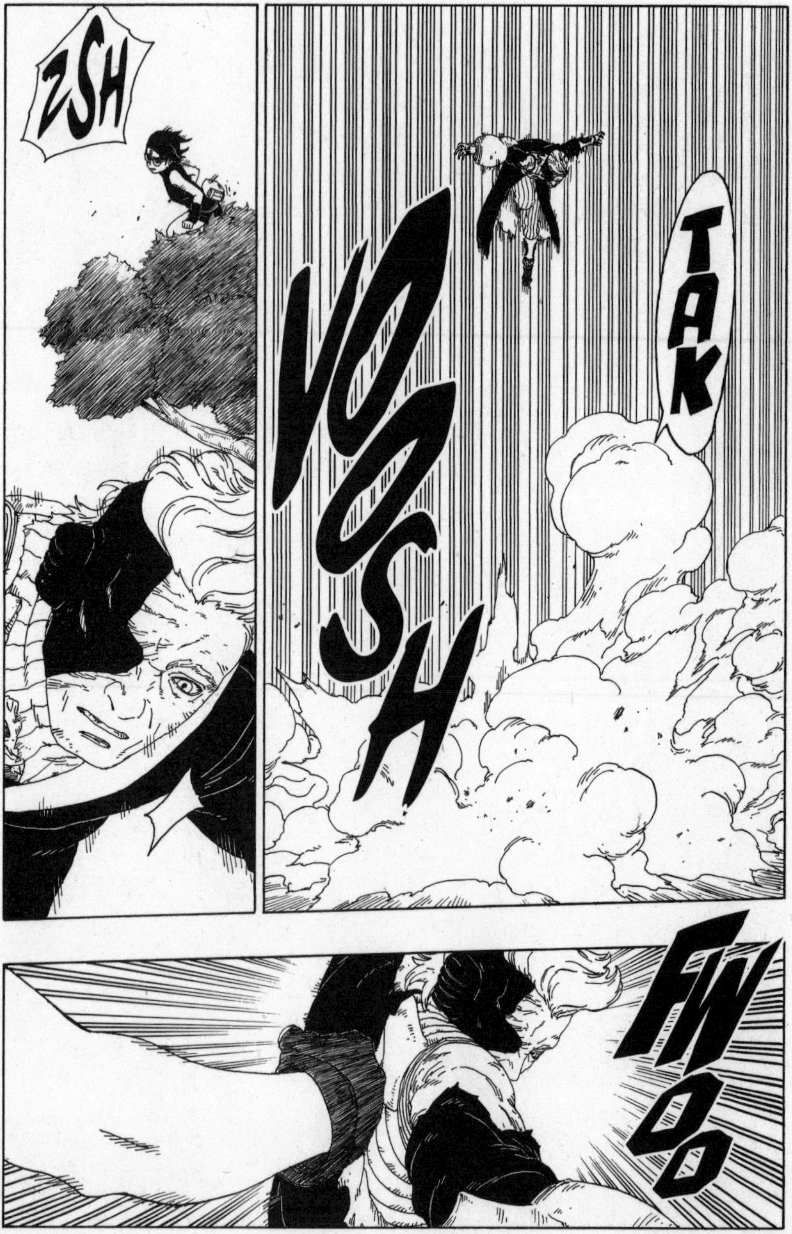
TAK
VOOSH
ZSH
FWOO

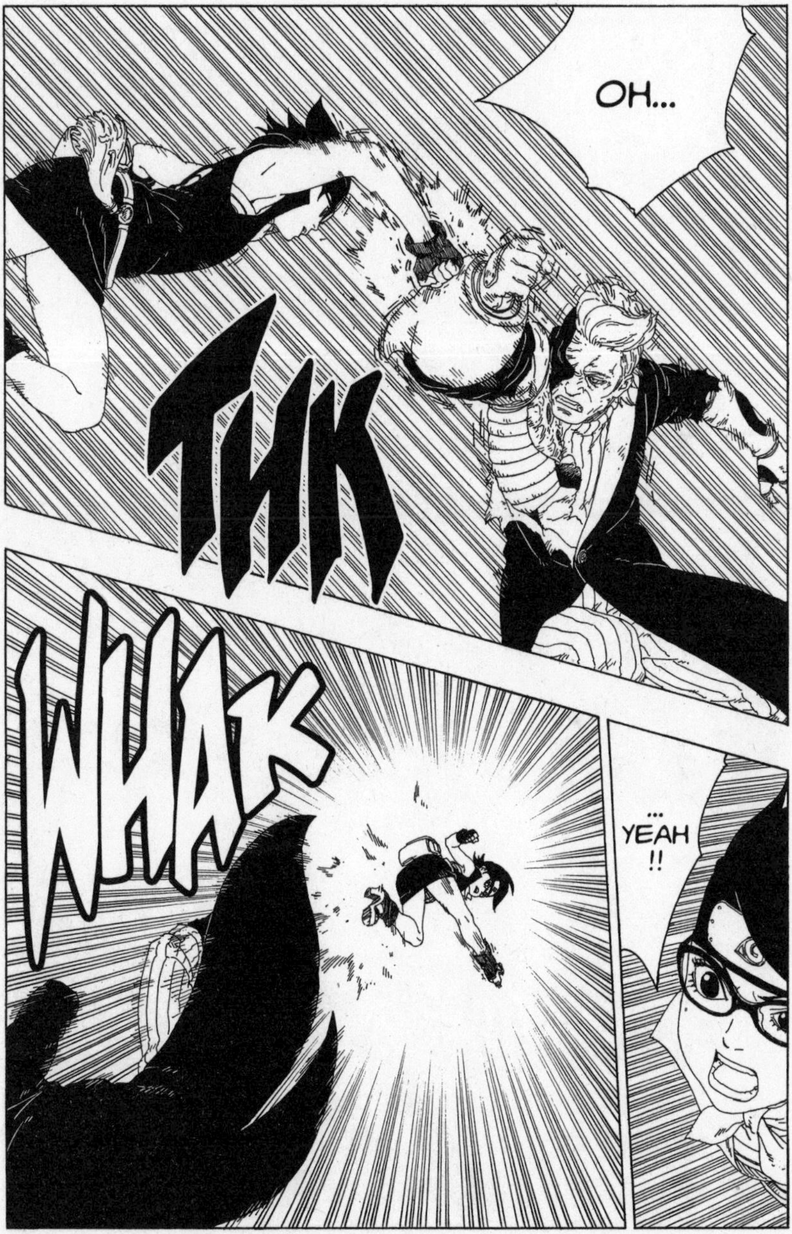
OH...
THK
...YEAH!!
WHAK

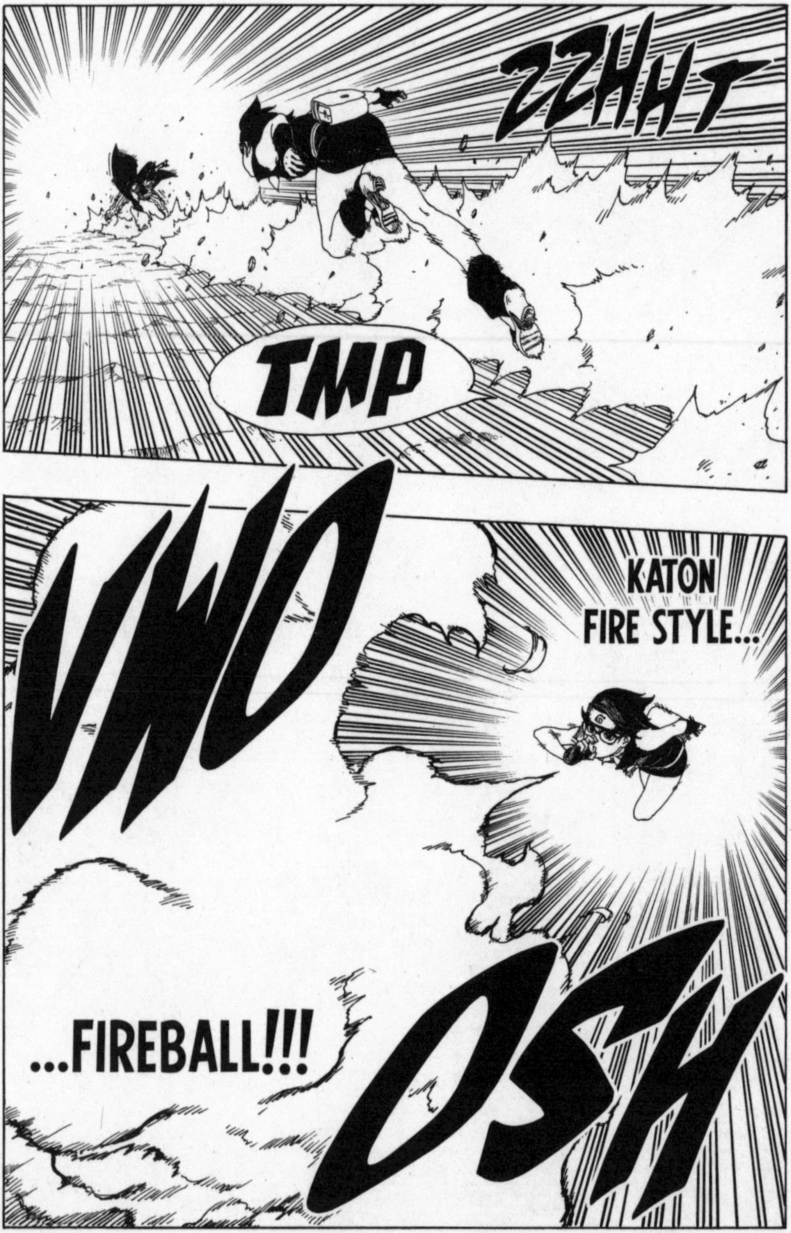
ZZHHT
TMP
KATON FIRE STYLE...
VWO
OSH
...FIREBALL!!!

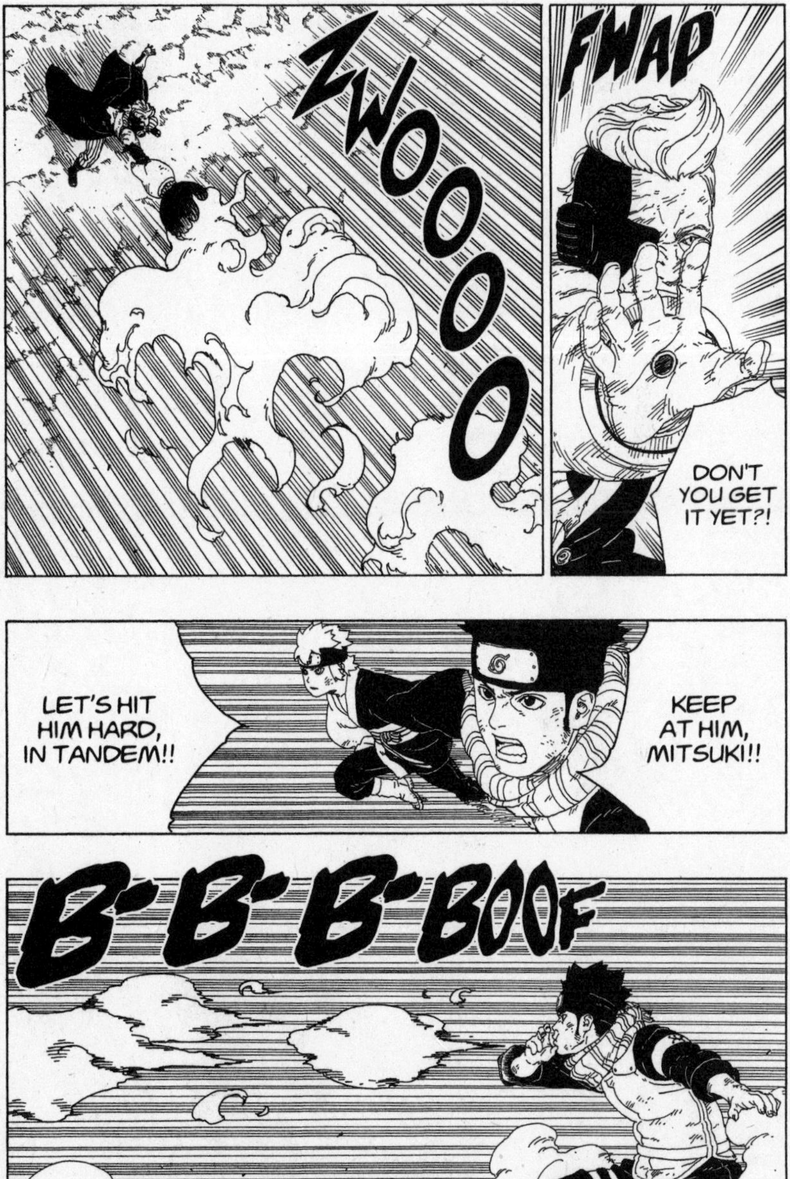
FWAP
DON'T YOU GET IT YET?!
ZWOOOOO
KEEP AT HIM, MITSUKI!!
LET'S HIT HIM HARD, IN TANDEM!!
B-B-B-BOOF

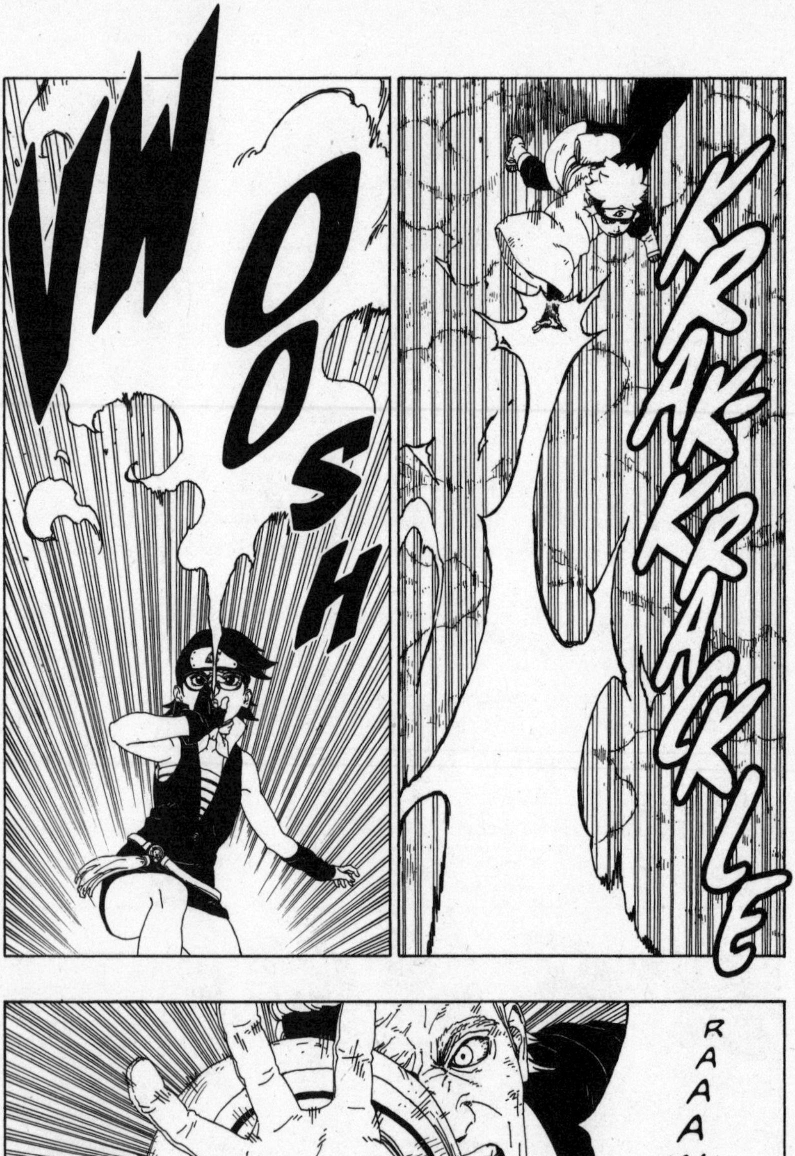
KRAKKRACKLE
VWOOSH
RAAAWR!!

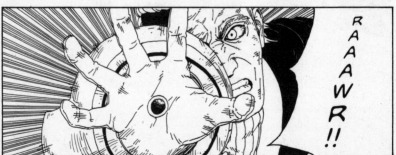

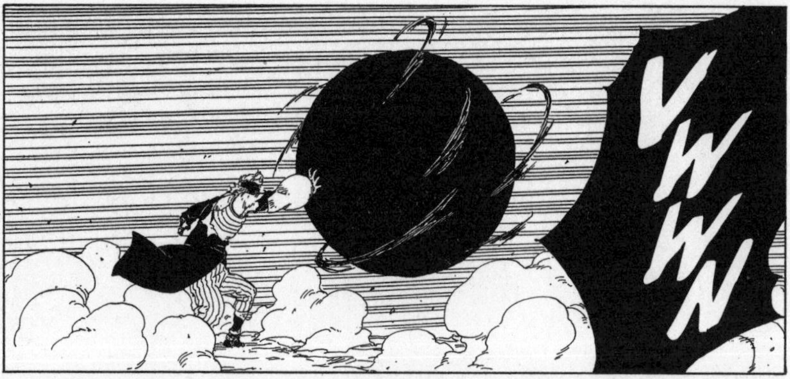
VWWN

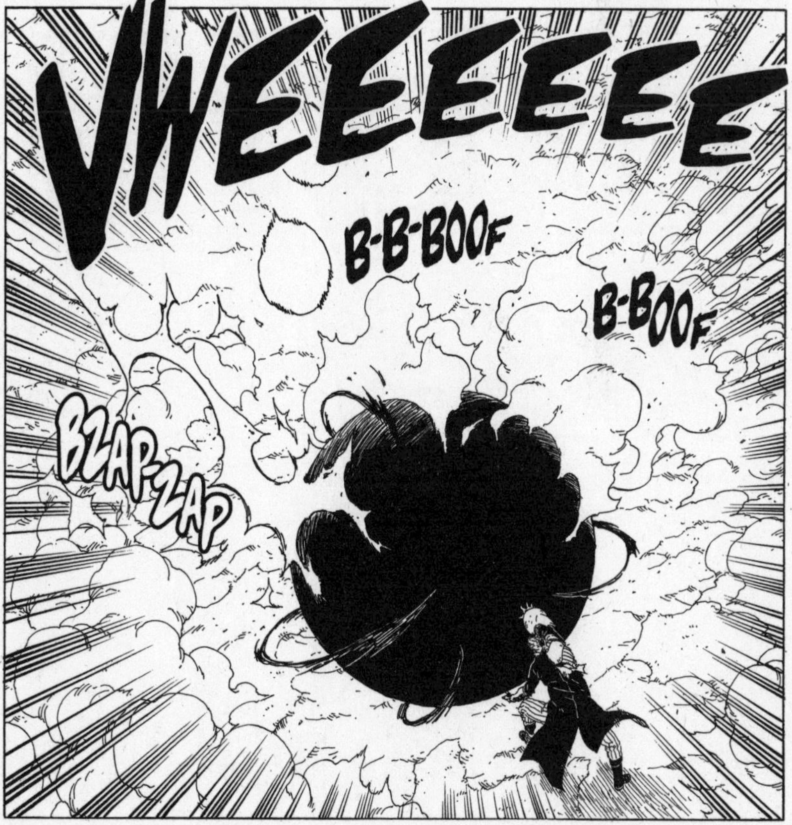
VWEEEEEE
B-B-BOOF
B-BOOF
BZAP-ZAP

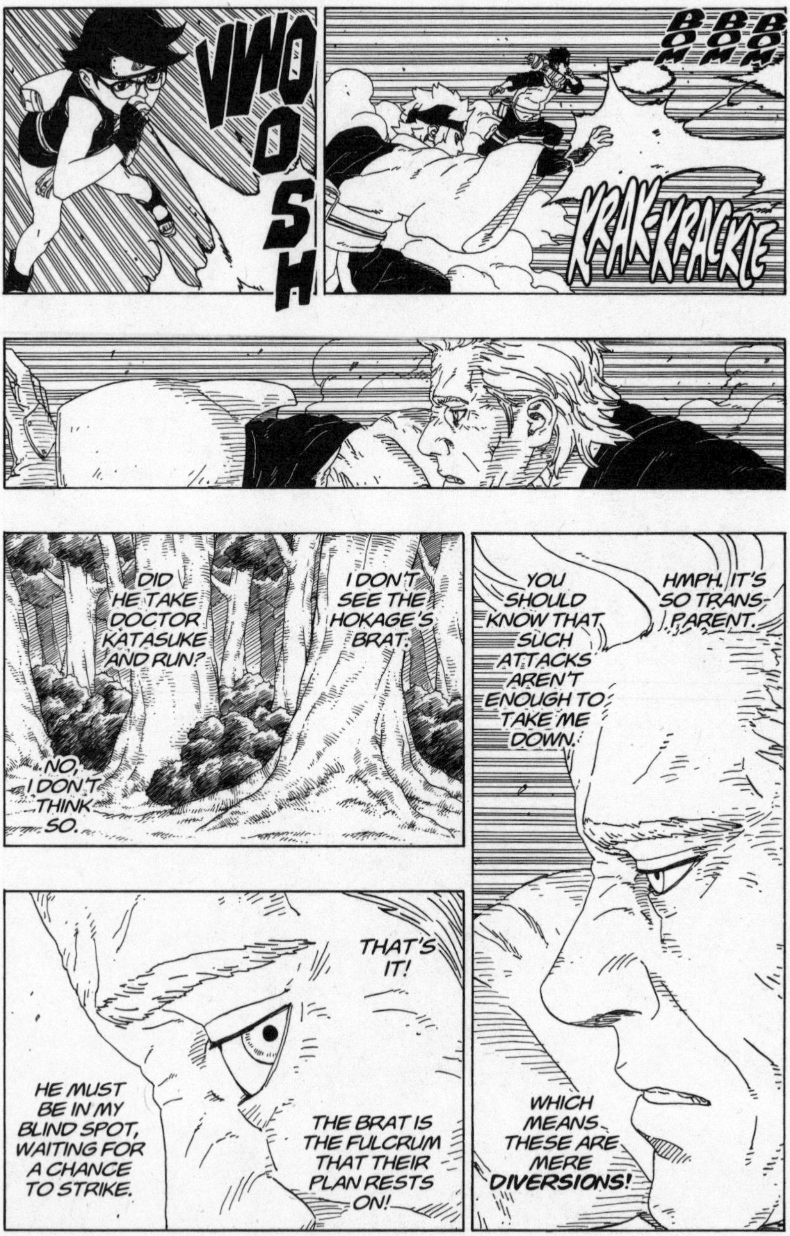
BOOM BOOM BOOM
KRAK-KRACKLE
VWOOSH
HMPH. IT'S SO TRANS-PARENT.
YOU SHOULD KNOW THAT SUCH ATTACKS AREN'T ENOUGH TO TAKE ME DOWN.
WHICH MEANS THESE ARE MERE **DIVERSIONS!**
I DON'T SEE THE HOKAGE'S BRAT.
DID HE TAKE DOCTOR KATASUKE AND RUN?
NO, I DON'T THINK SO.
THAT'S IT!
THE BRAT IS THE FULCRUM THAT THEIR PLAN RESTS ON!
HE MUST BE IN MY BLIND SPOT, WAITING FOR A CHANCE TO STRIKE.

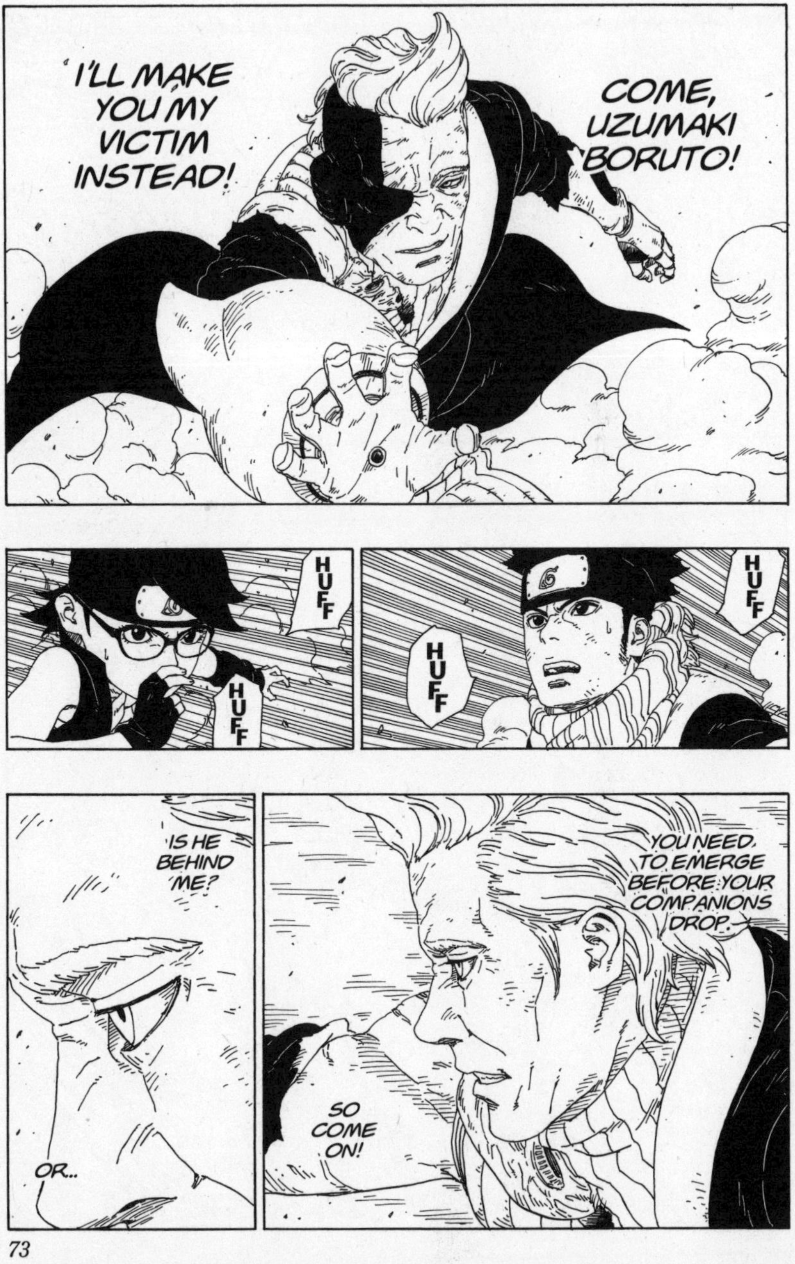
COME, UZUMAKI BORUTO!
I'LL MAKE YOU MY VICTIM INSTEAD!
HUFF
HUFF
HUFF
HUFF
YOU NEED TO EMERGE BEFORE YOUR COMPANIONS DROP.
SO COME ON!
IS HE BEHIND ME?
OR...

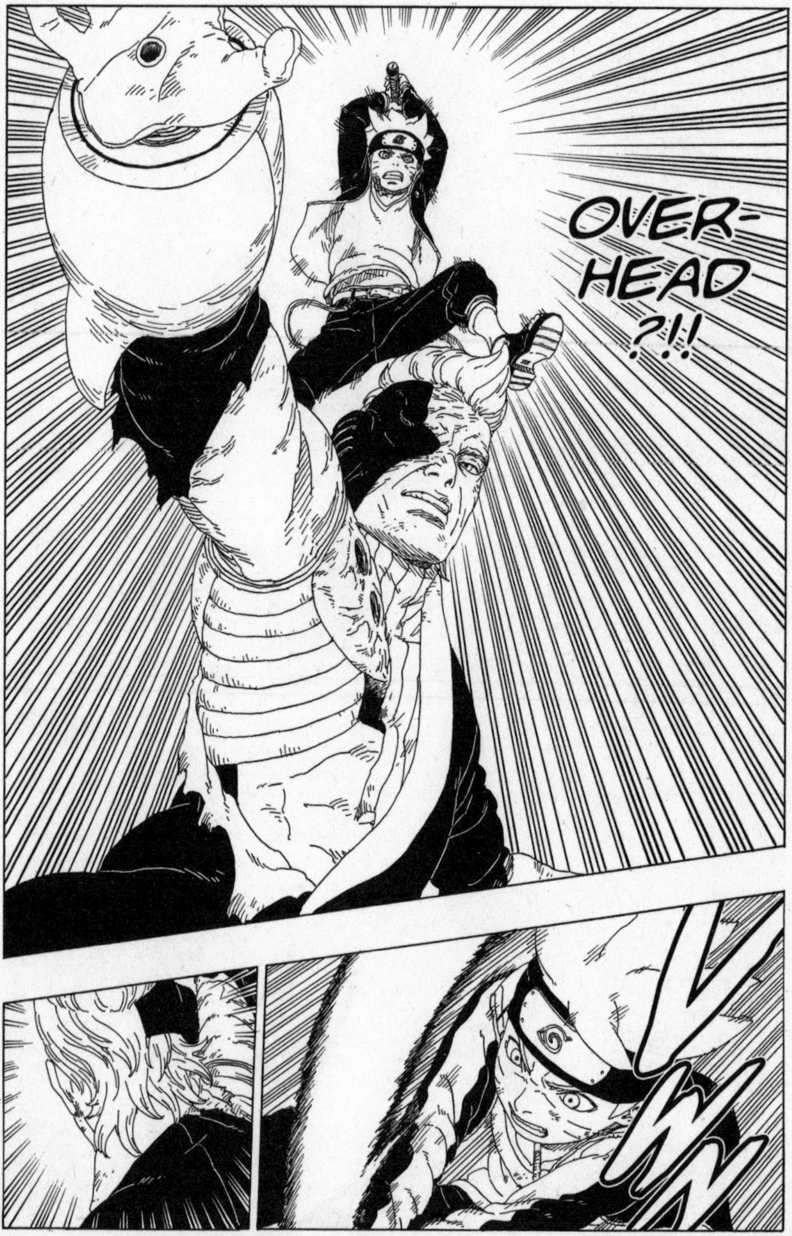
OVER-HEAD ?!!

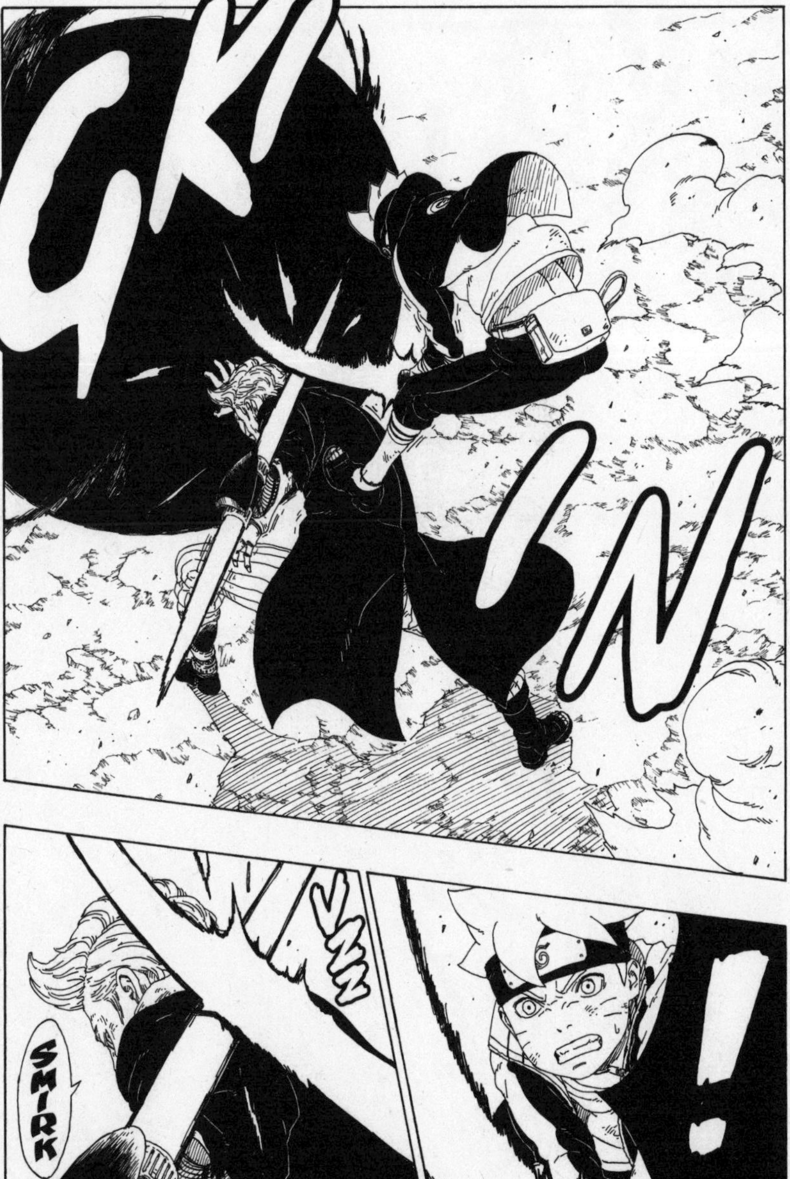
!
SMIRK

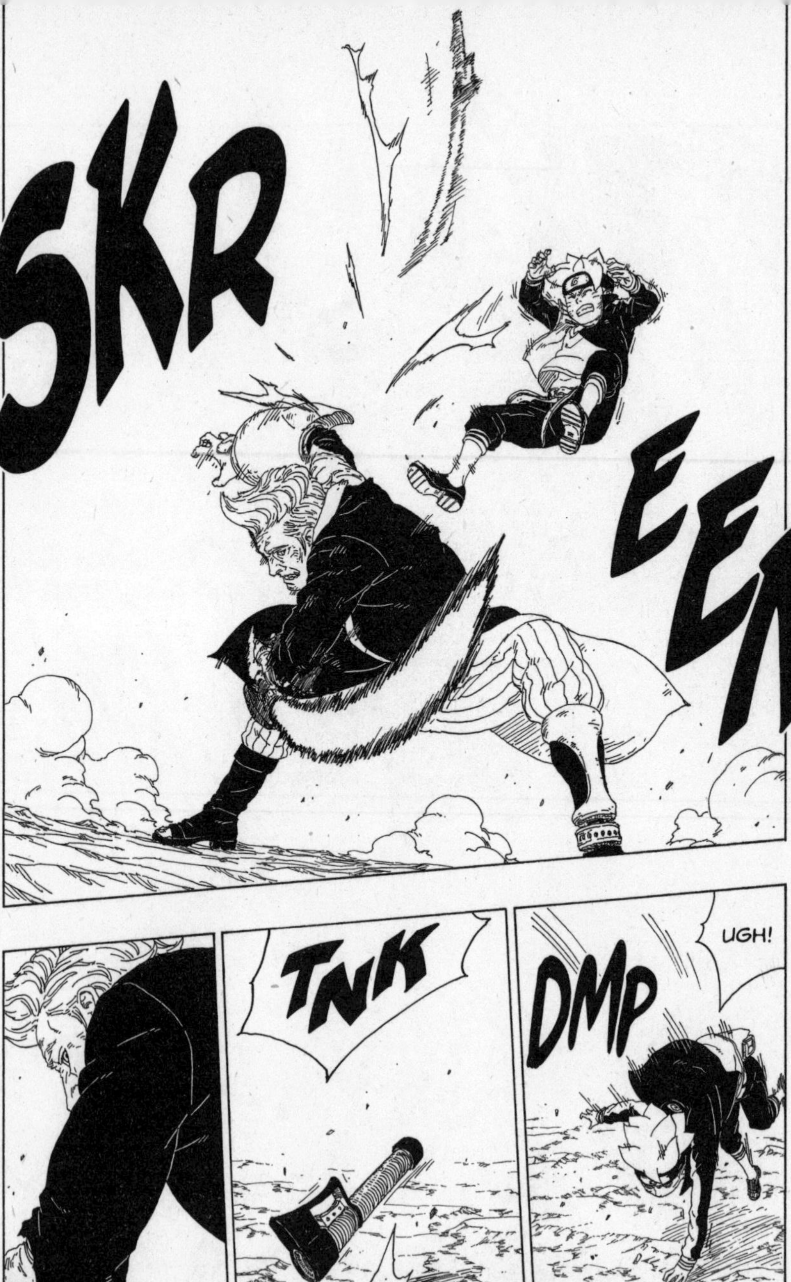
SKR
EEN
UGH!
DMP
TNK

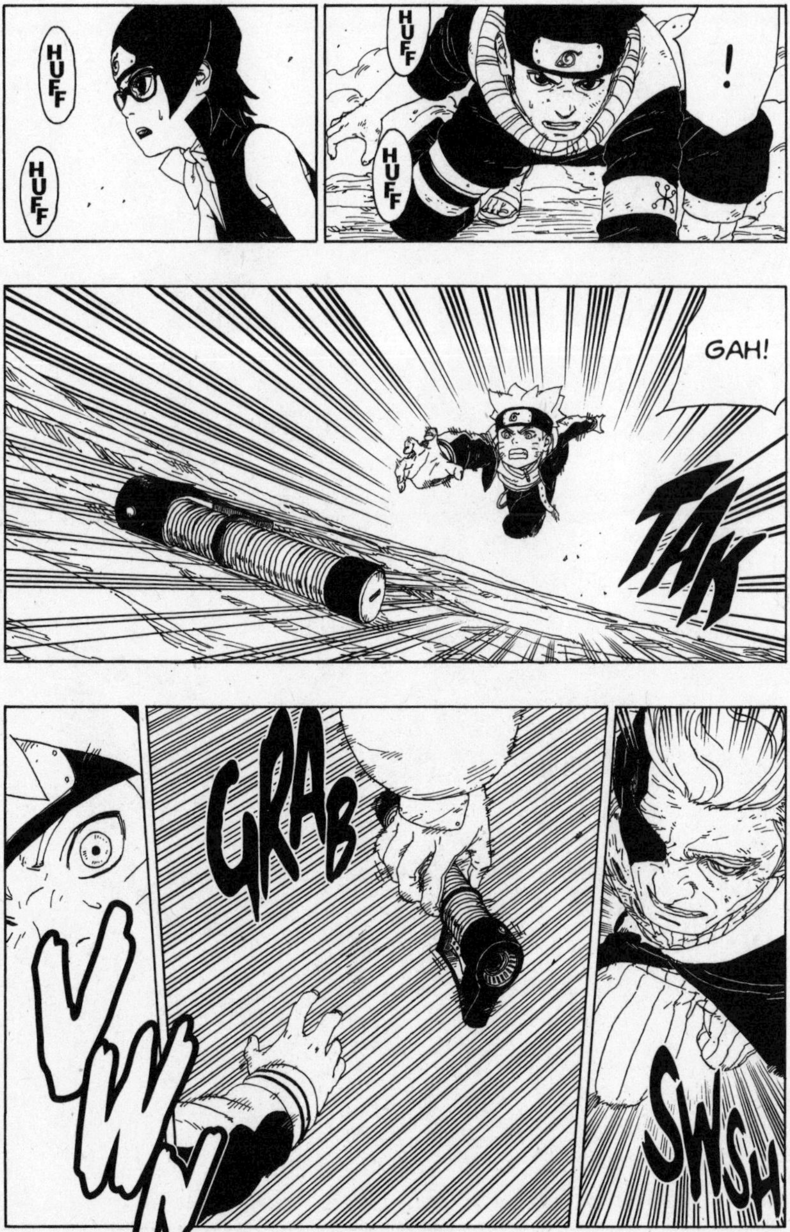
HUFF
HUFF
!
HUFF
HUFF
GAH!
TAK
SWSH
GRAB
VWN

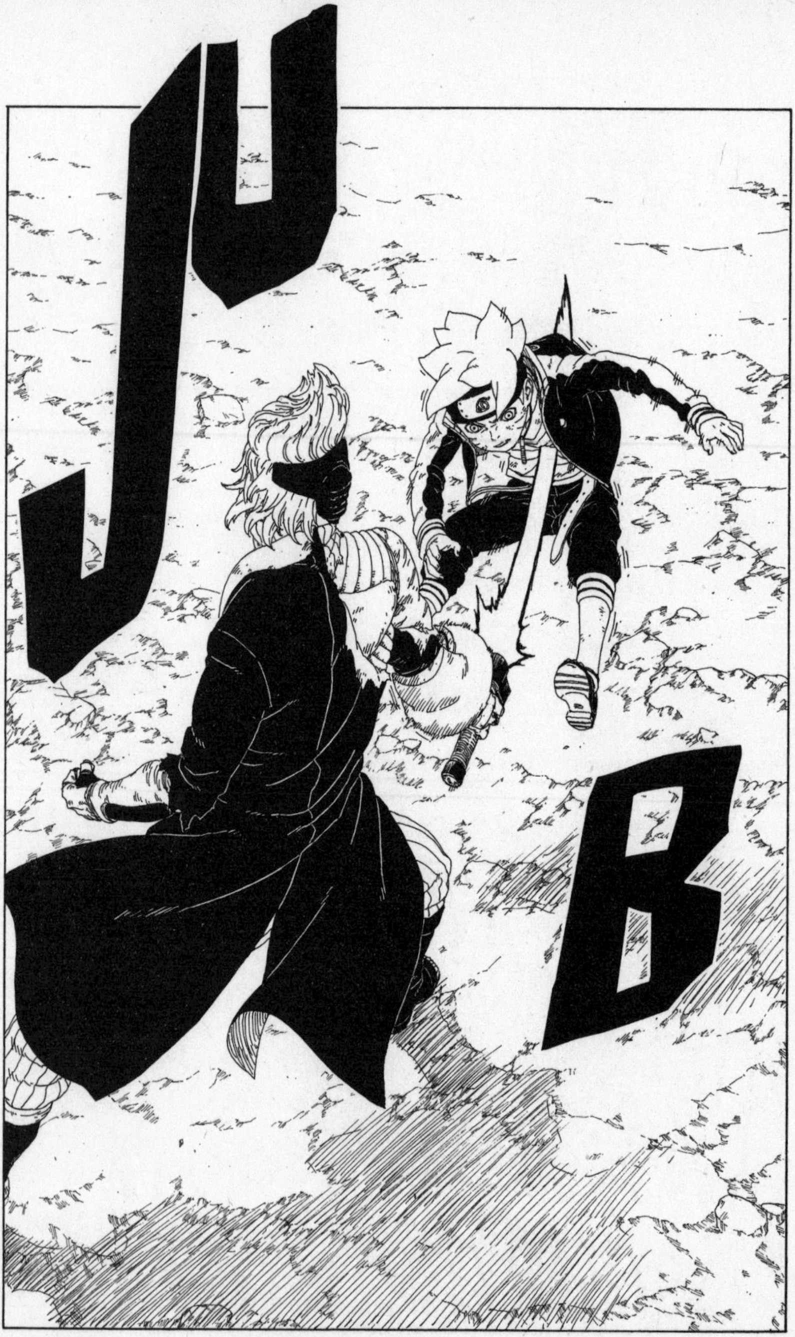
JU
B

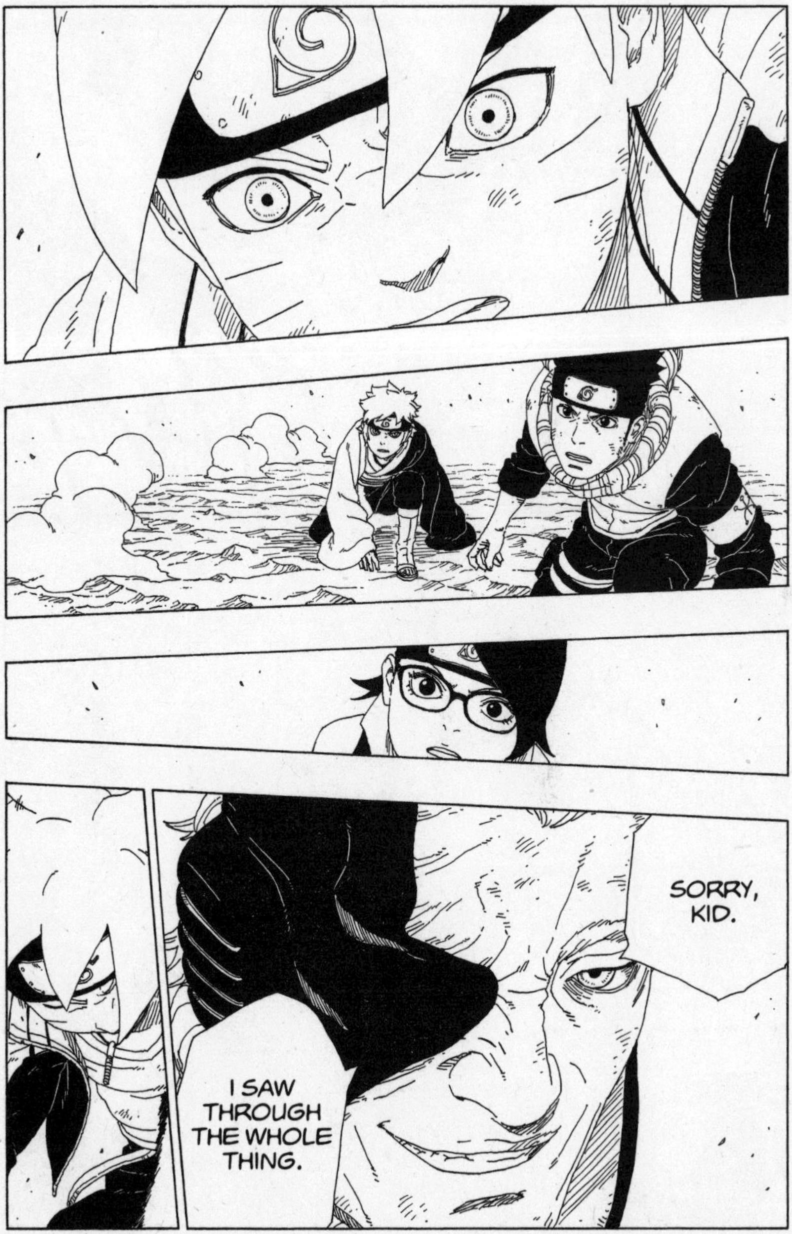
SORRY, KID.
I SAW THROUGH THE WHOLE THING.

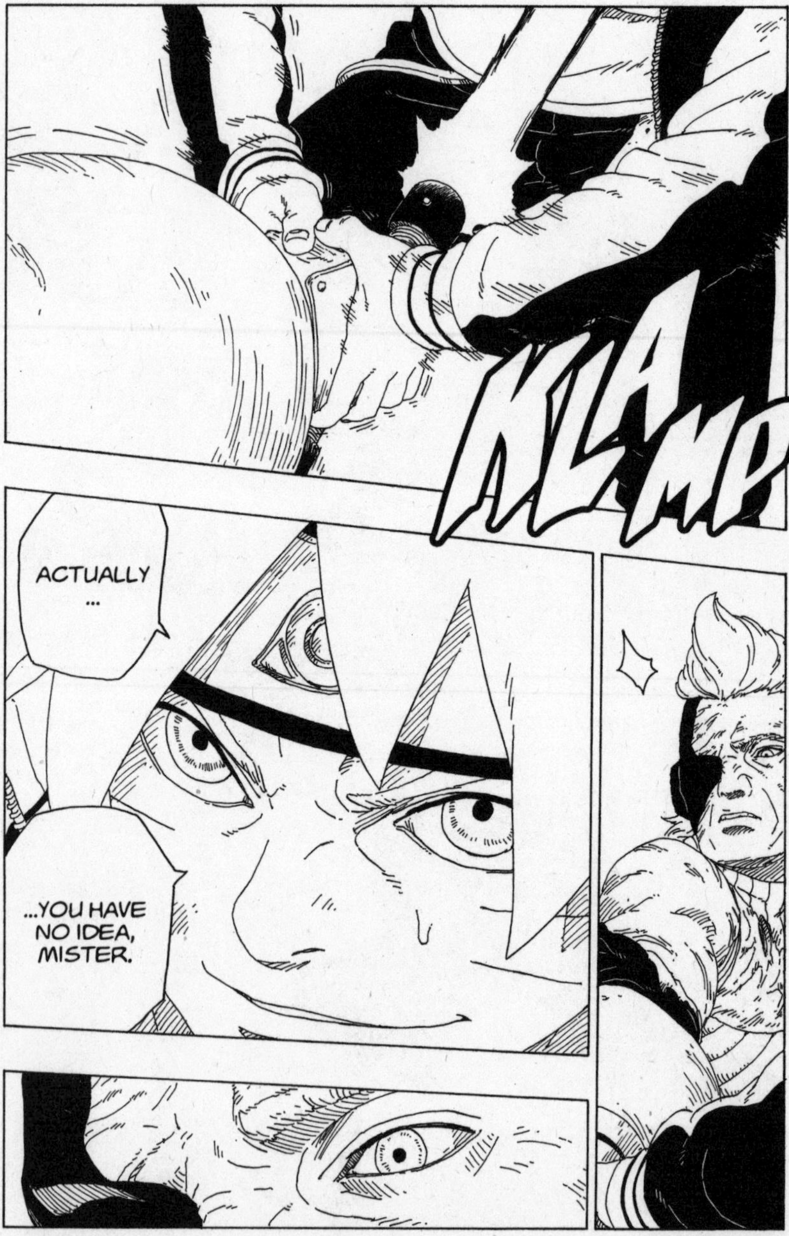
KLAMP
ACTUALLY ...
...YOU HAVE NO IDEA, MISTER.

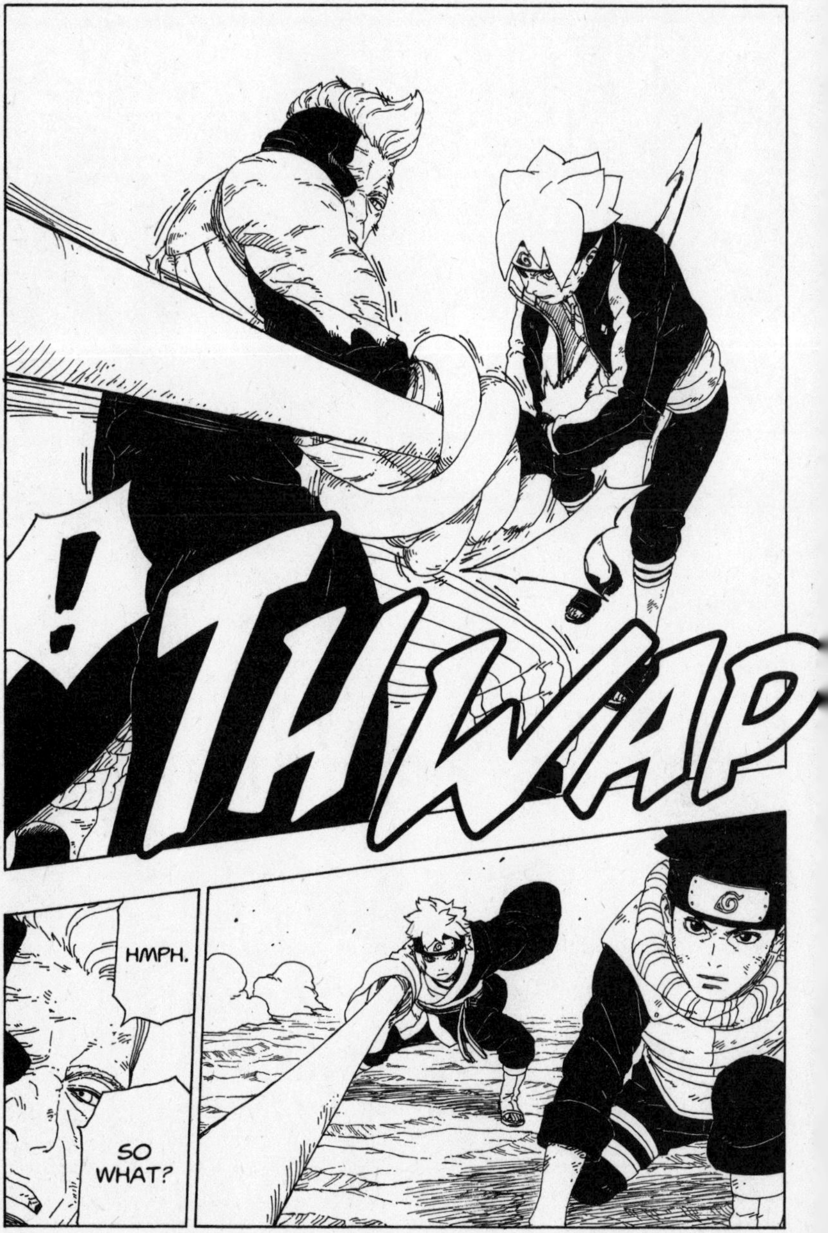
!
THWAP
HMPH.
SO WHAT?

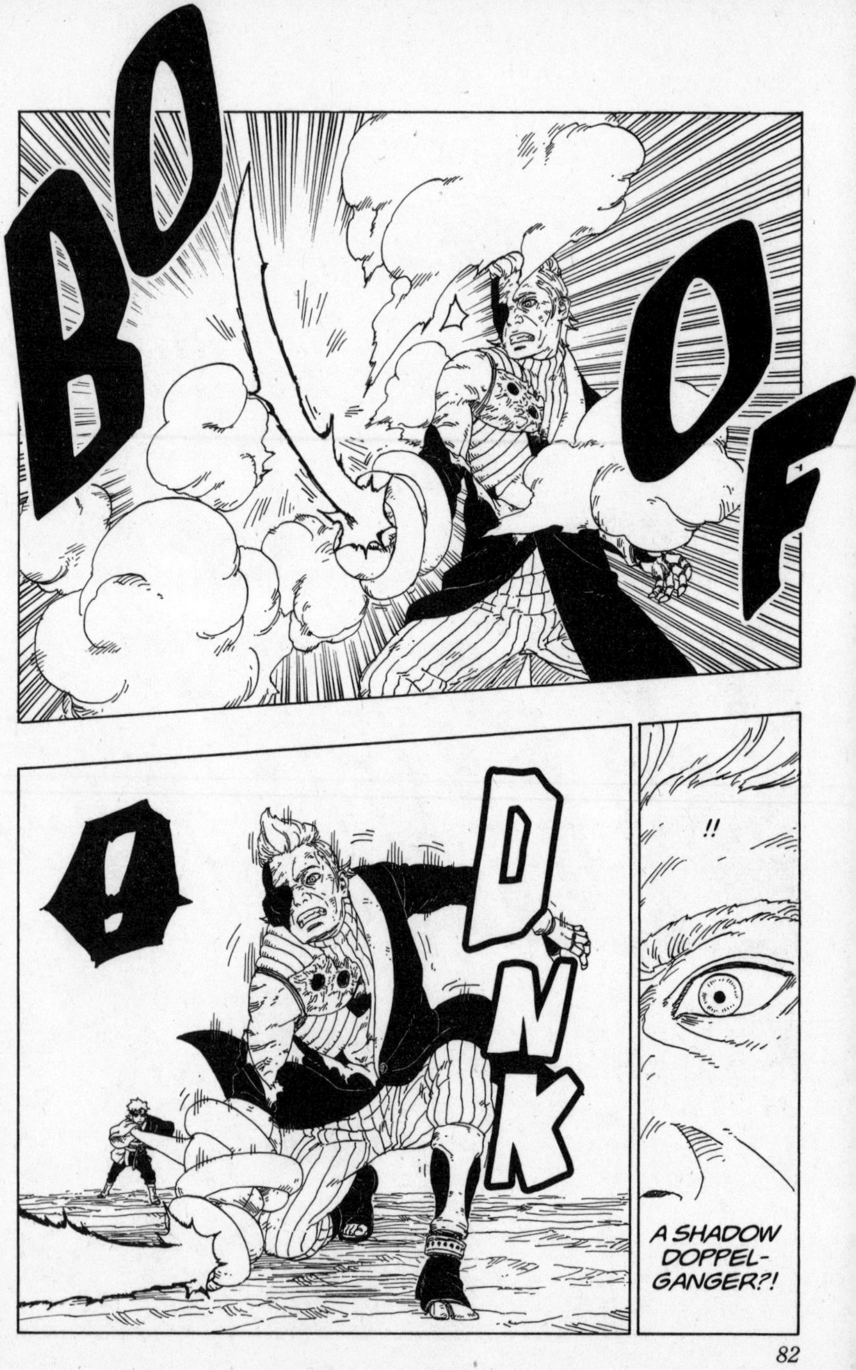
BOOF
!!
A SHADOW DOPPEL-GANGER?!
DNK
!

WHAT THE...?!
THIS SCIENTIFIC NINJA TOOL...
IT'S DRAINING...
...MY STRENGTH?!
GAH!
KACHK
B-BOOM
UNH!
SSSH

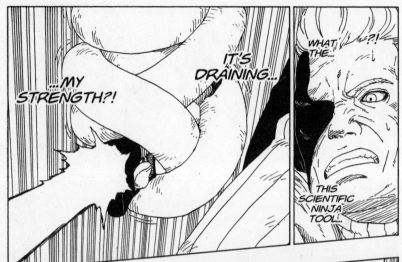

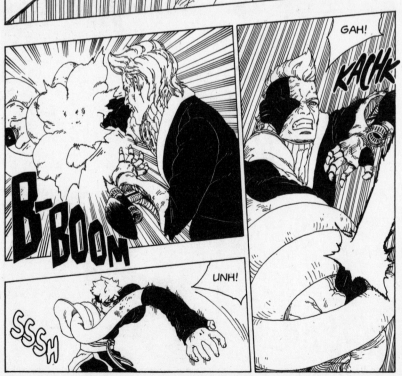

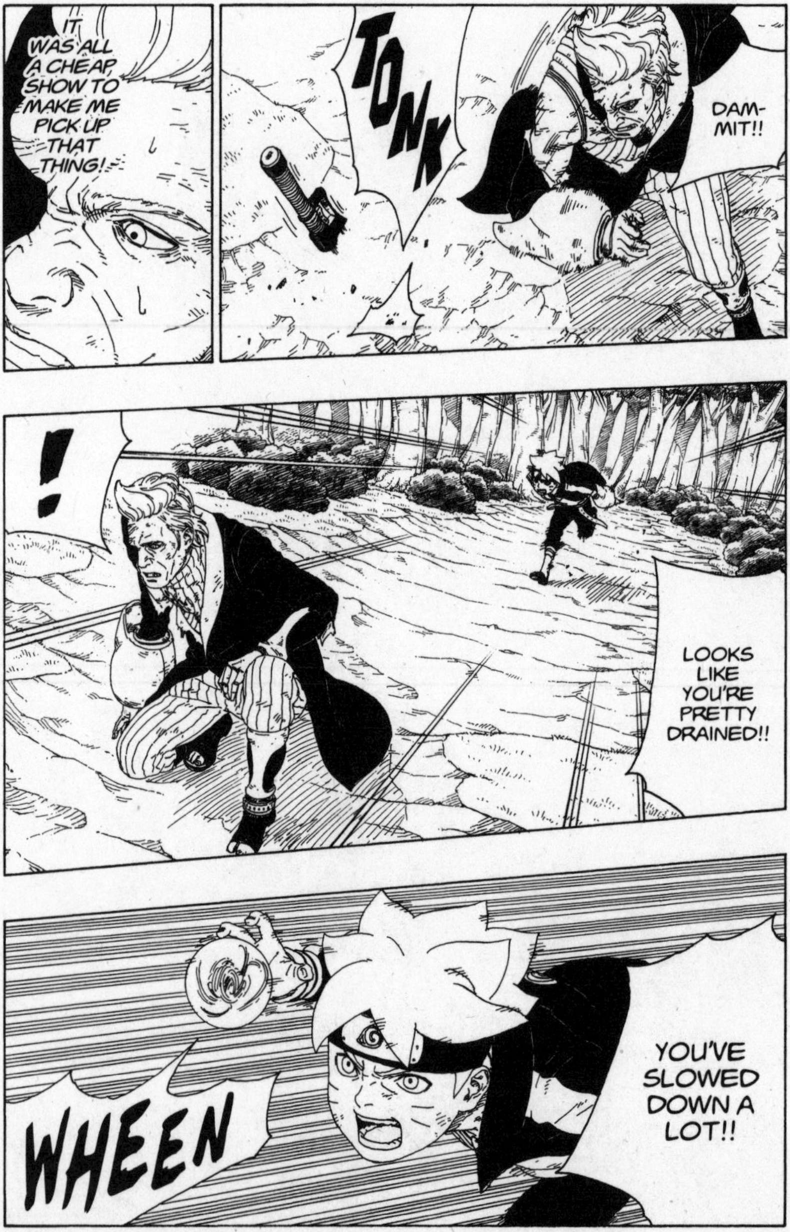
TONK
DAM-MIT!!
IT WAS ALL A CHEAP SHOW TO MAKE ME PICK UP THAT THING!
!
LOOKS LIKE YOU'RE PRETTY DRAINED!!
YOU'VE SLOWED DOWN A LOT!!
WHEEN

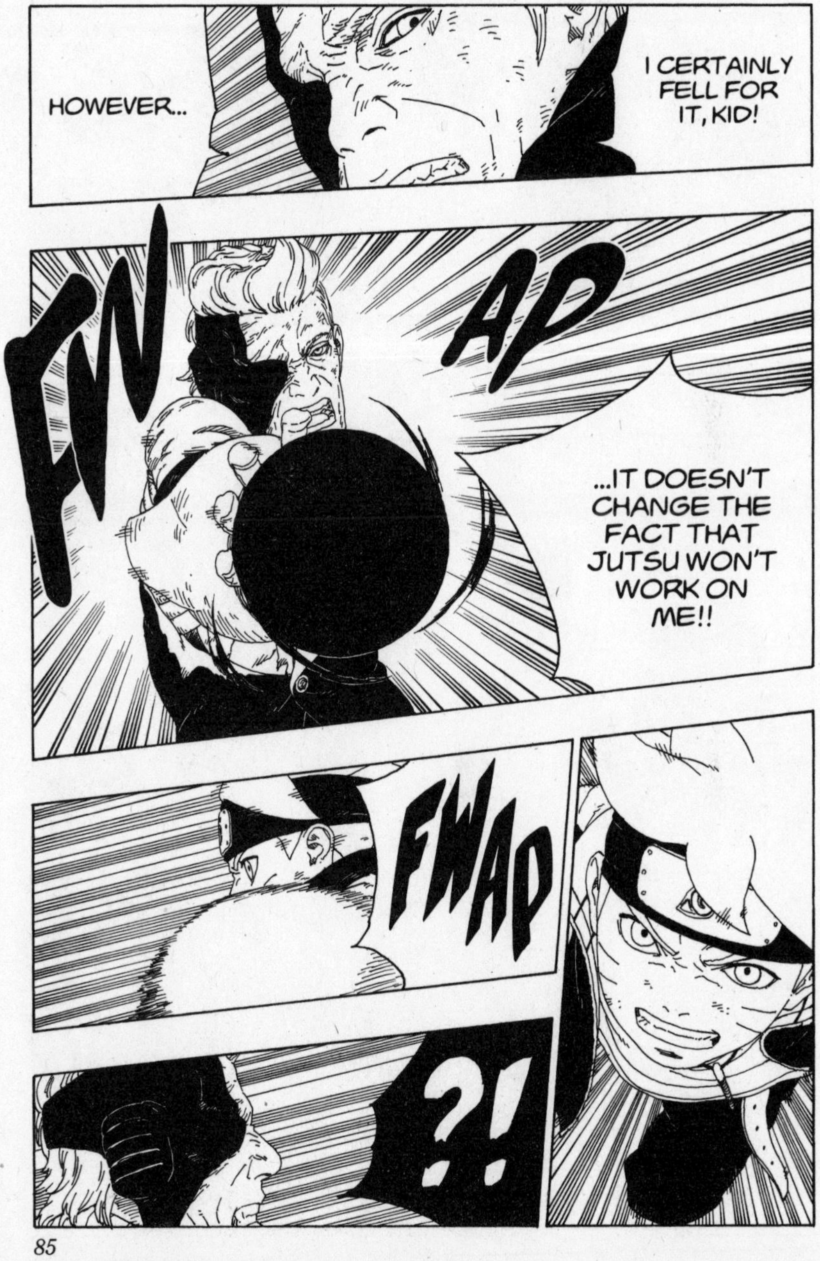
I CERTAINLY FELL FOR IT, KID!
HOWEVER...
FWAP
...IT DOESN'T CHANGE THE FACT THAT JUTSU WON'T WORK ON ME!!
FWAP
?!

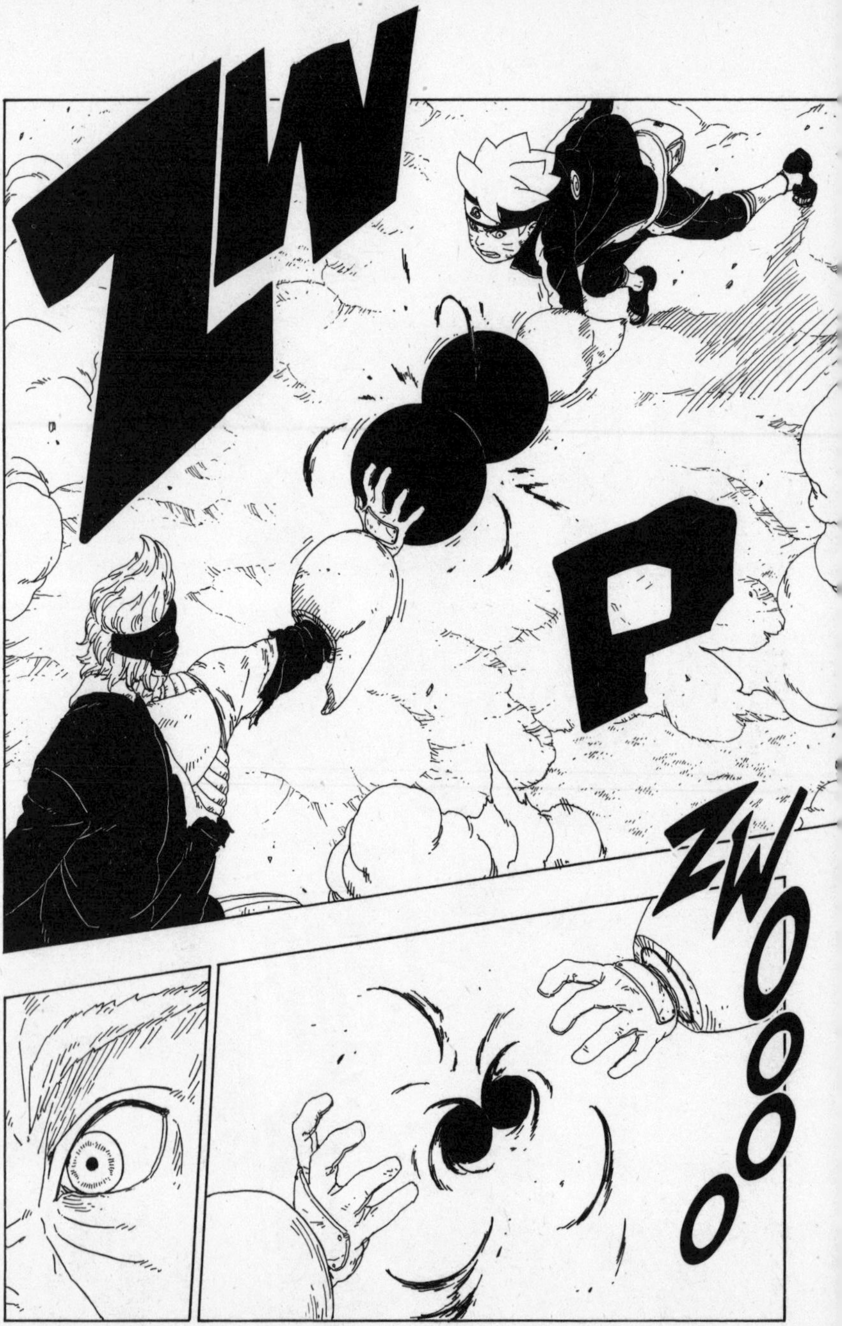
ZWP
ZWOOOOOO

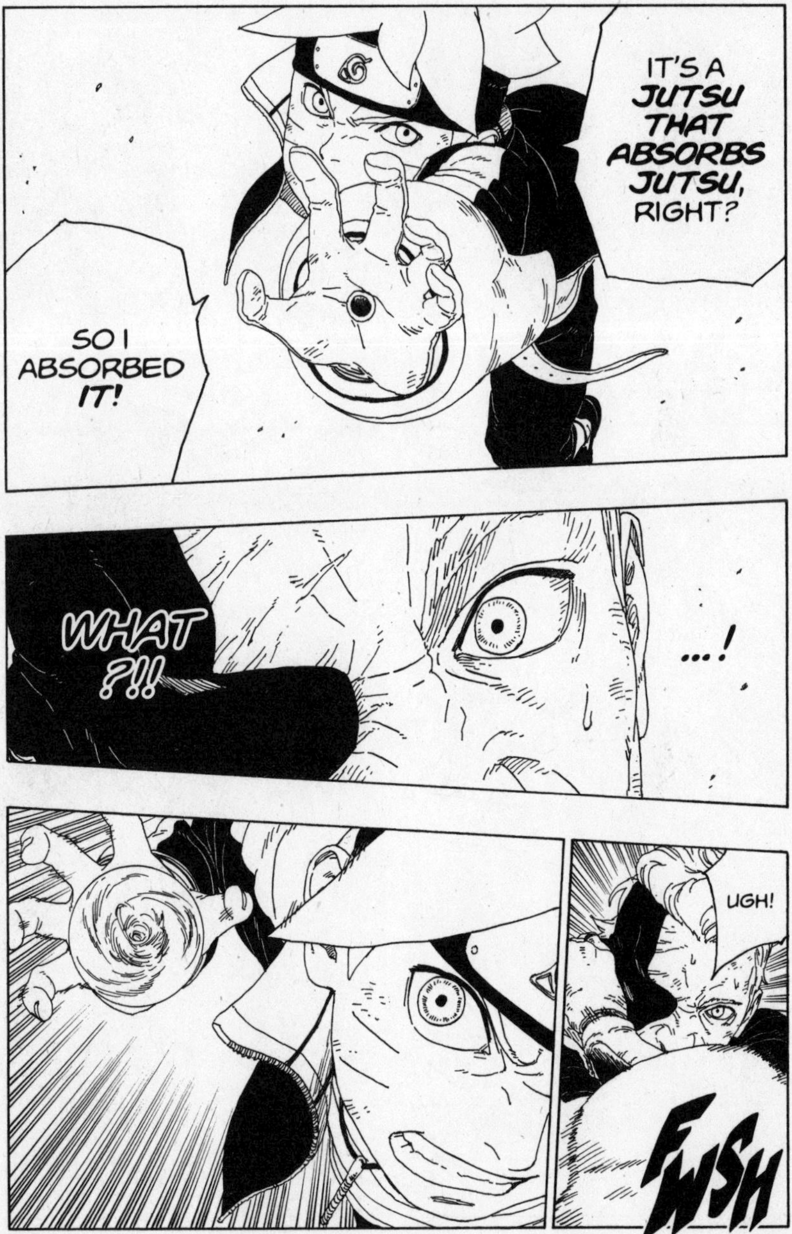

IT'S A JUTSU THAT ABSORBS JUTSU, RIGHT?
SO I ABSORBED IT!
...!
WHAT ?!!
UGH!
FWSH

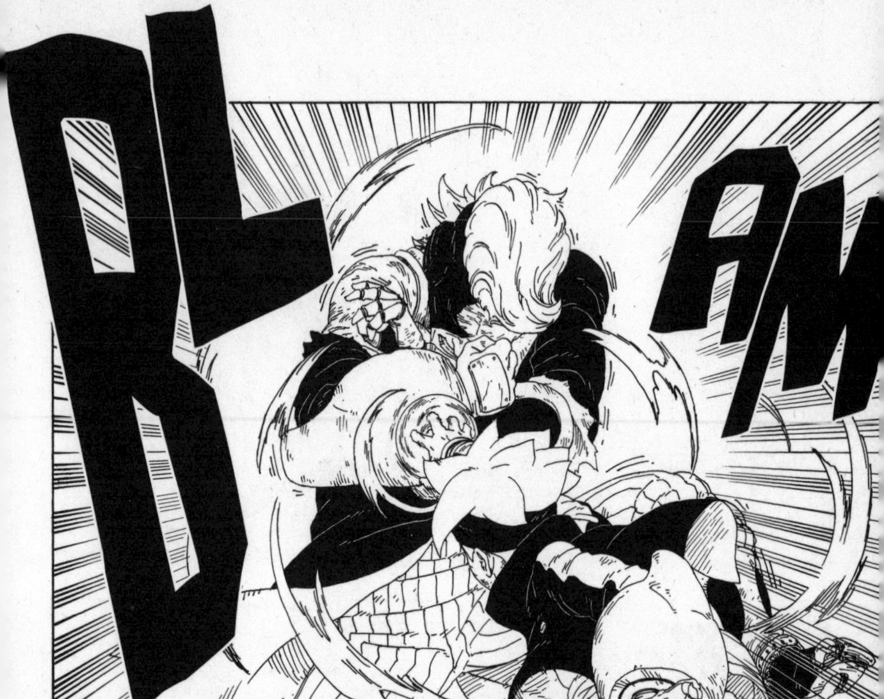
BL-
AM
RASENGAN!!!

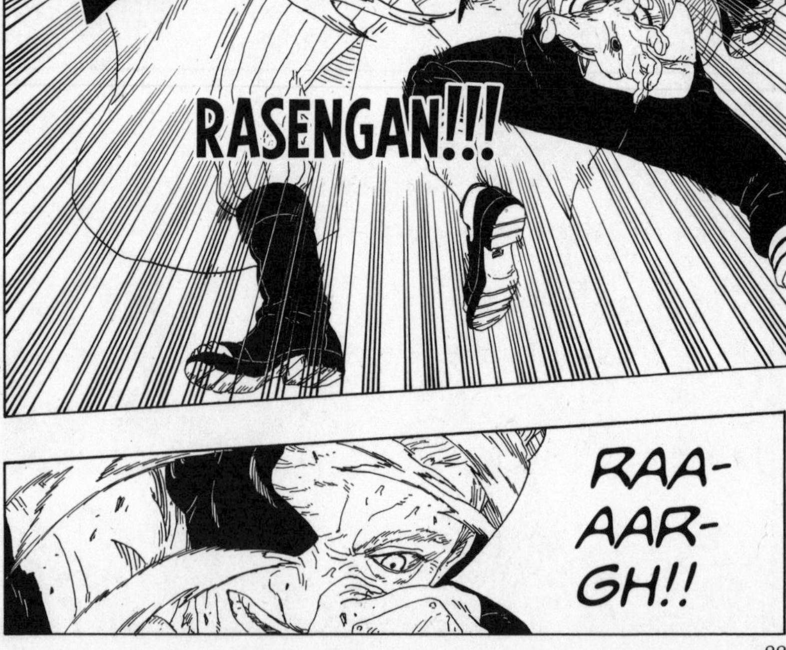
RAA-
AAR-
GH!!

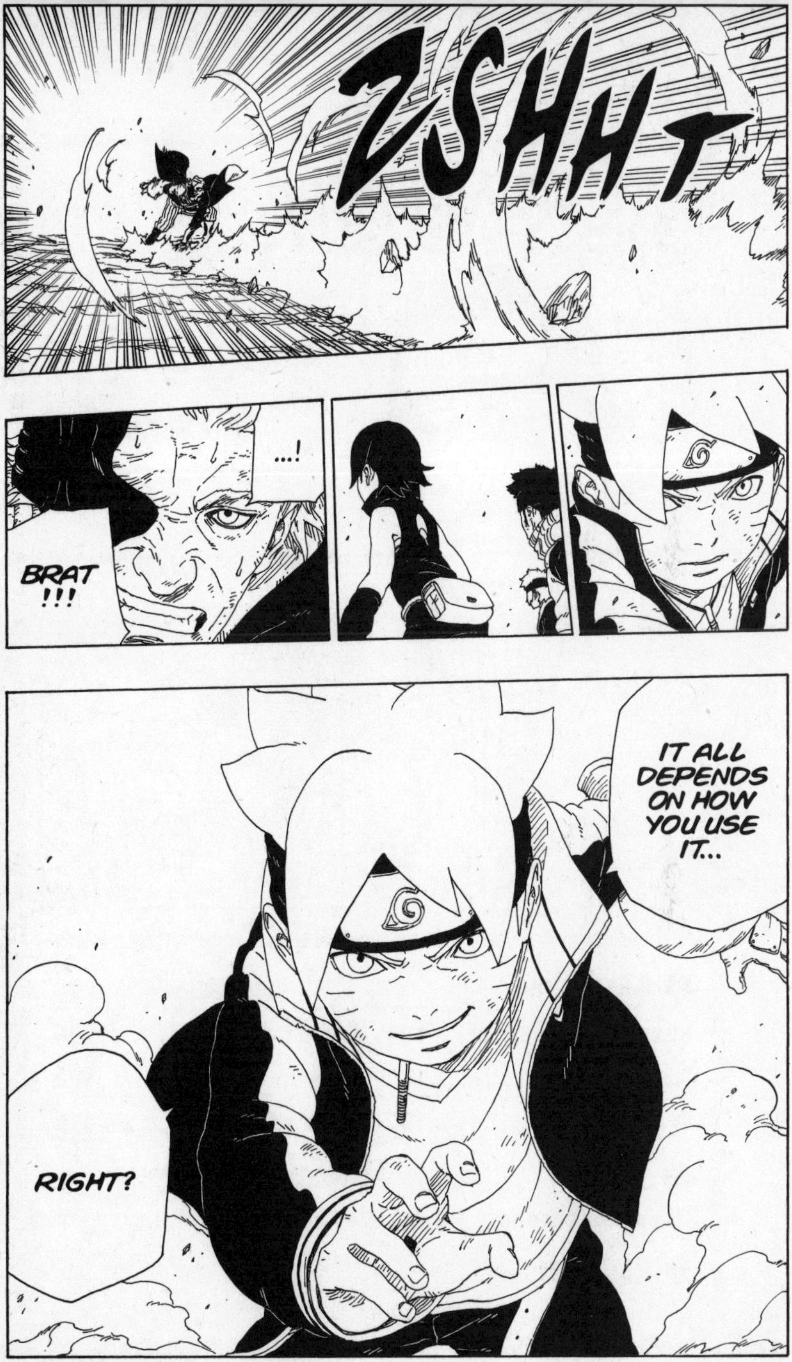
ZSHHT
...!
BRAT!!!
IT ALL DEPENDS ON HOW YOU USE IT...
RIGHT?

NINJA ENCYCLOPEDIA · ENTRY 17

MORINO IBIKI

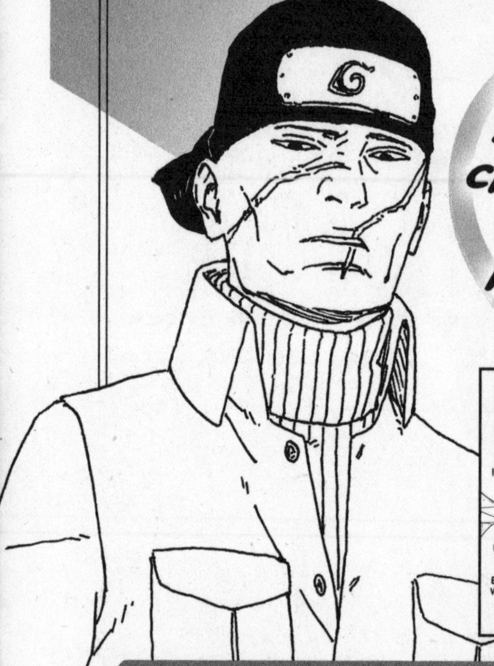

"Hurry up and spill it, for it won't change what comes next, eh?"

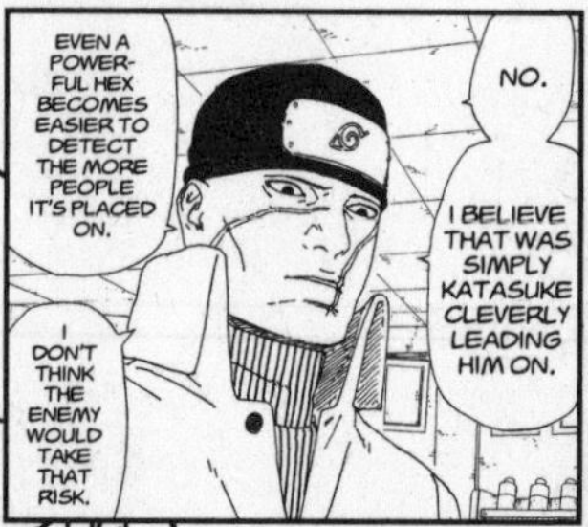
NO.
I BELIEVE THAT WAS SIMPLY KATASUKE CLEVERLY LEADING HIM ON.
EVEN A POWER-FUL HEX BECOMES EASIER TO DETECT THE MORE PEOPLE IT'S PLACED ON.
I DON'T THINK THE ENEMY WOULD TAKE THAT RISK.

● Attributes

Strength	100	Dexterity	98
Intelligence	120	Chakra	100
Perception	130	Negotiation	120

● Skills

Interrogation & Torture ☆☆☆☆☆ Medicine ☆☆☆ Psychology ☆☆☆

● Ninja Arts

Art of the Ebi-zeme (Shrimp Tie), Summoning: Torture Chamber, etc.

*Average attribute value is 60 for ordinary people and 90 for genin. Skill values range from 1 to 5☆ with 5☆ signifying super top-notch.

Number 22: Fierce Battle Conclusion!

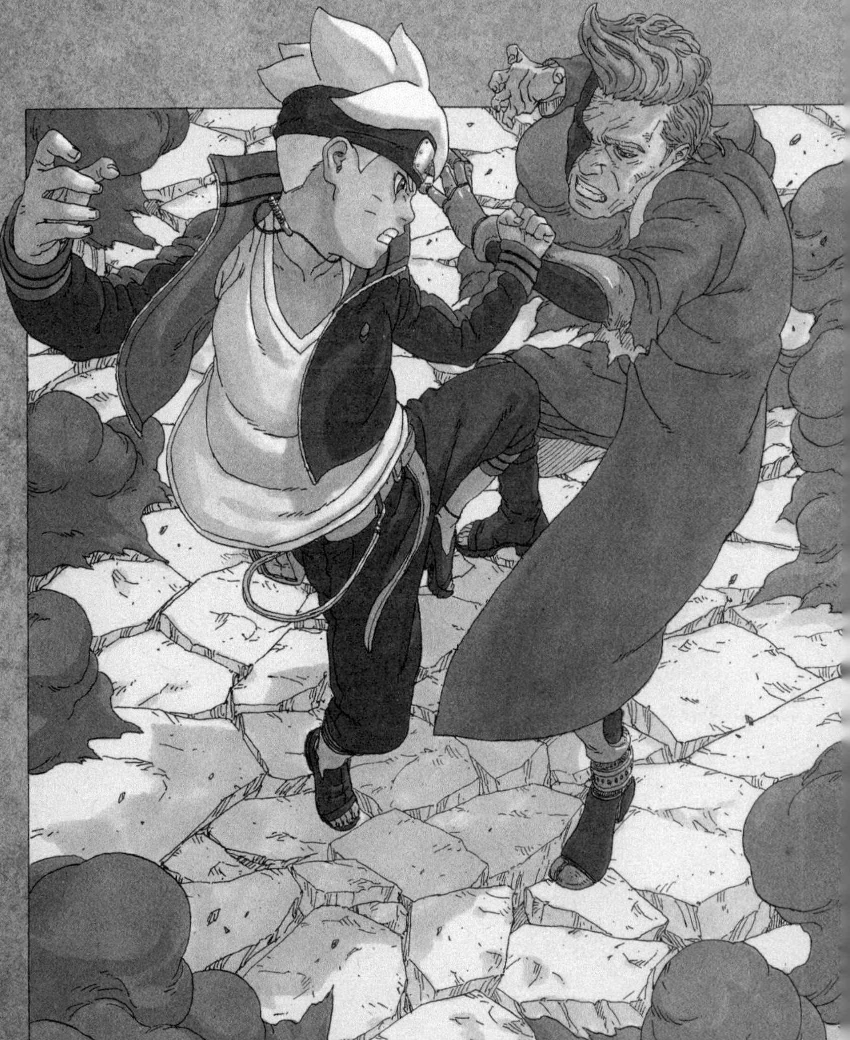

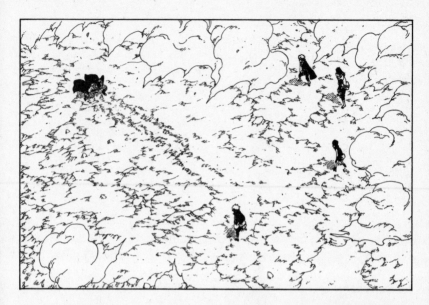

YOUNG MASTER!

TMp

IT WORKED, DOCTOR KATASUKE.

I WASN'T ABLE TO FINISH HIM, BUT...

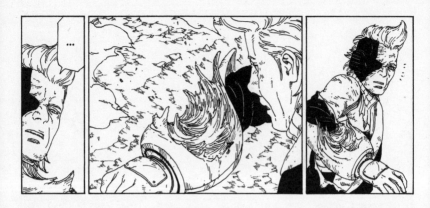

...

YOU WON'T BE USING THAT ANYMORE.

NO MORE ABSORBING JUTSU FOR YOU!

...

HMPH.

ZRP

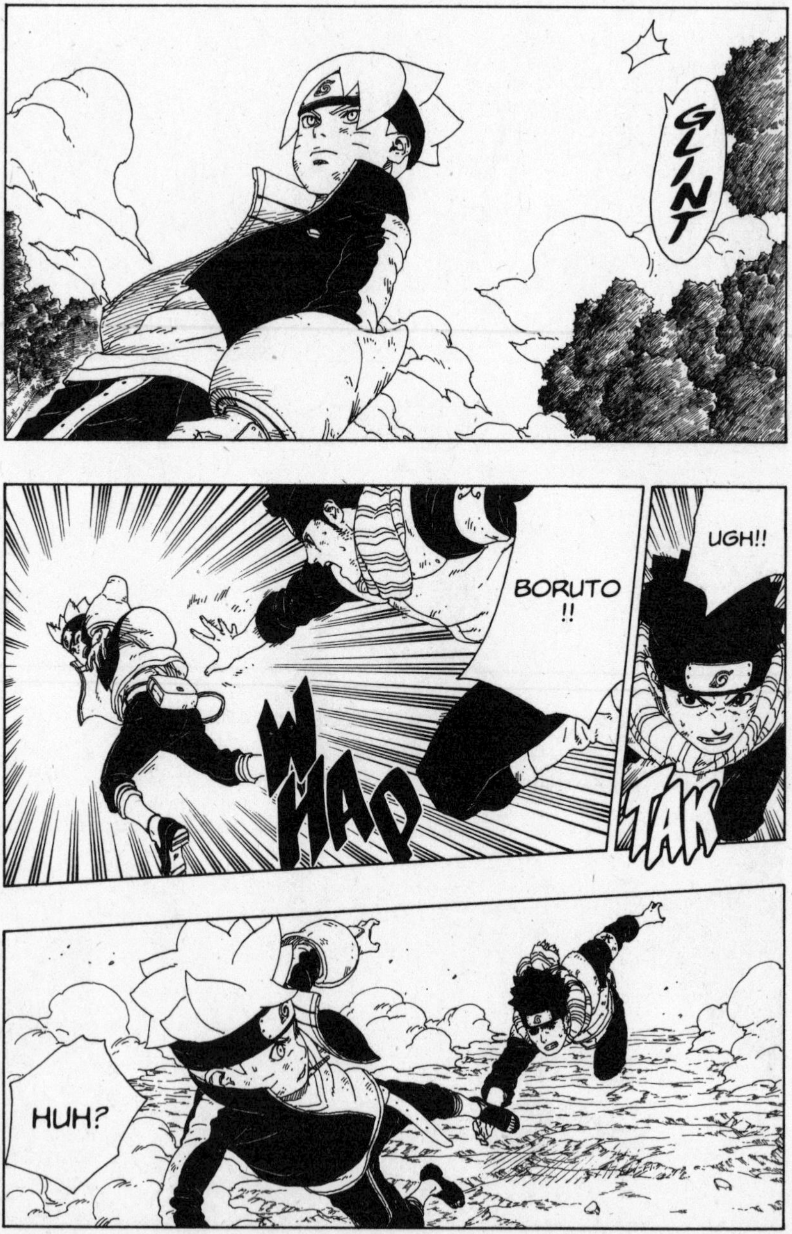
GLINT
UGH!!
TAK
BORUTO !!
WHAP
HUH?

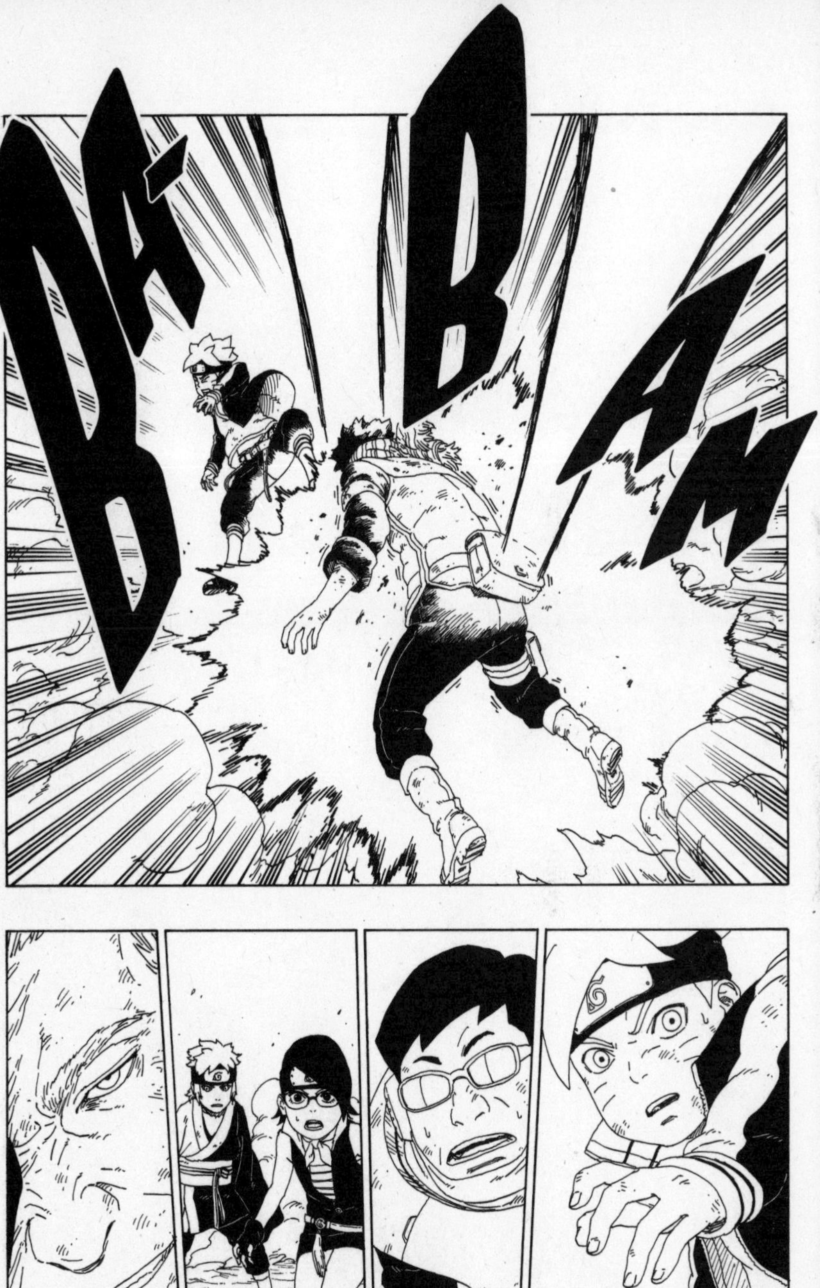
BA-BAM

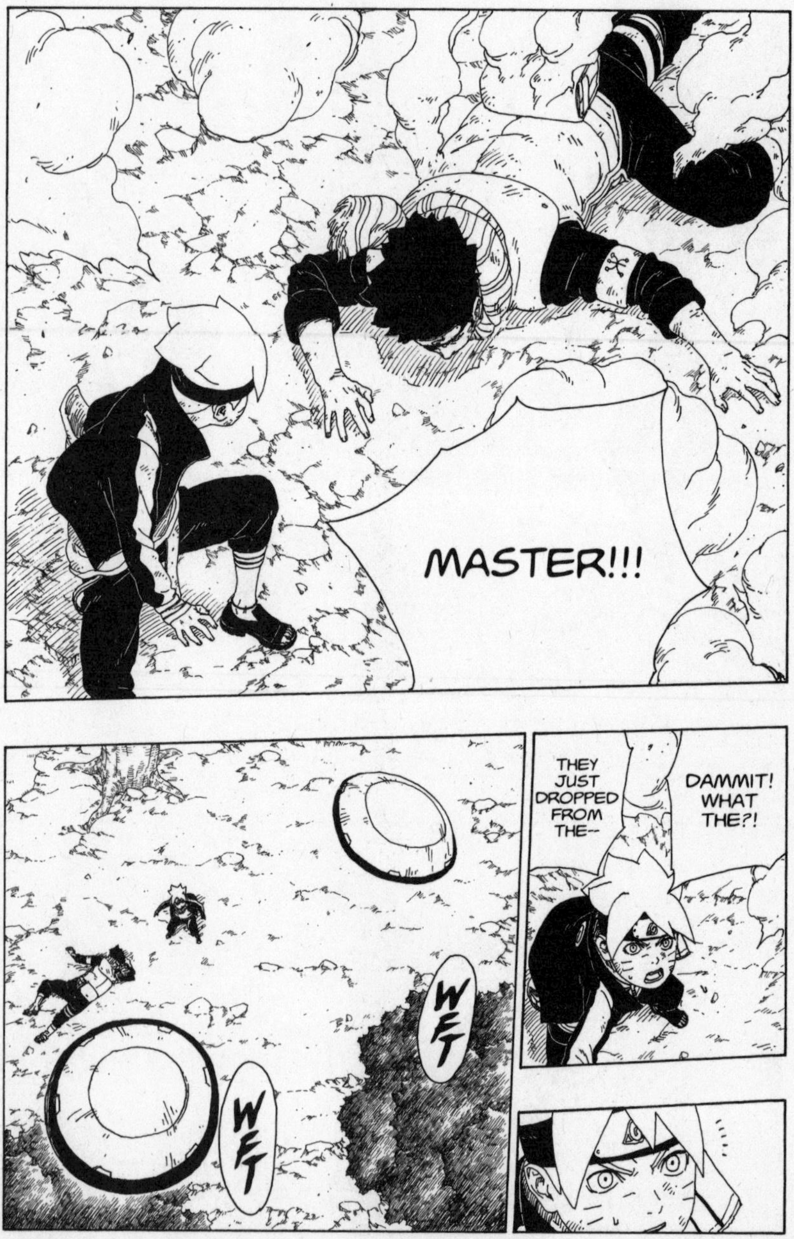
MASTER!!!
DAMMIT! WHAT THE?!
THEY JUST DROPPED FROM THE--
...
WFT
WFT

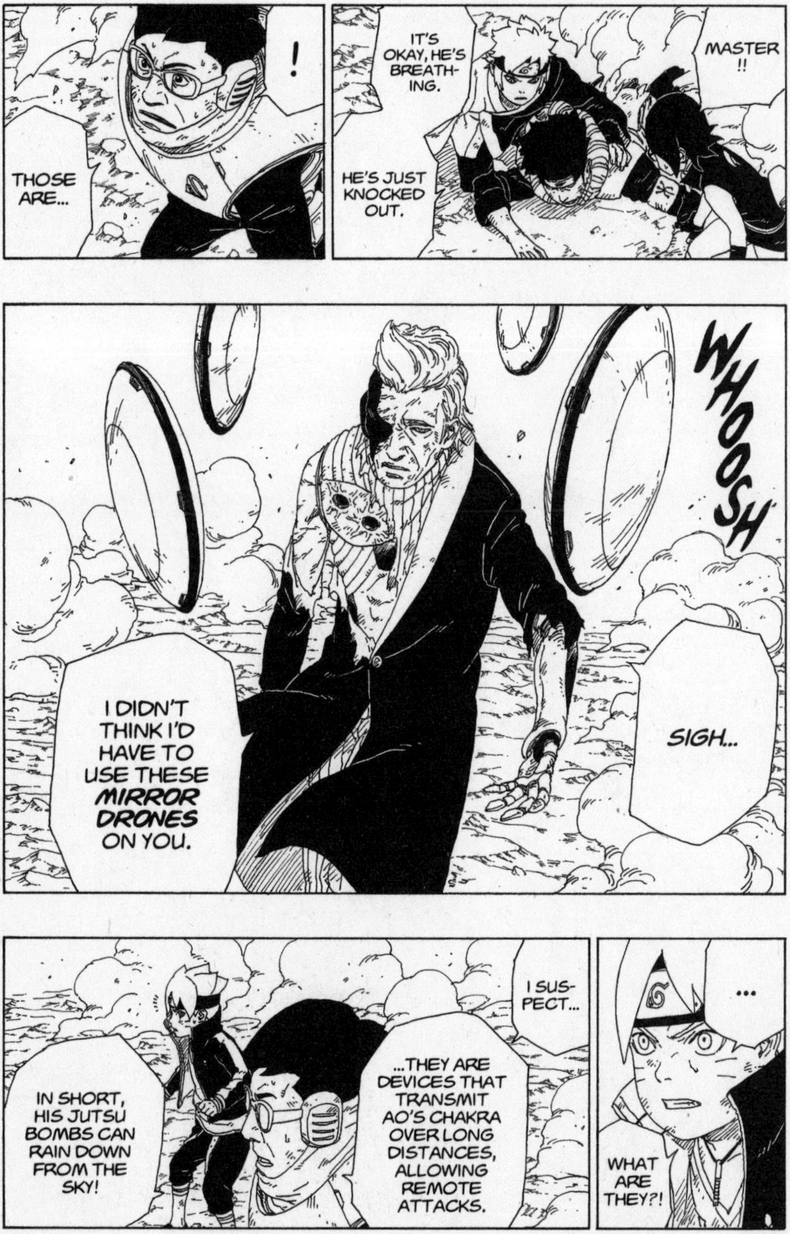
MASTER !!
IT'S OKAY, HE'S BREATHING.
HE'S JUST KNOCKED OUT.
!
THOSE ARE...
WHOOOSH
SIGH...
I DIDN'T THINK I'D HAVE TO USE THESE ***MIRROR DRONES*** ON YOU.
...
WHAT ARE THEY?!
I SUSPECT...
...THEY ARE DEVICES THAT TRANSMIT AO'S CHAKRA OVER LONG DISTANCES, ALLOWING REMOTE ATTACKS.
IN SHORT, HIS JUTSU BOMBS CAN RAIN DOWN FROM THE SKY!

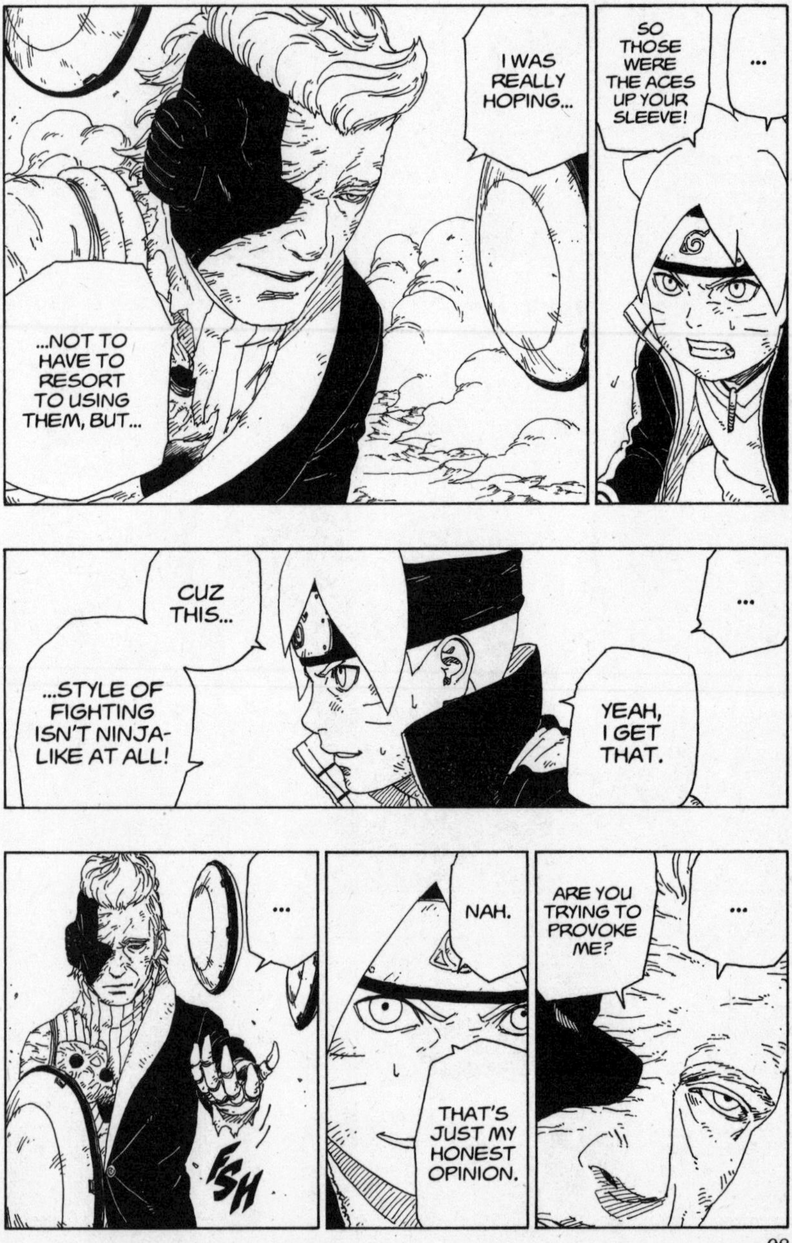
...
SO THOSE WERE THE ACES UP YOUR SLEEVE!
I WAS REALLY HOPING...
...NOT TO HAVE TO RESORT TO USING THEM, BUT...
...
YEAH, I GET THAT.
CUZ THIS...
...STYLE OF FIGHTING ISN'T NINJA-LIKE AT ALL!
...
ARE YOU TRYING TO PROVOKE ME?
NAH.
THAT'S JUST MY HONEST OPINION.
...
FSH

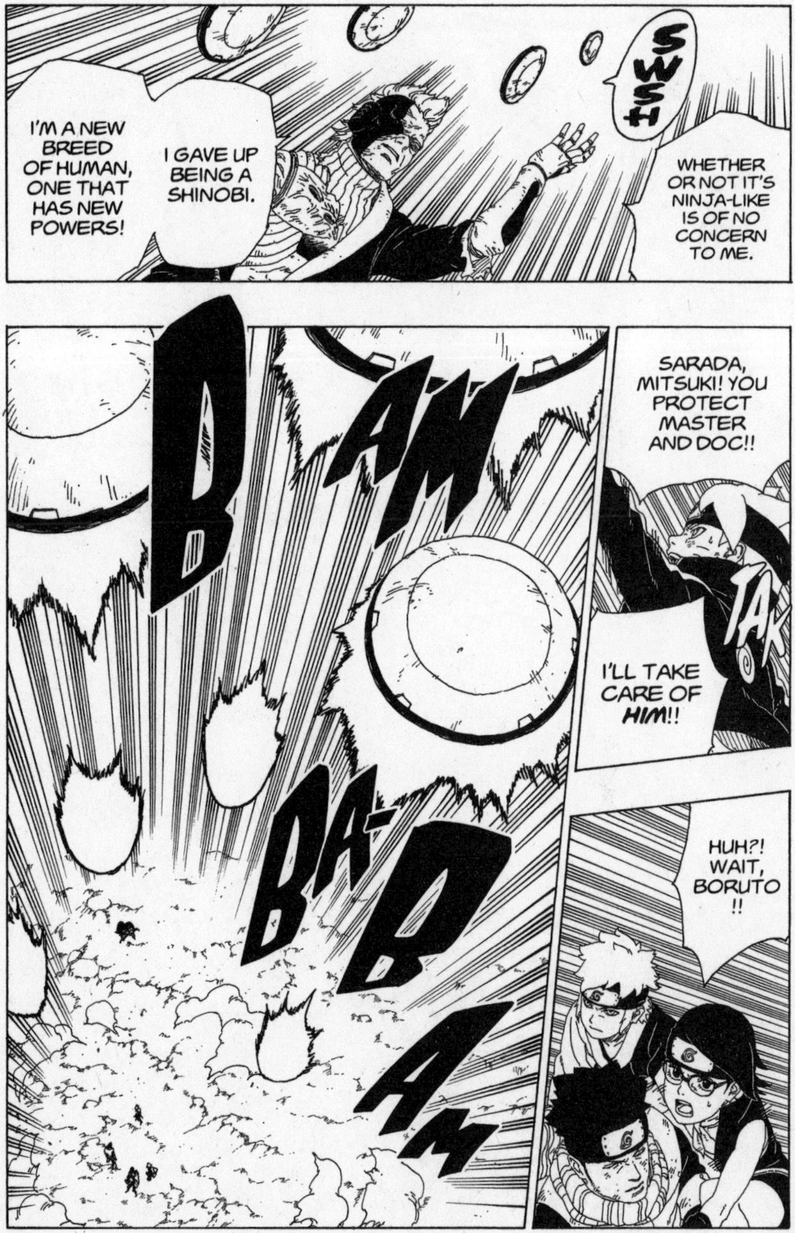
SWSH
WHETHER OR NOT IT'S NINJA-LIKE IS OF NO CONCERN TO ME.
I GAVE UP BEING A SHINOBI.
I'M A NEW BREED OF HUMAN, ONE THAT HAS NEW POWERS!
SARADA, MITSUKI! YOU PROTECT MASTER AND DOC!!
TAK
I'LL TAKE CARE OF HIM!!
HUH?! WAIT, BORUTO!!
BAM
BA-BAM

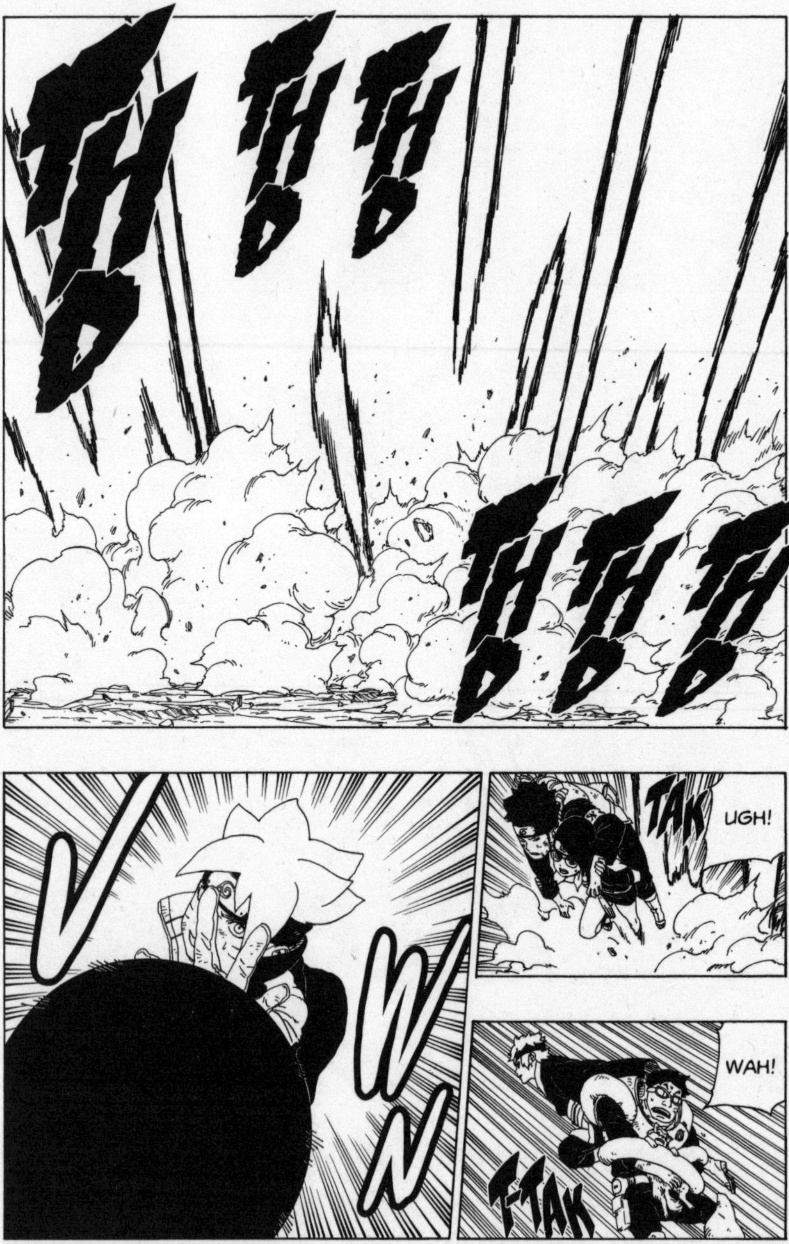
THD
THD
THD
THD
THD
THD
TAK
UGH!
WAH!
T-TAK

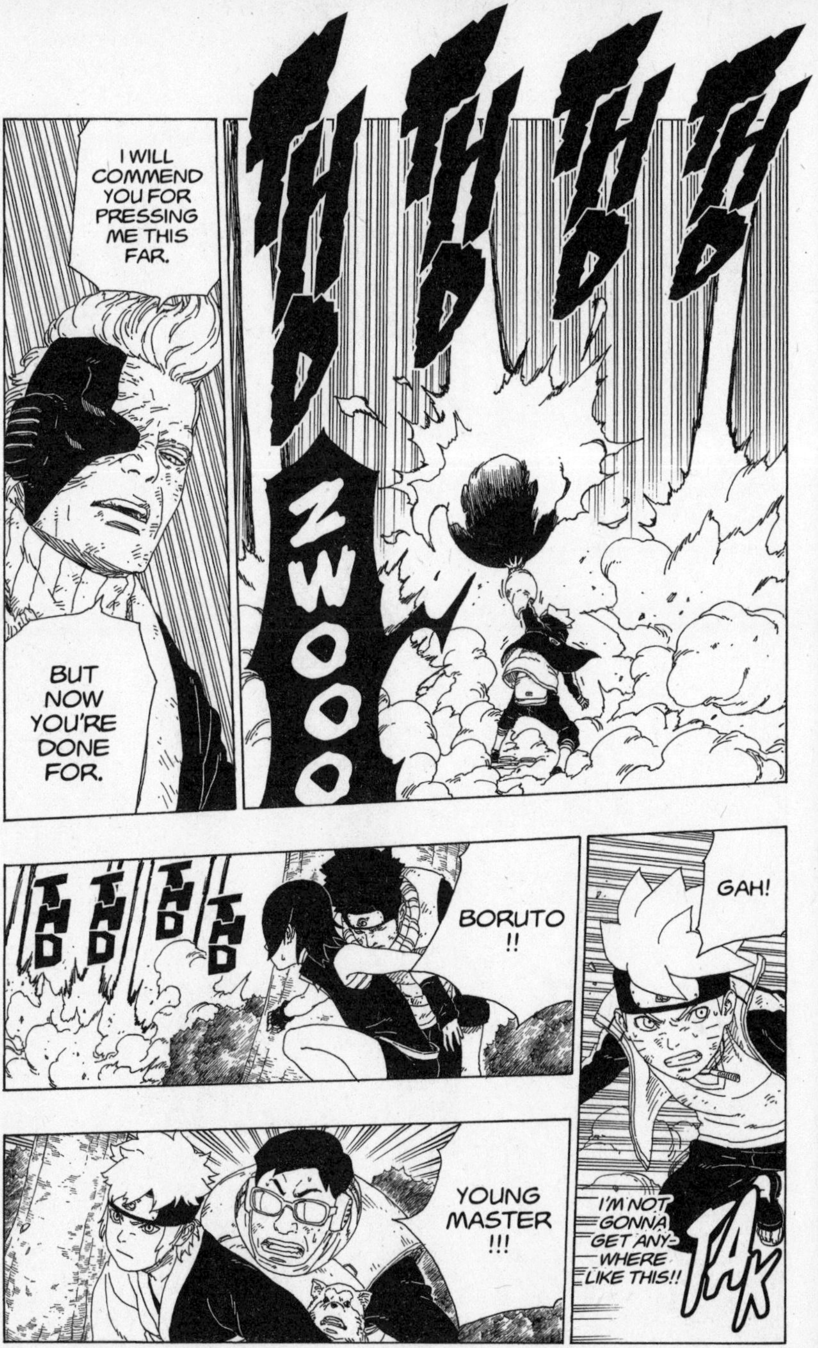

ZWOOO
I WILL COMMEND YOU FOR PRESSING ME THIS FAR.
BUT NOW YOU'RE DONE FOR.
GAH!
I'M NOT GONNA GET ANYWHERE LIKE THIS!!
TAK
THD THD THD THD
BORUTO!!
YOUNG MASTER!!!

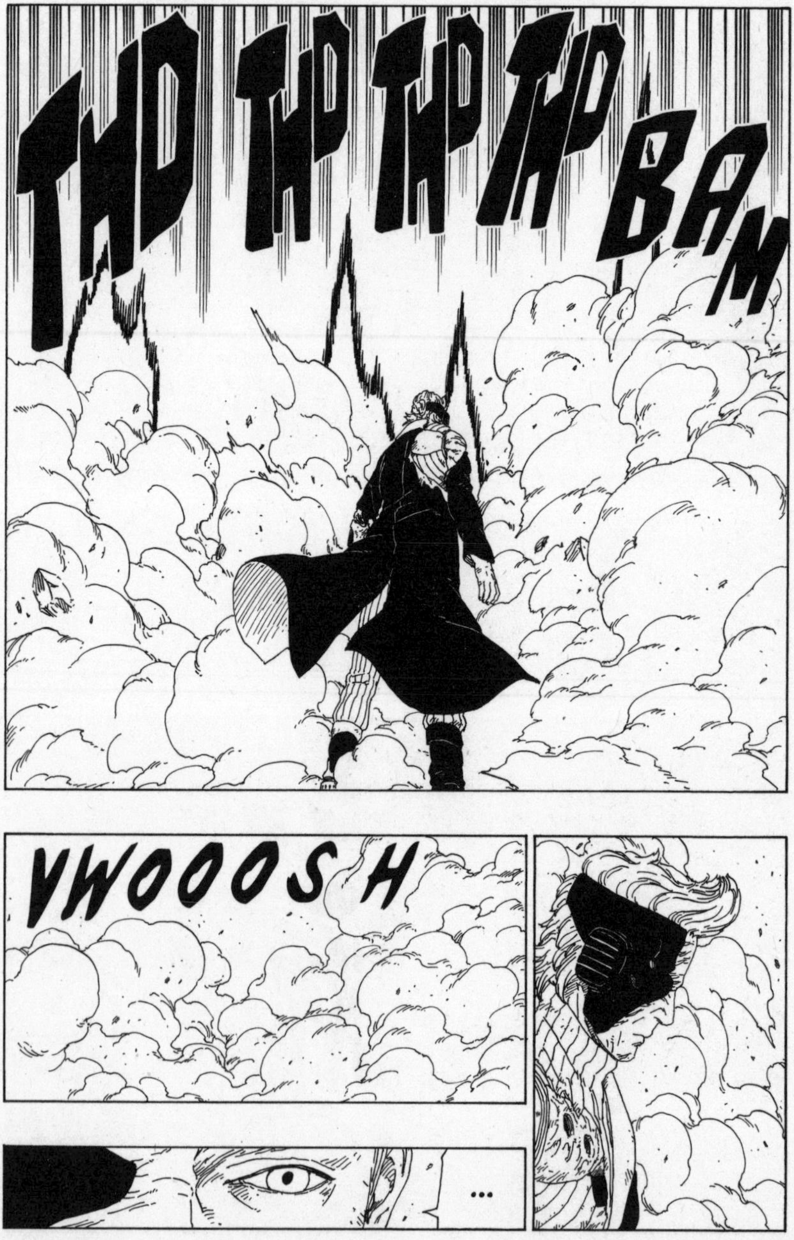
THD THD THD THD BAM
VWOOOSH
...

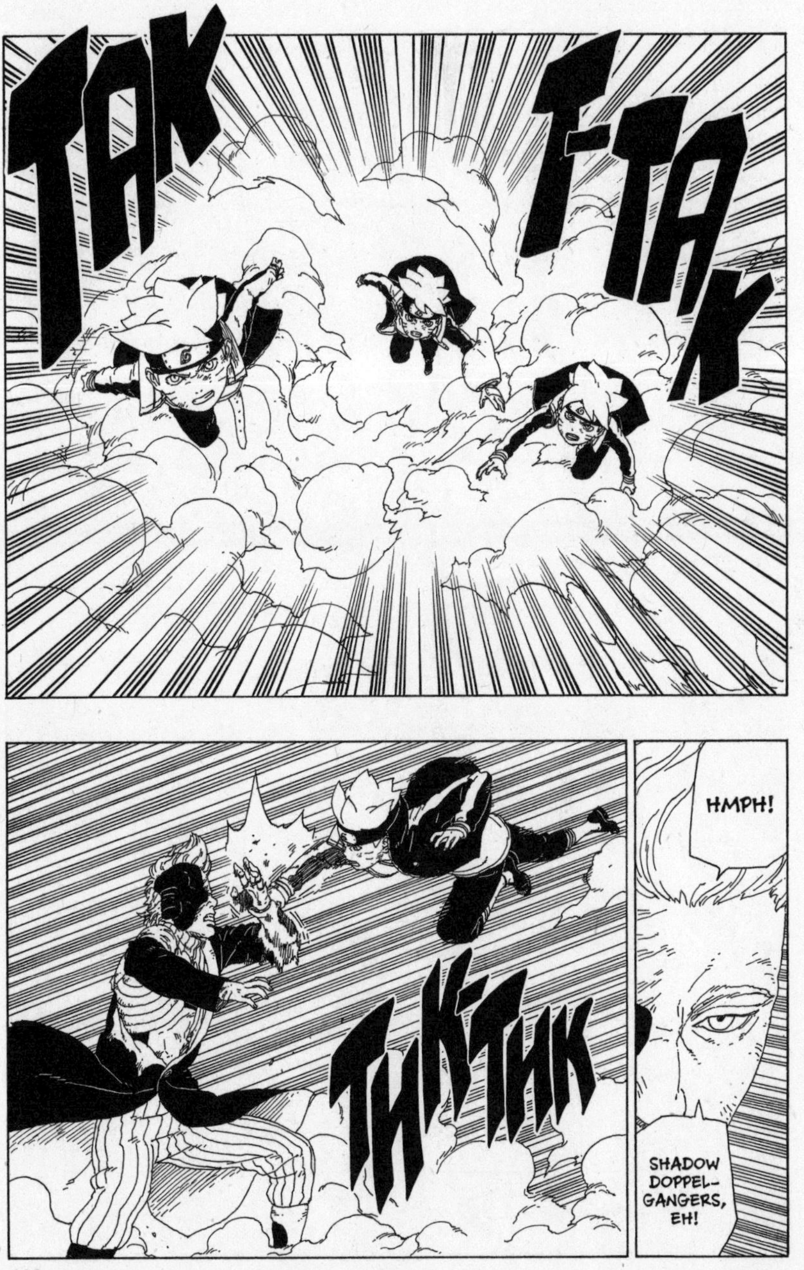
T-TAK
TAK
HMPH!
SHADOW DOPPEL-GANGERS, EH!
THK-THK

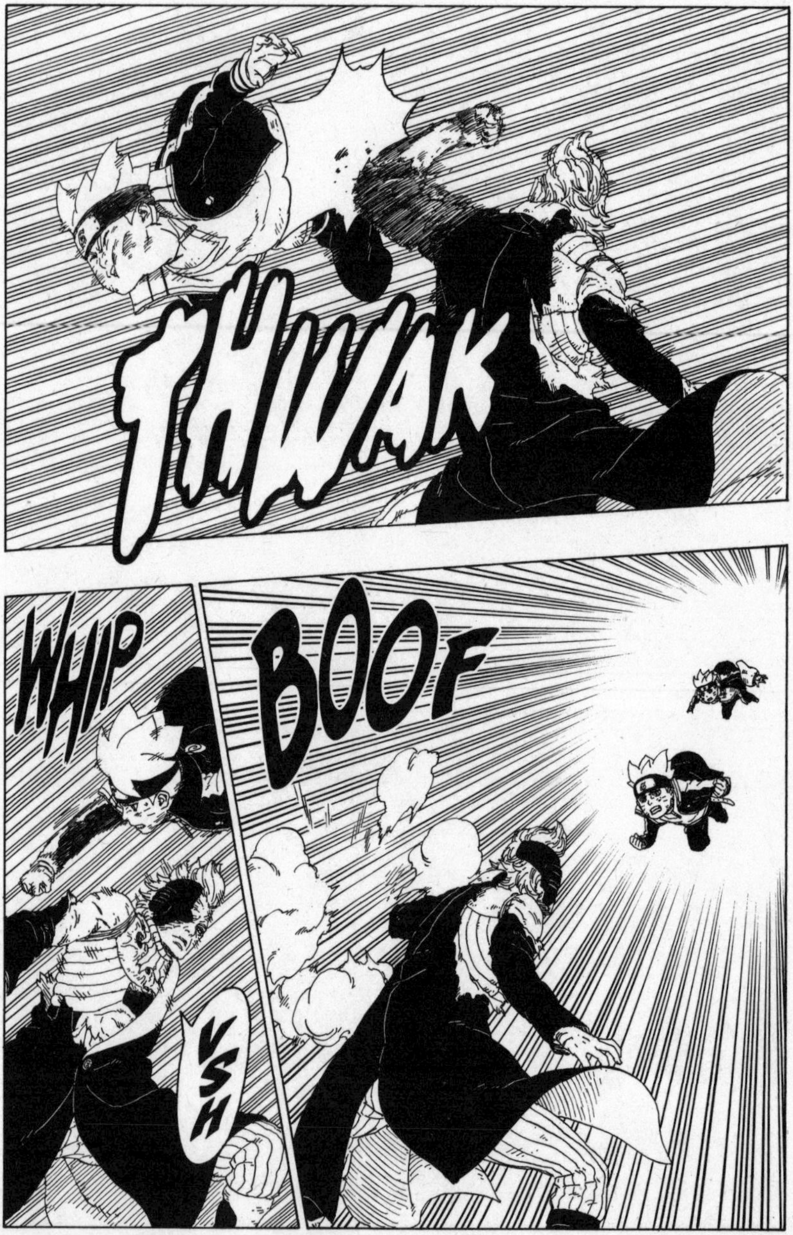
THWAK
BOOF
WHIP
VSH

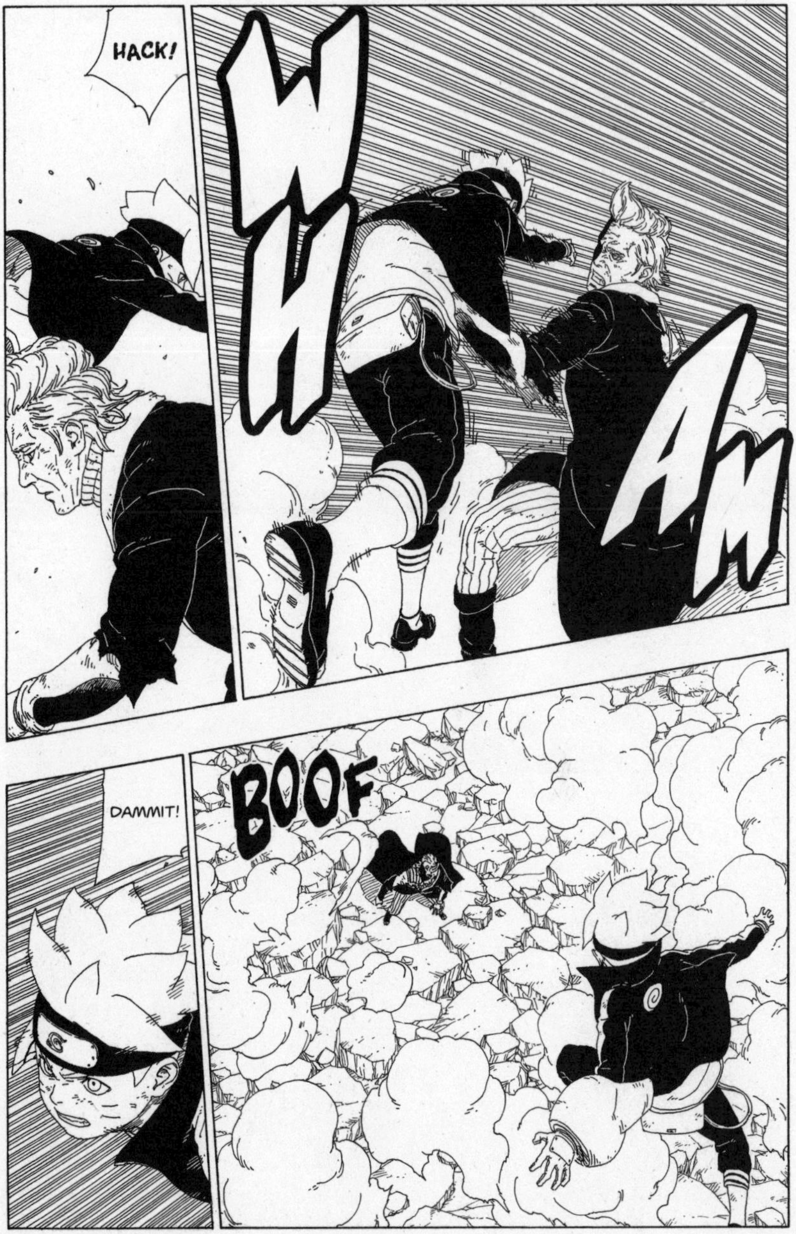

WHAM
HACK!
BOOF
DAMMIT!

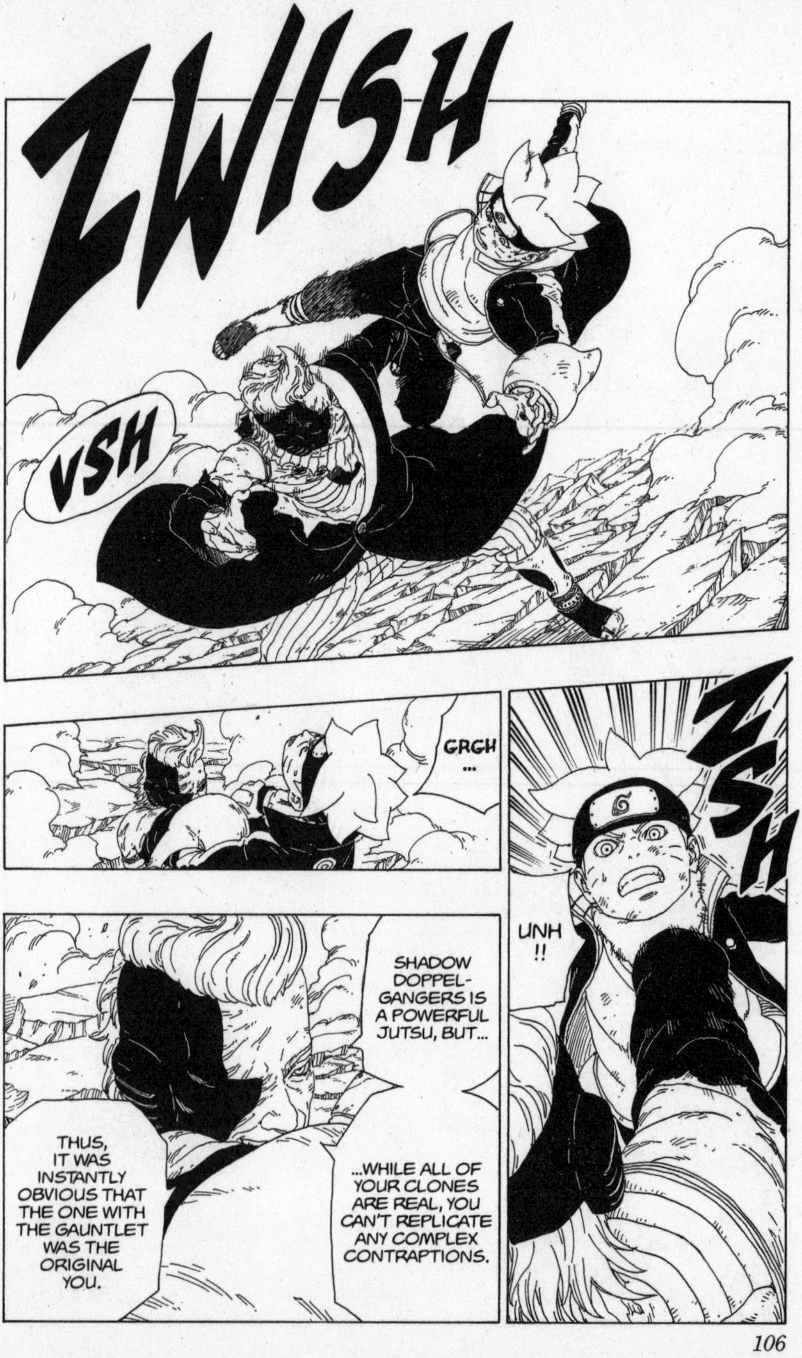
ZWISH
VSH
ZSH
UNH !!
GRGH ...
SHADOW DOPPEL-GANGERS IS A POWERFUL JUTSU, BUT...
...WHILE ALL OF YOUR CLONES ARE REAL, YOU CAN'T REPLICATE ANY COMPLEX CONTRAPTIONS.
THUS, IT WAS INSTANTLY OBVIOUS THAT THE ONE WITH THE GAUNTLET WAS THE ORIGINAL YOU.

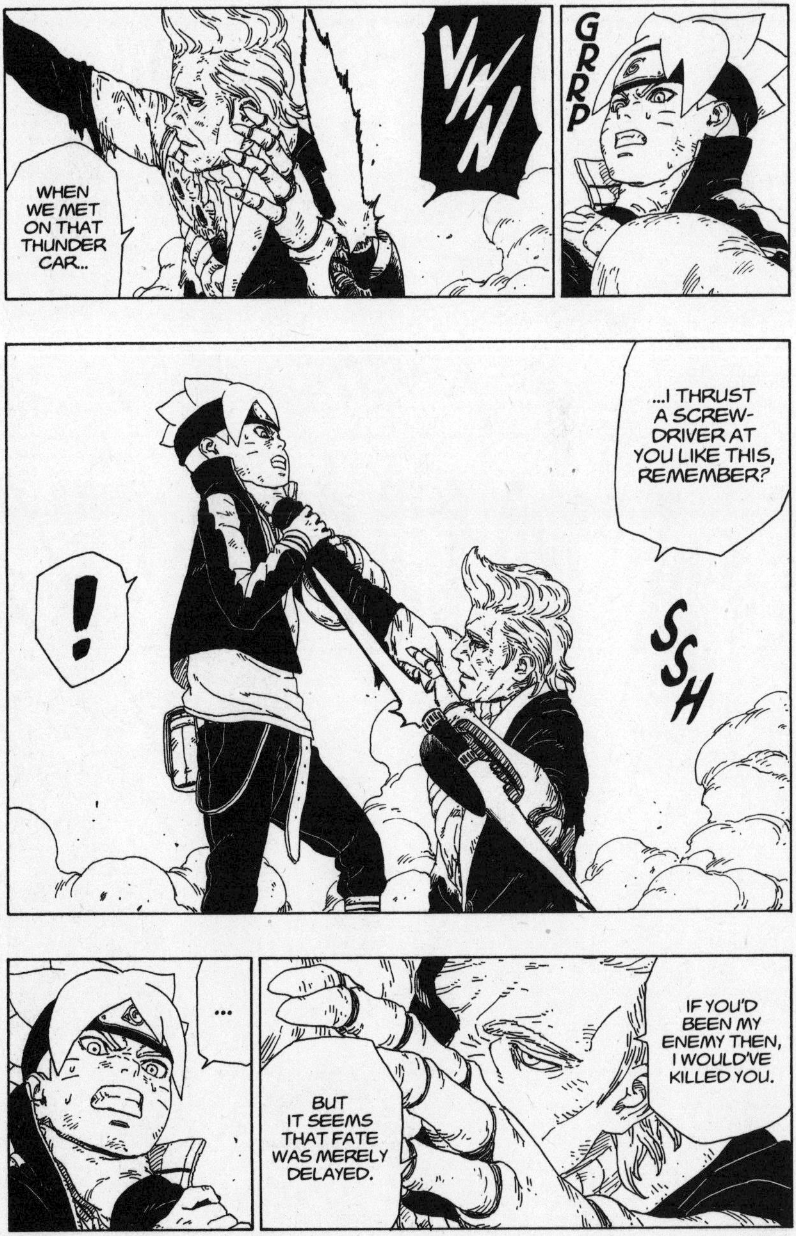

GRRP
VWN
WHEN WE MET ON THAT THUNDER CAR...
...I THRUST A SCREW-DRIVER AT YOU LIKE THIS, REMEMBER?
SSH
!
IF YOU'D BEEN MY ENEMY THEN, I WOULD'VE KILLED YOU.
BUT IT SEEMS THAT FATE WAS MERELY DELAYED.
...

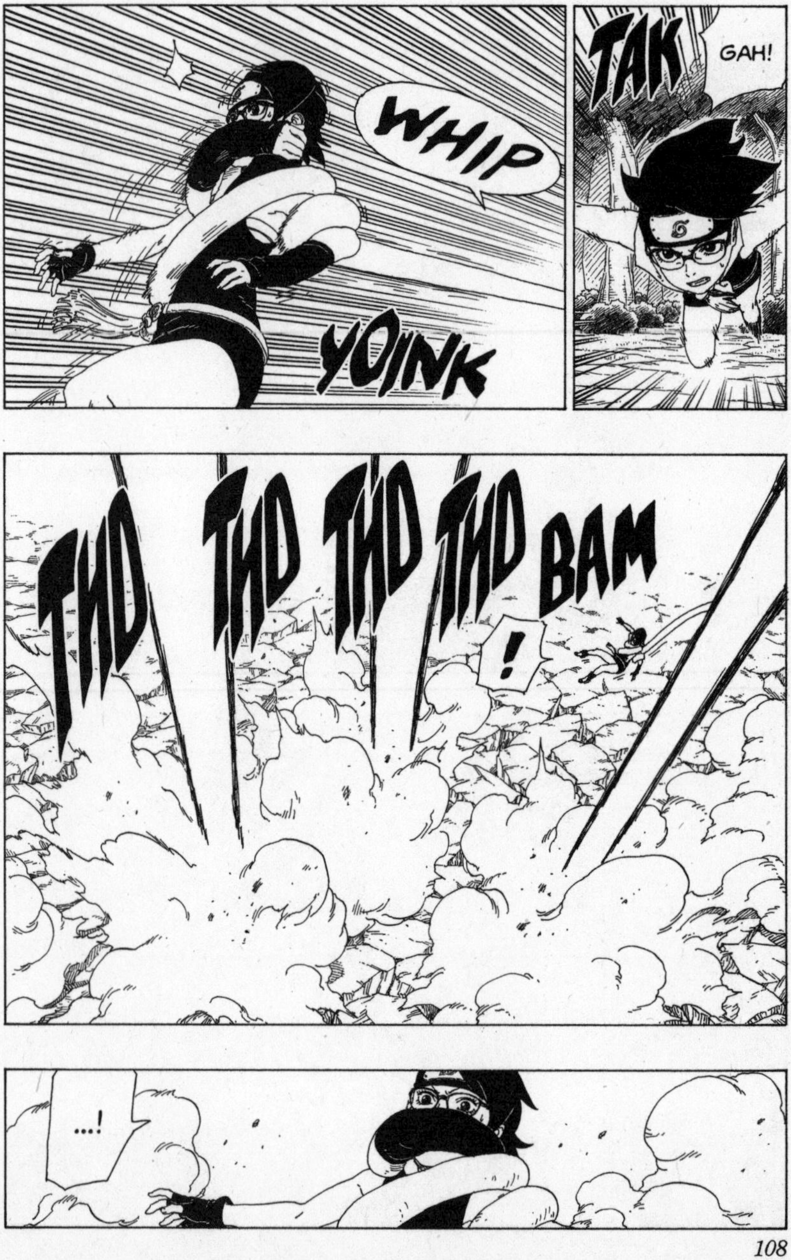
TAK
GAH!
WHIP
YOINK
THD THD THD THD
BAM
!
...!

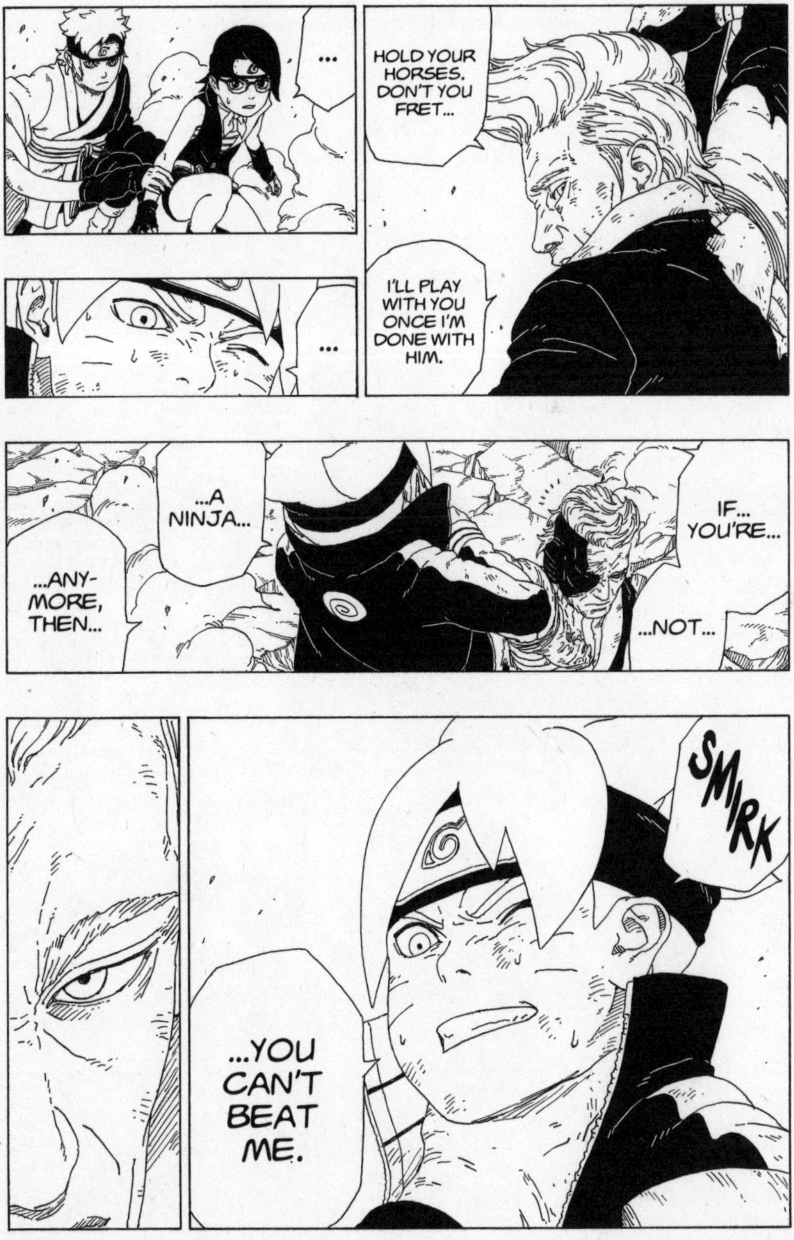
HOLD YOUR HORSES. DON'T YOU FRET...
I'LL PLAY WITH YOU ONCE I'M DONE WITH HIM.
...
...
IF... YOU'RE...
...NOT...
...A NINJA...
...ANY-MORE, THEN...
SMIRK
...YOU CAN'T BEAT ME.

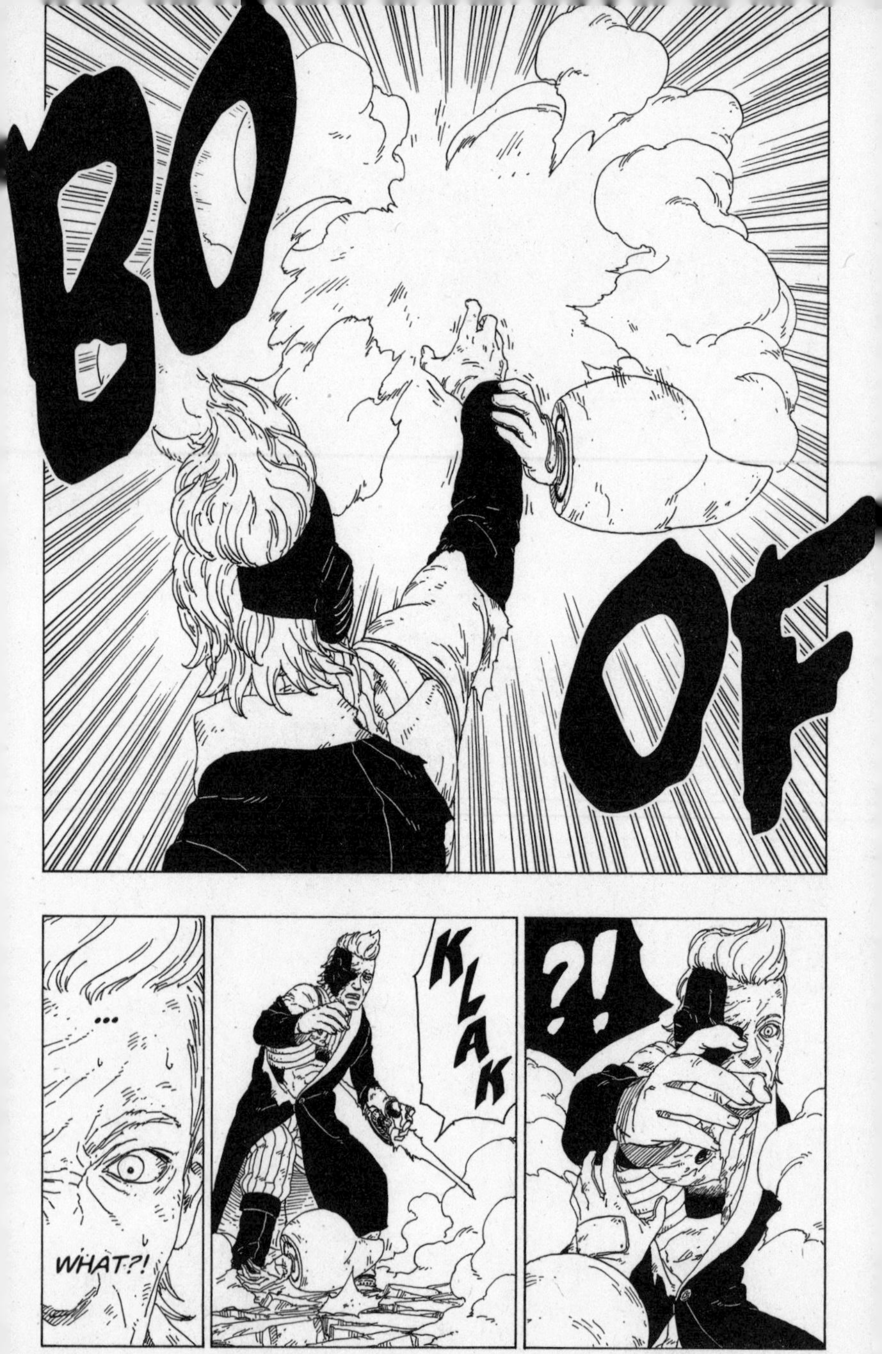
BOOF
?!
KLAK
...
WHAT?!

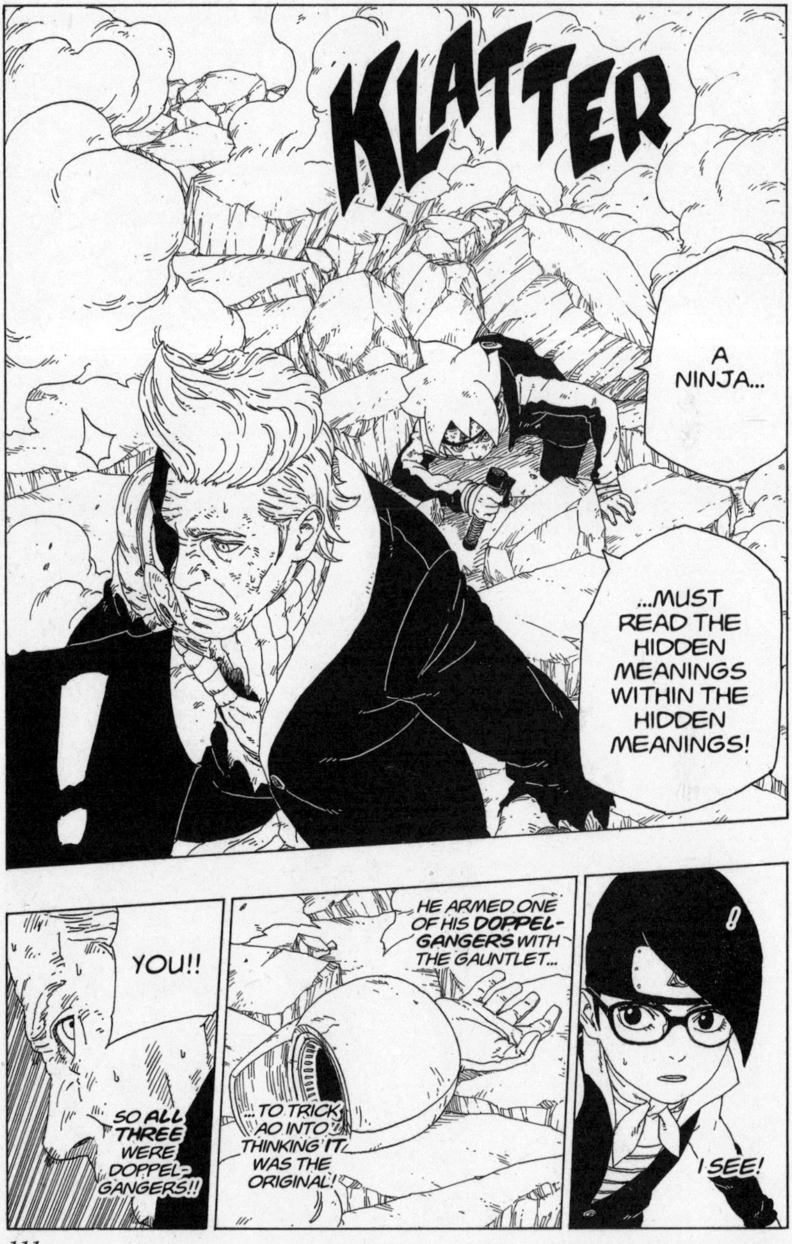
KLATTER
A NINJA...
...MUST READ THE HIDDEN MEANINGS WITHIN THE HIDDEN MEANINGS!
I SEE!
HE ARMED ONE OF HIS DOPPELGANGERS WITH THE GAUNTLET...
...TO TRICK AO INTO THINKING IT WAS THE ORIGINAL!
YOU!!
SO ALL THREE WERE DOPPELGANGERS!!

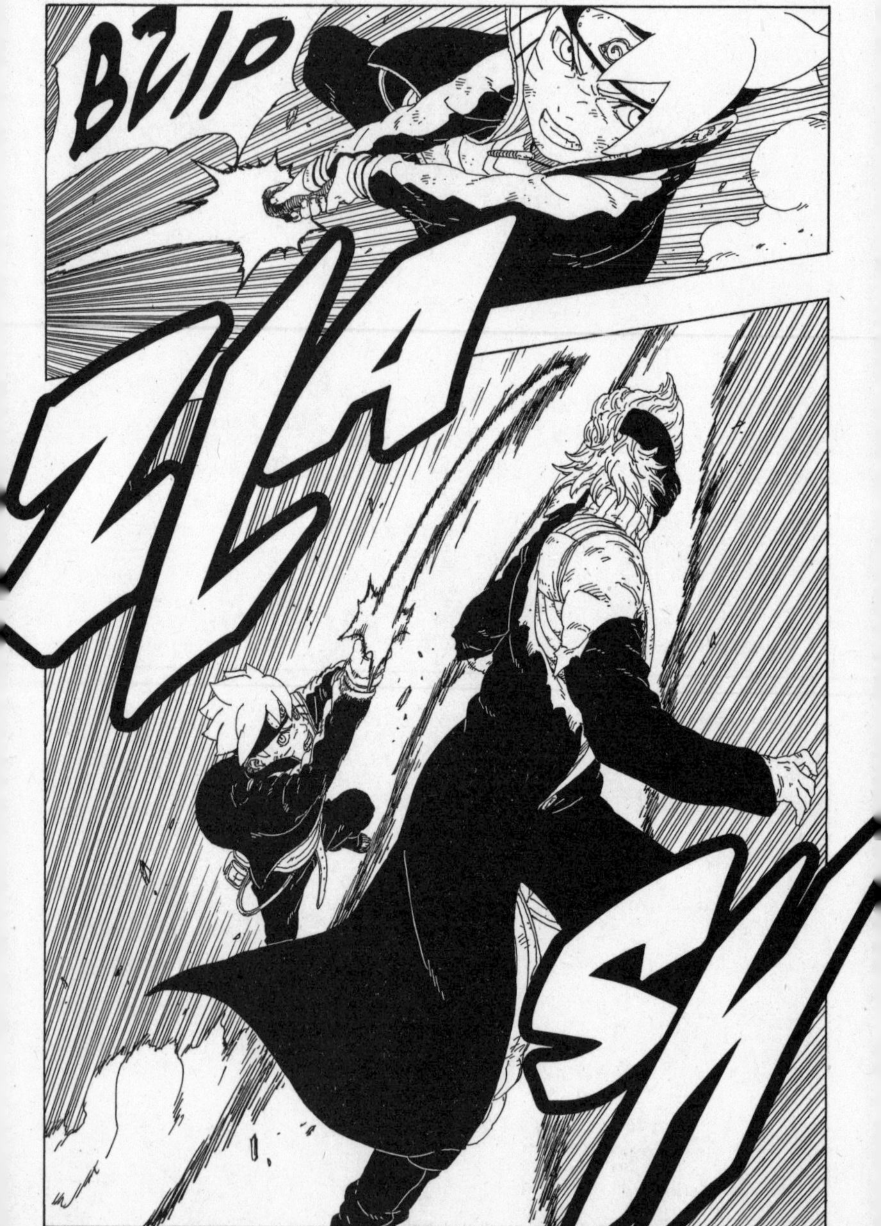
BZIP
ZA
SH

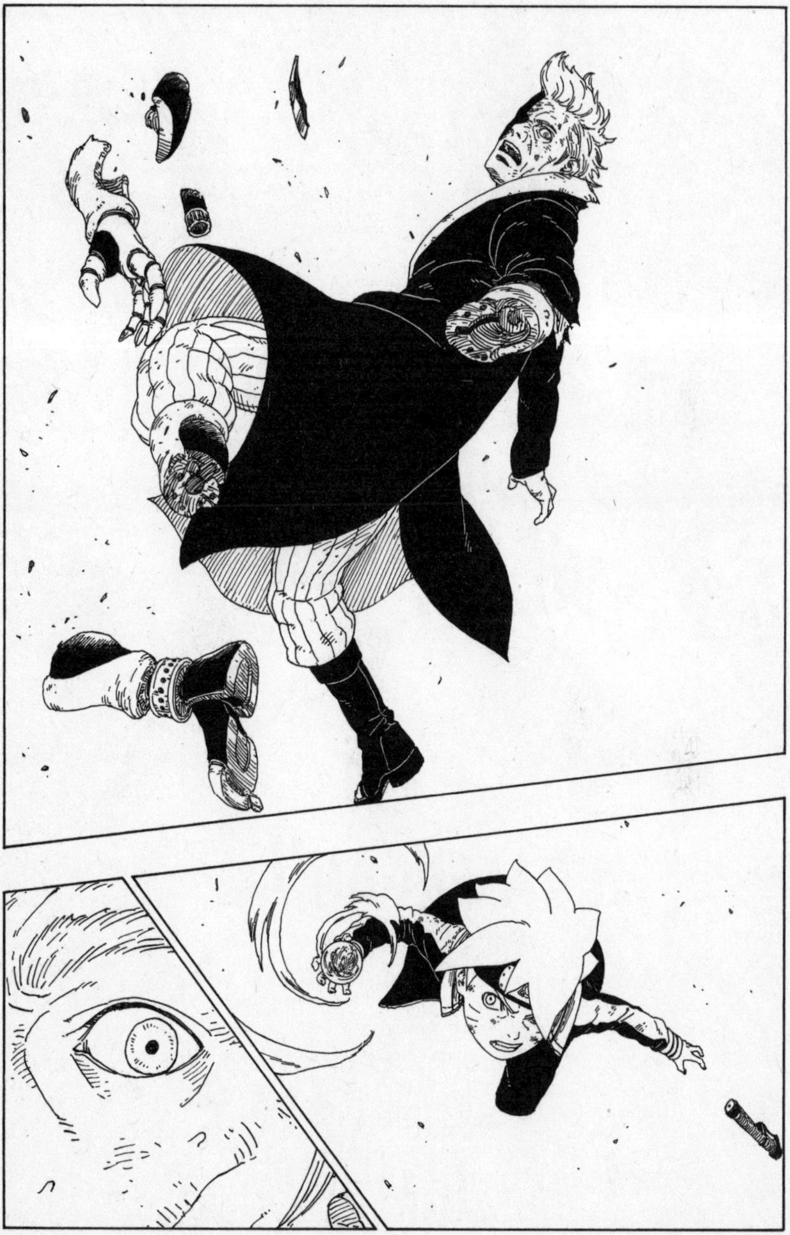

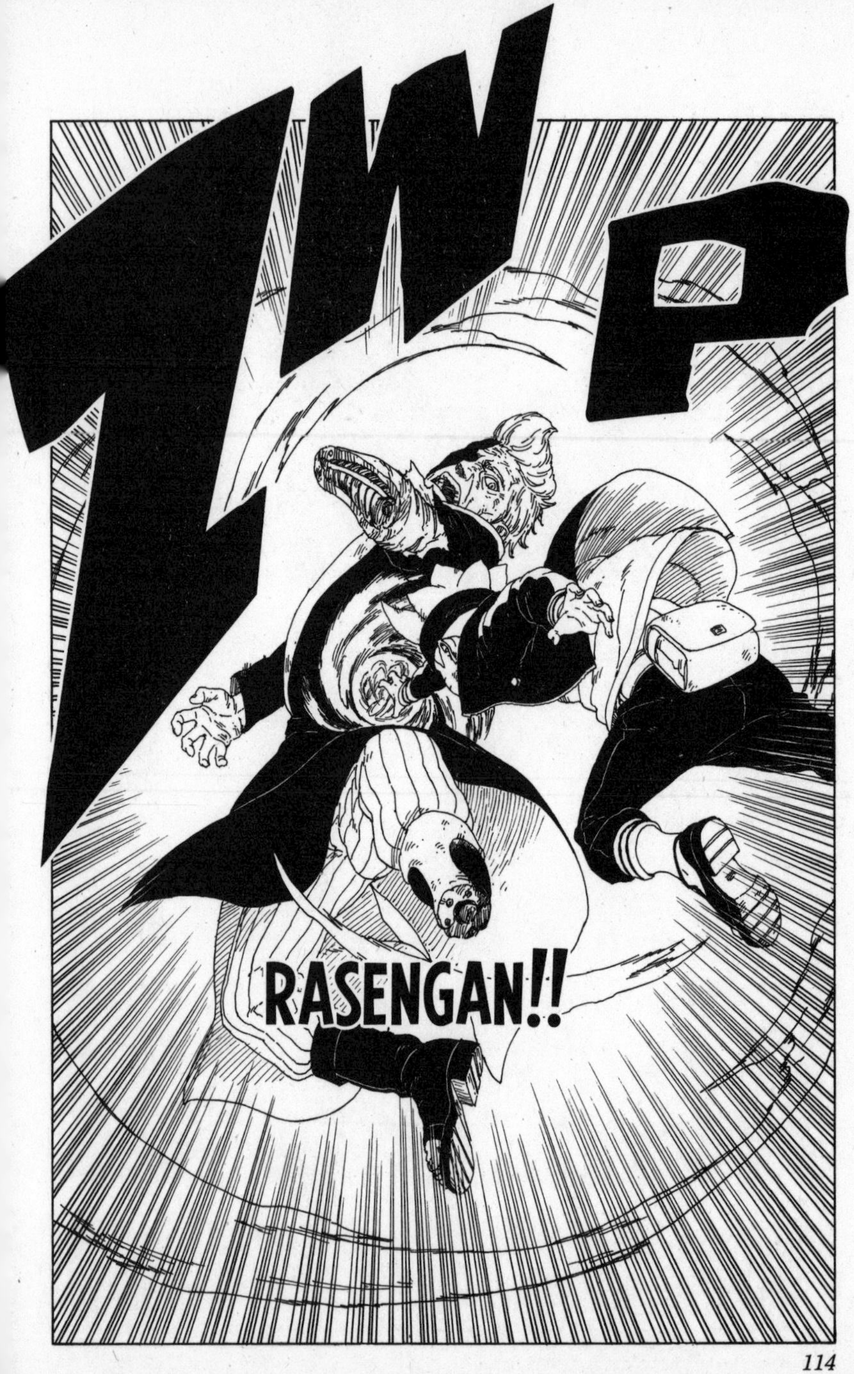
ZWP
RASENGAN!!

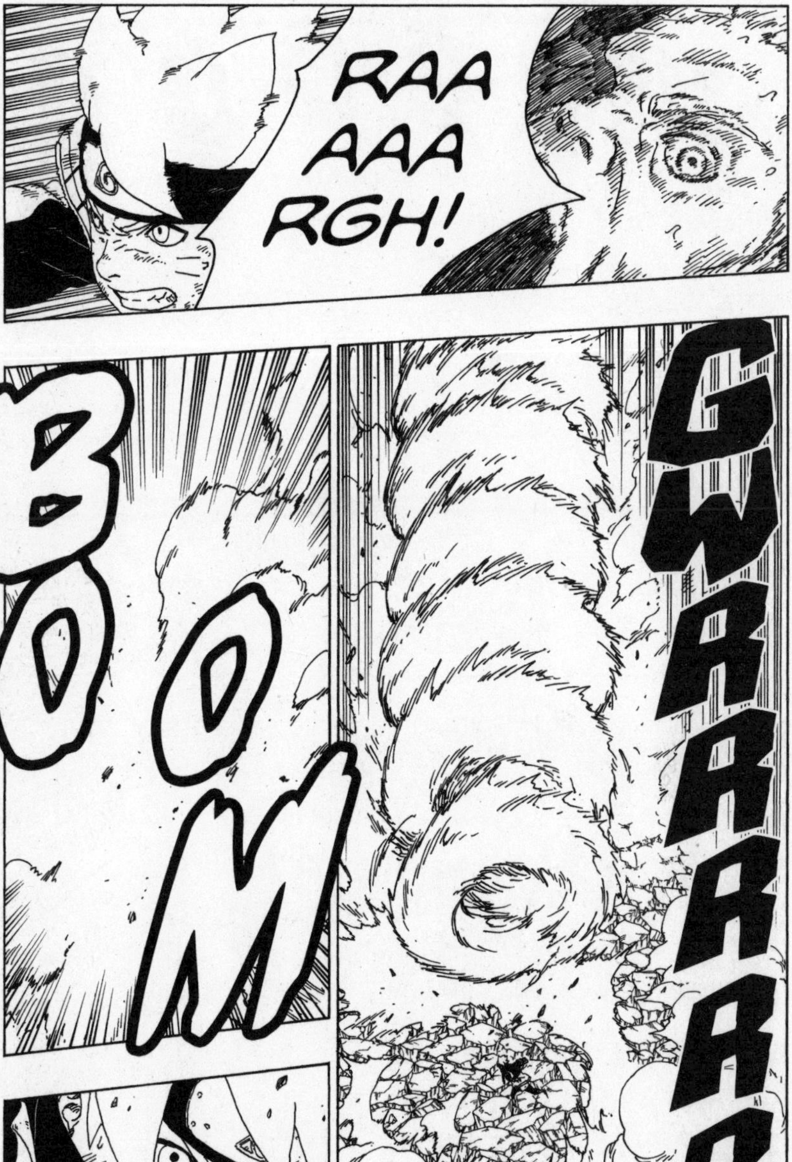
RAAAAARGH!
GWRRRRRR
BOOM

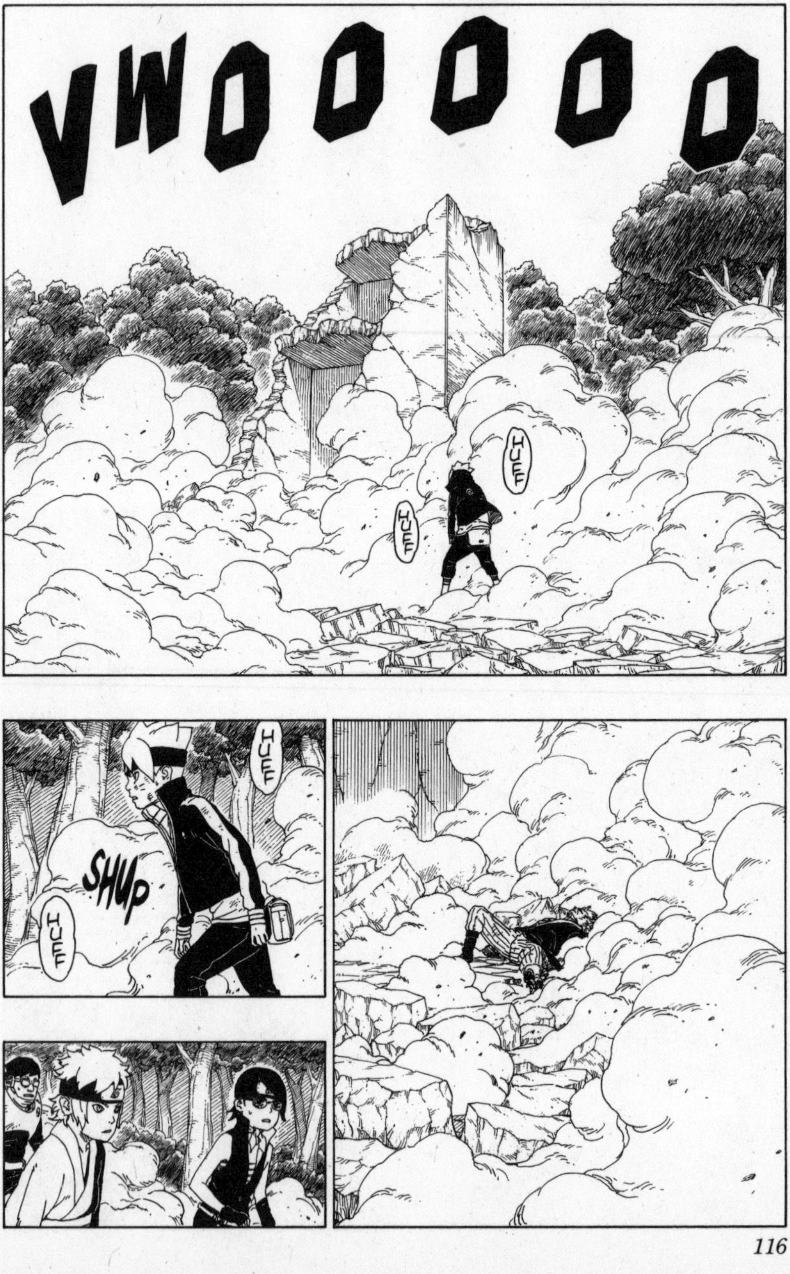
VWOOOOOO
HUFF
HUFF
HUFF
SHUP
HUFF

...

WELL DONE.

YOU WIN.

...

RSTL

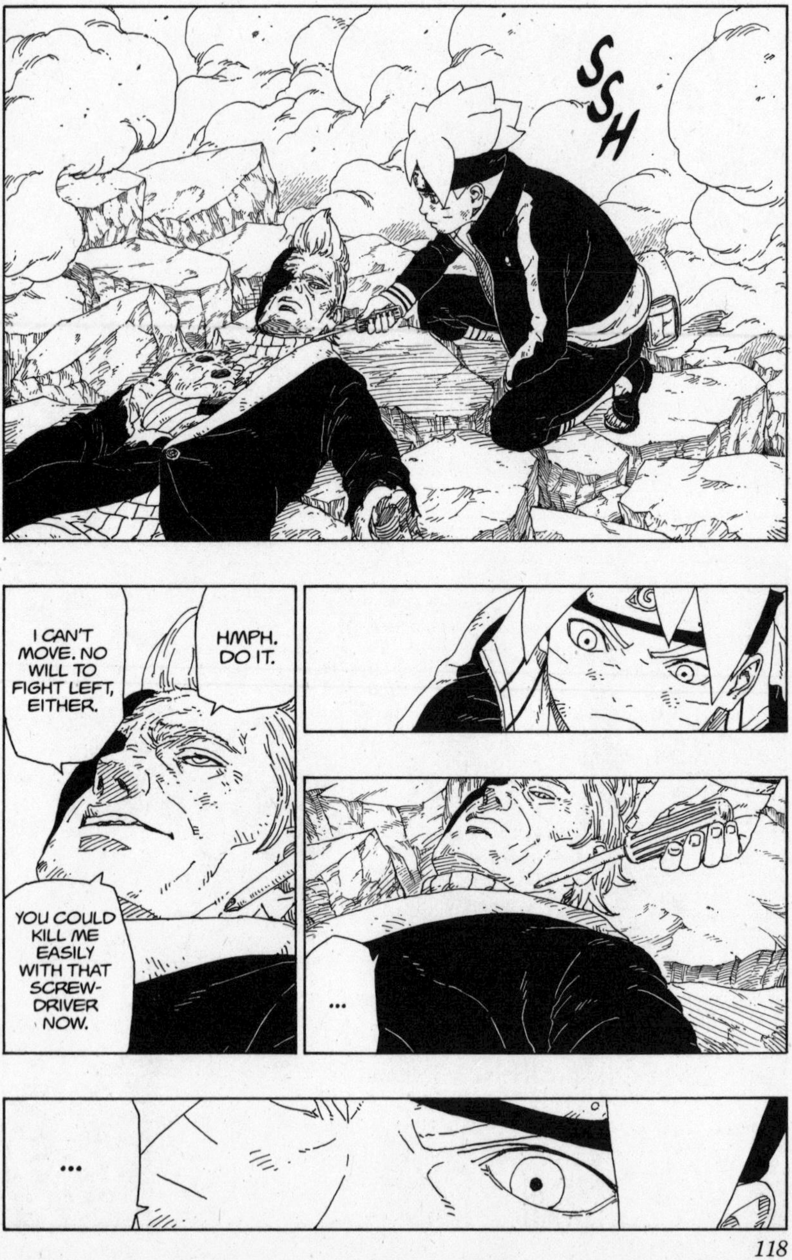
SSH
...
HMPH. DO IT.
I CAN'T MOVE. NO WILL TO FIGHT LEFT, EITHER.
YOU COULD KILL ME EASILY WITH THAT SCREW-DRIVER NOW.
...

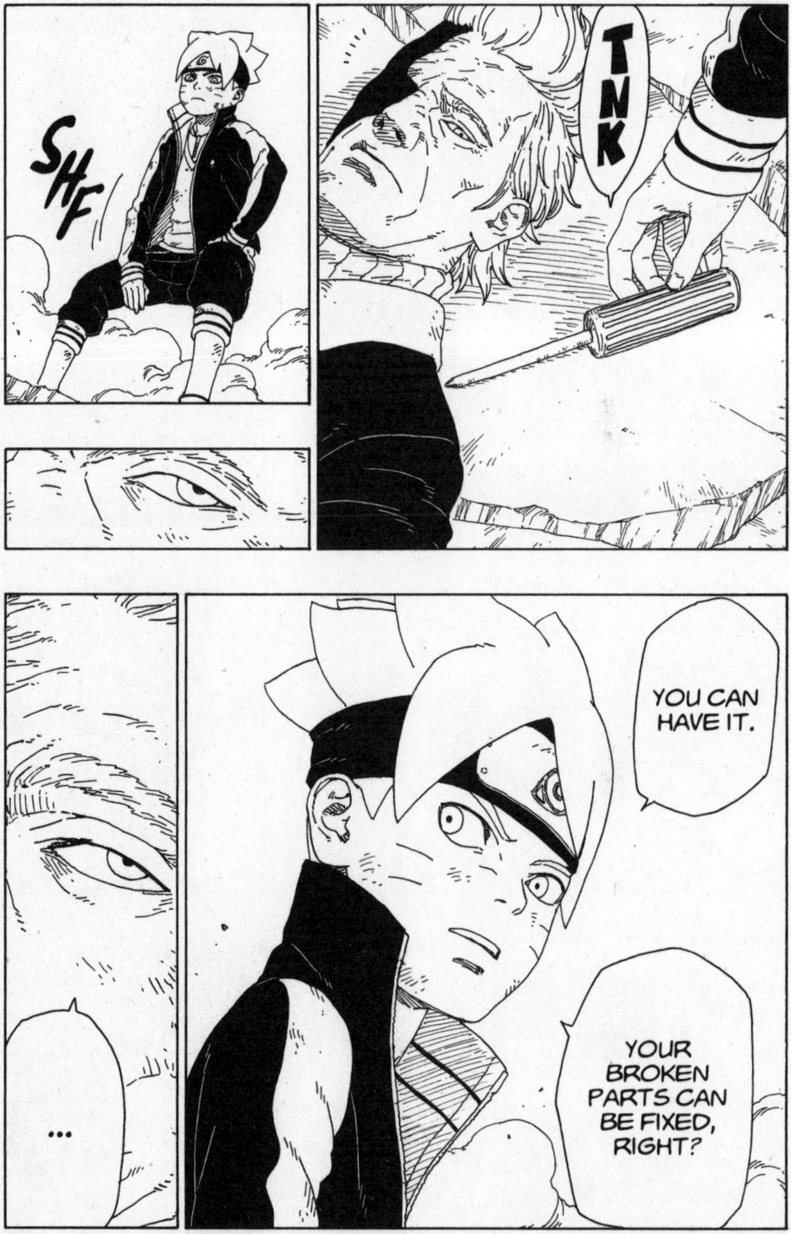
TNK
SHF
YOU CAN HAVE IT.
YOUR BROKEN PARTS CAN BE FIXED, RIGHT?
...

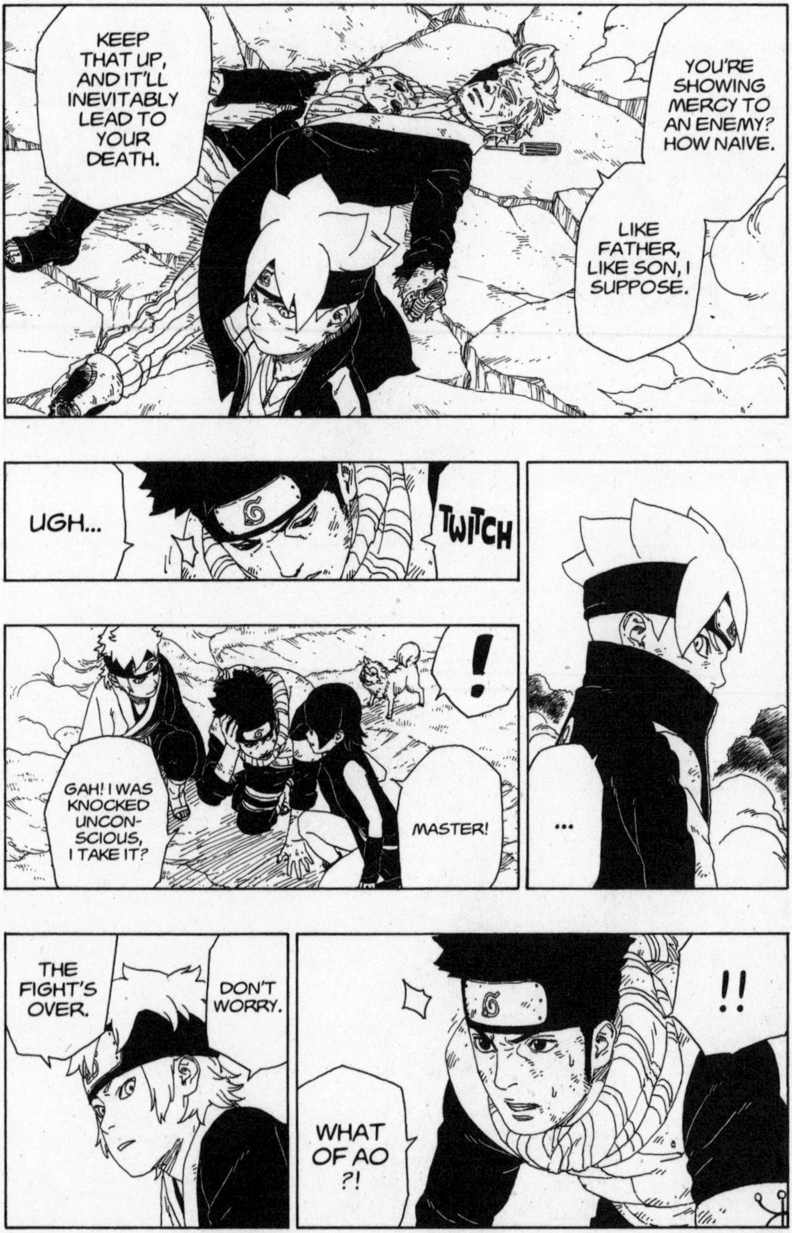
YOU'RE SHOWING MERCY TO AN ENEMY? HOW NAIVE.
LIKE FATHER, LIKE SON, I SUPPOSE.
KEEP THAT UP, AND IT'LL INEVITABLY LEAD TO YOUR DEATH.
...
TWITCH
UGH...
!
MASTER!
GAH! I WAS KNOCKED UNCON-SCIOUS, I TAKE IT?
!!
WHAT OF AO ?!
DON'T WORRY.
THE FIGHT'S OVER.

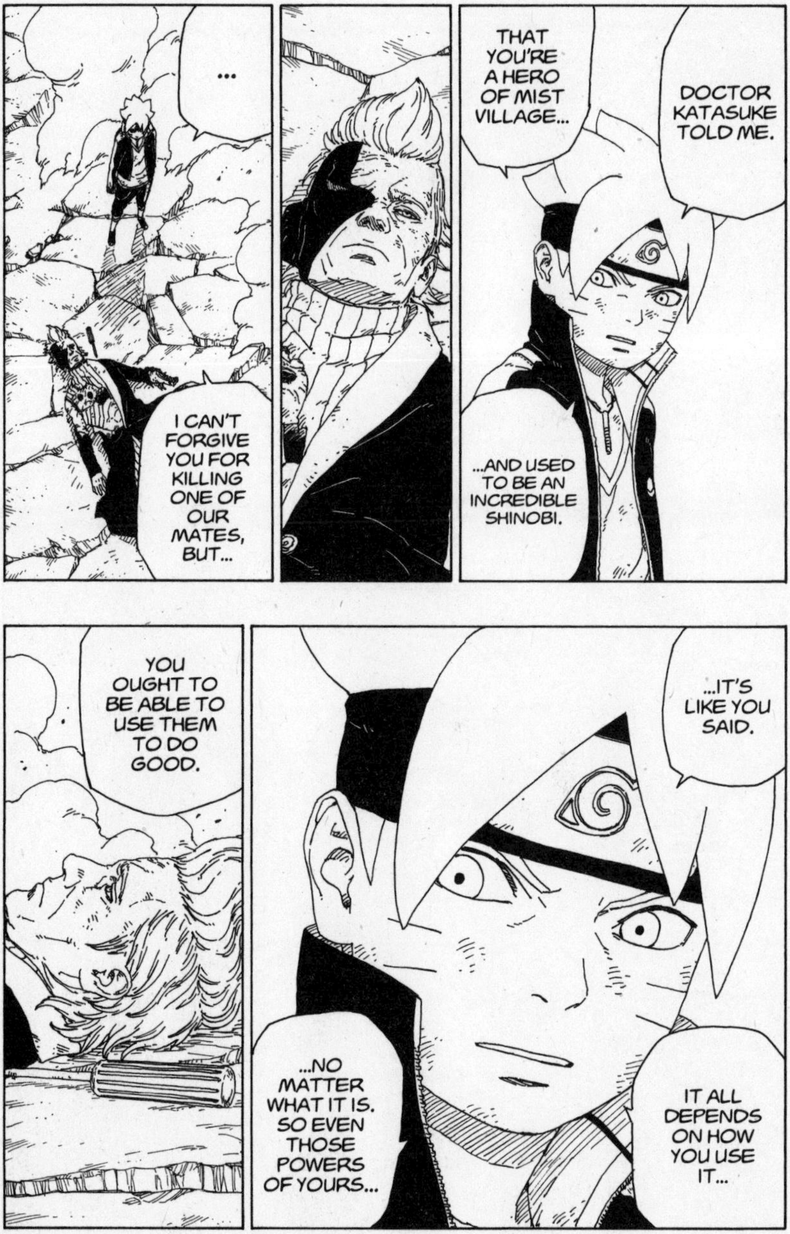
DOCTOR KATASUKE TOLD ME.
THAT YOU'RE A HERO OF MIST VILLAGE...
...AND USED TO BE AN INCREDIBLE SHINOBI.
...
I CAN'T FORGIVE YOU FOR KILLING ONE OF OUR MATES, BUT...
...IT'S LIKE YOU SAID.
IT ALL DEPENDS ON HOW YOU USE IT...
...NO MATTER WHAT IT IS. SO EVEN THOSE POWERS OF YOURS...
YOU OUGHT TO BE ABLE TO USE THEM TO DO GOOD.

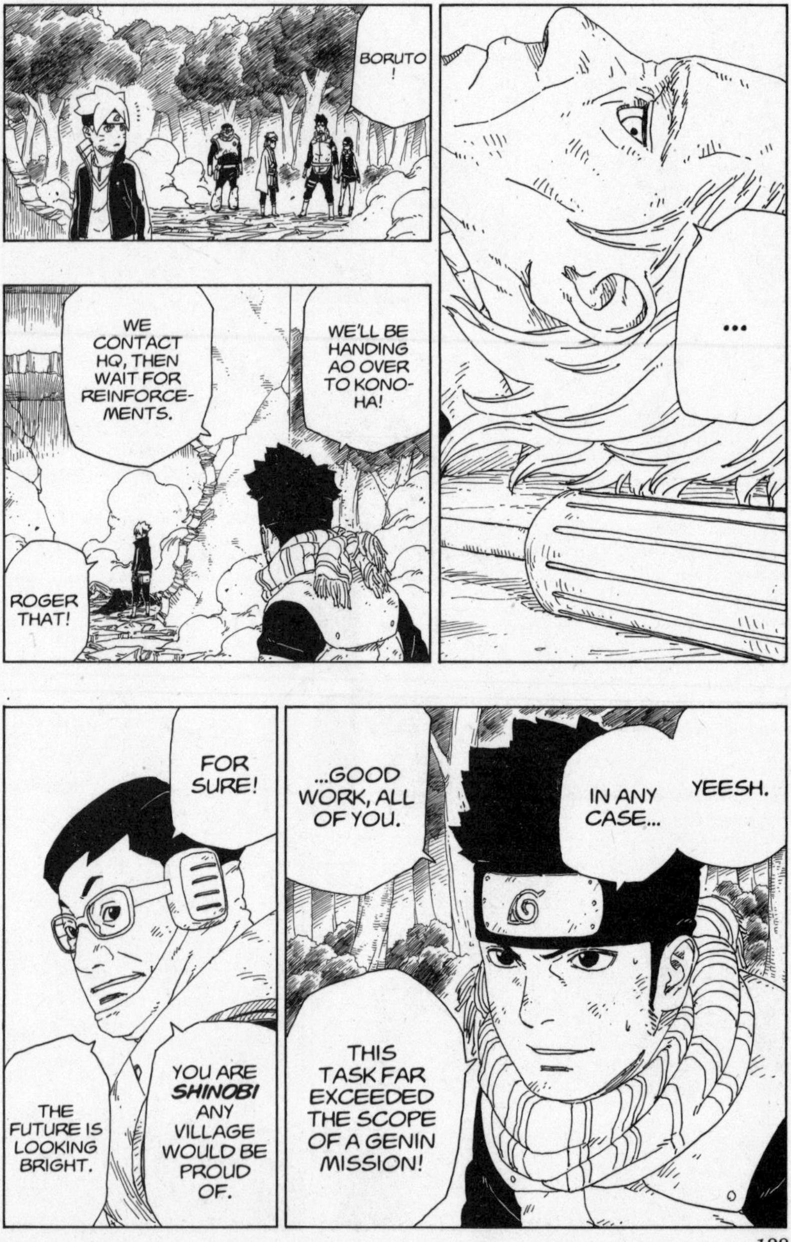
...
BORUTO!
WE'LL BE HANDING AO OVER TO KONOHA!
WE CONTACT HQ, THEN WAIT FOR REINFORCEMENTS.
ROGER THAT!
YEESH.
IN ANY CASE...
...GOOD WORK, ALL OF YOU.
THIS TASK FAR EXCEEDED THE SCOPE OF A GENIN MISSION!
FOR SURE!
YOU ARE *SHINOBI* ANY VILLAGE WOULD BE PROUD OF.
THE FUTURE IS LOOKING BRIGHT.

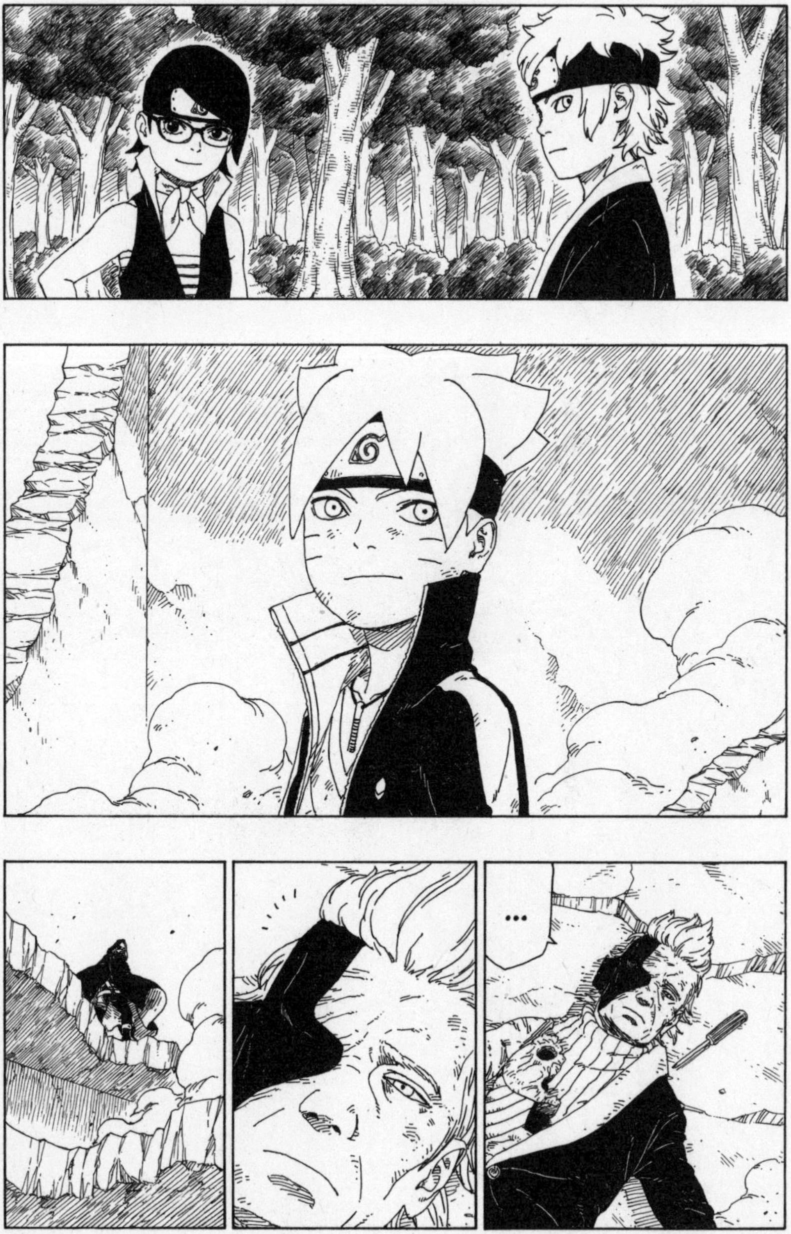
...

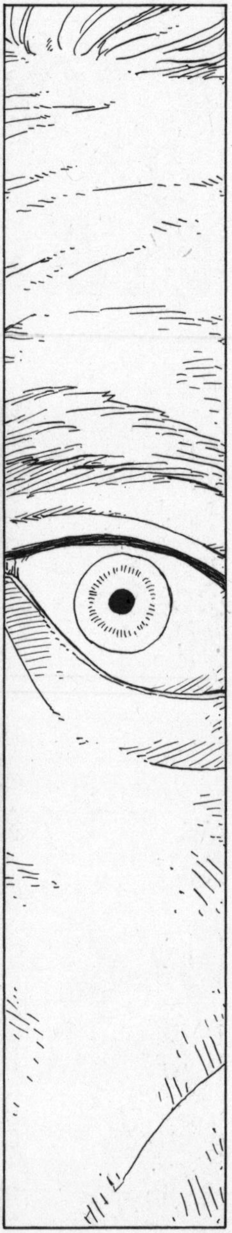

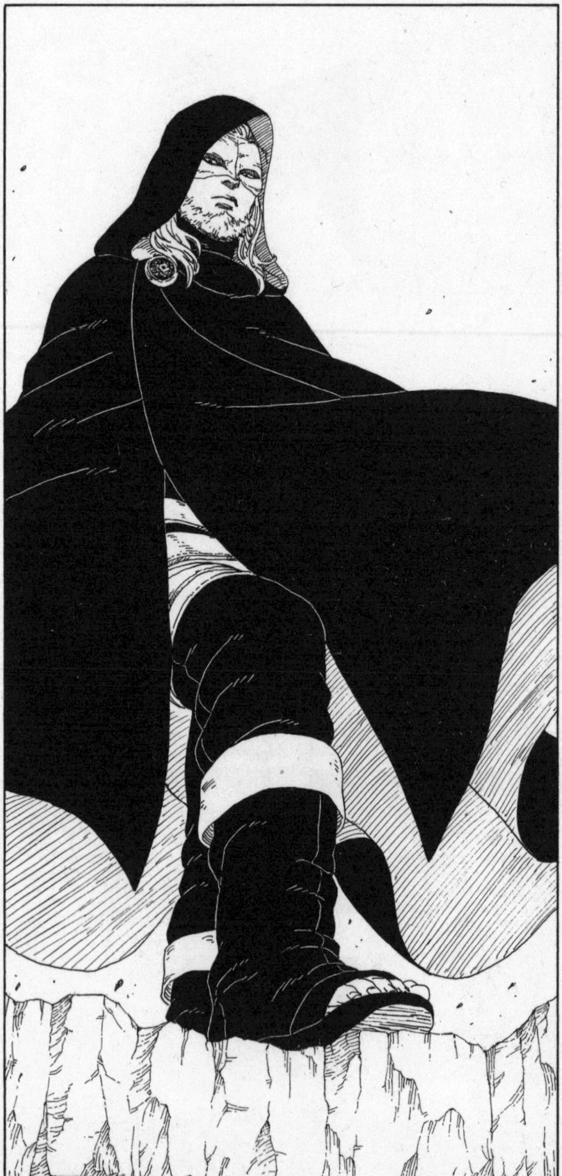

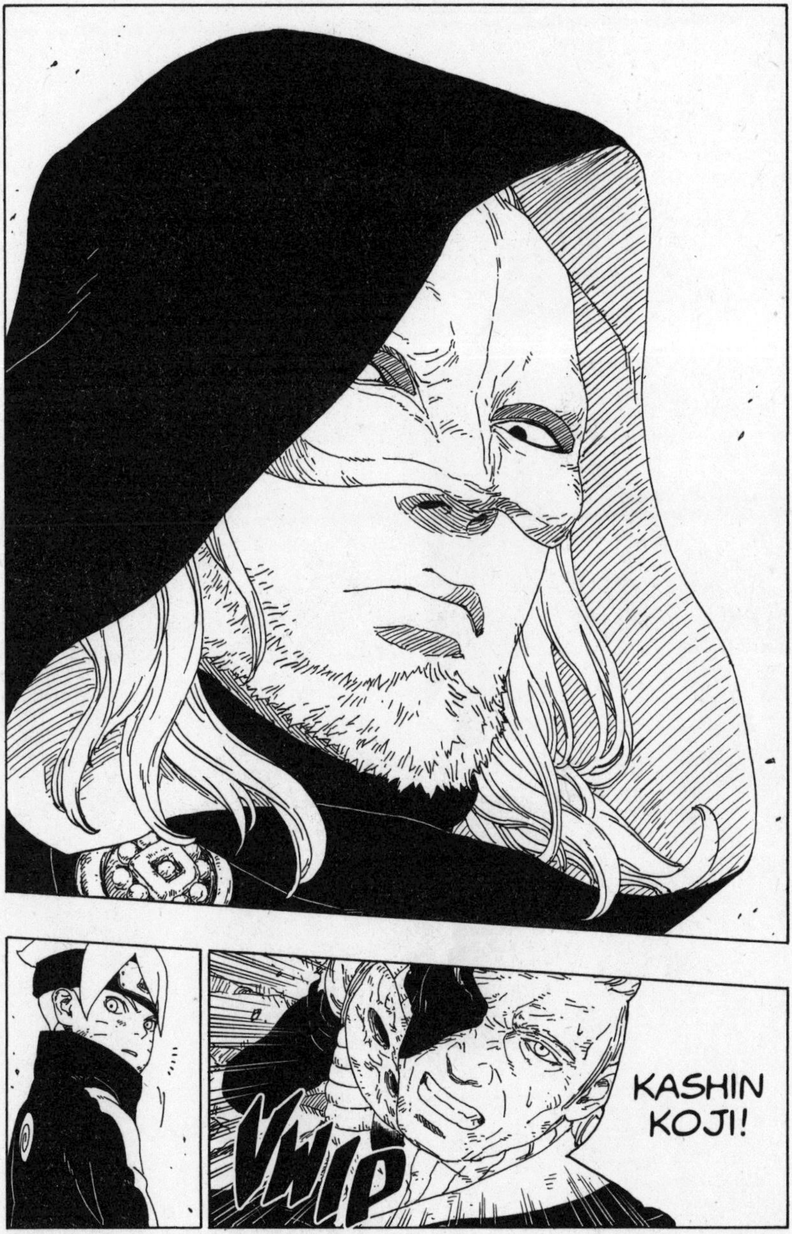
KASHIN KOJI!
VWIP

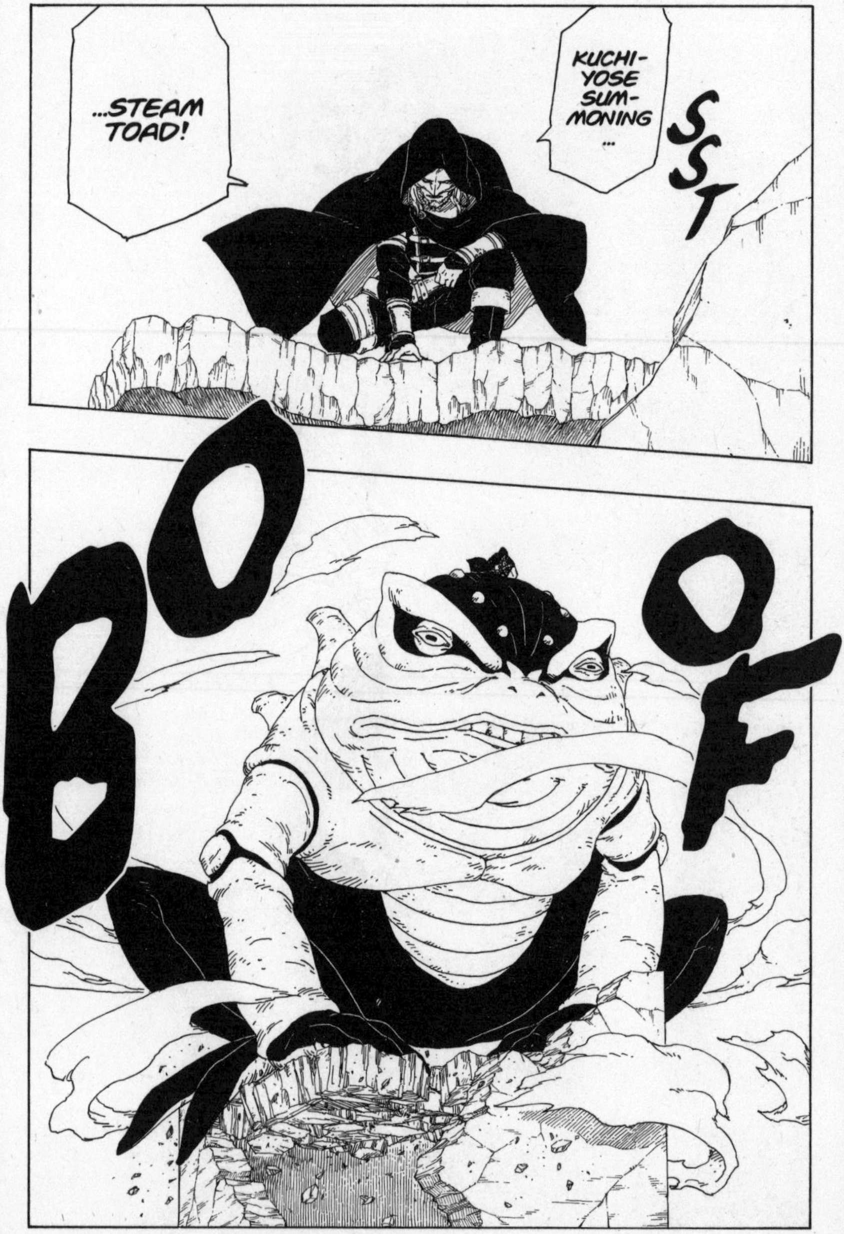
KUCHI-YOSE SUMMONING...
SST
...STEAM TOAD!
BOOF

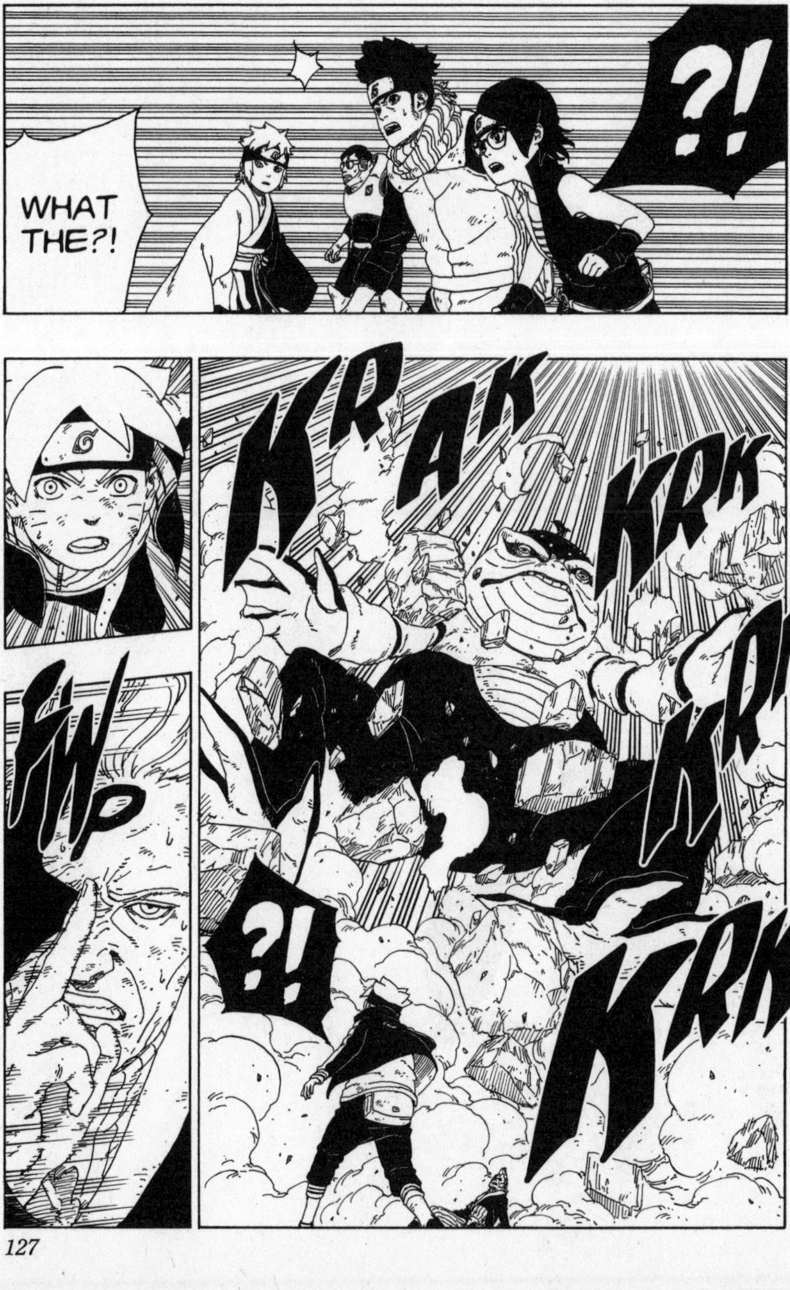
?!
WHAT THE?!
KRAK
KRK
KRK
KRK
?!
FWP

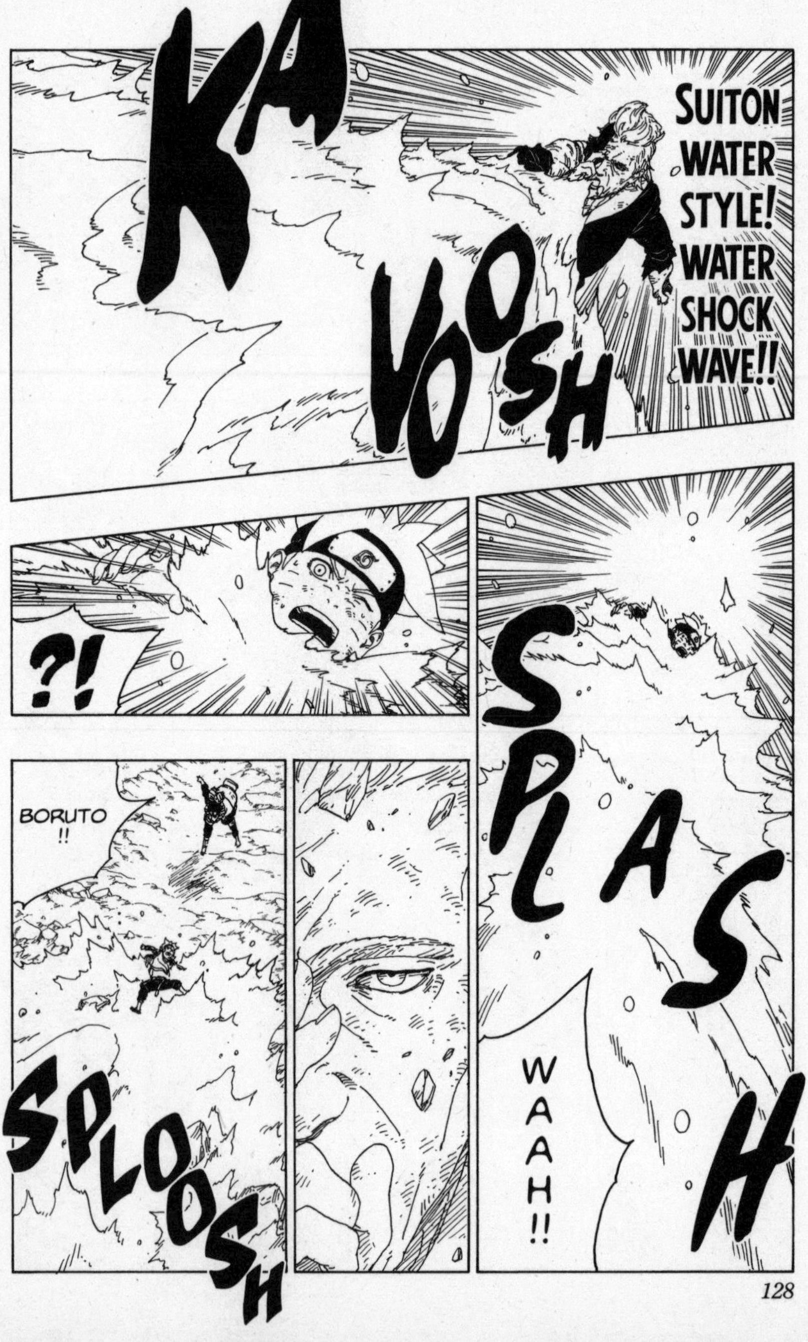
KA
VOOSH
SUITON WATER STYLE! WATER SHOCK WAVE!!
SPLASH
WAAH!!
?!
BORUTO!!
SPLOOSH

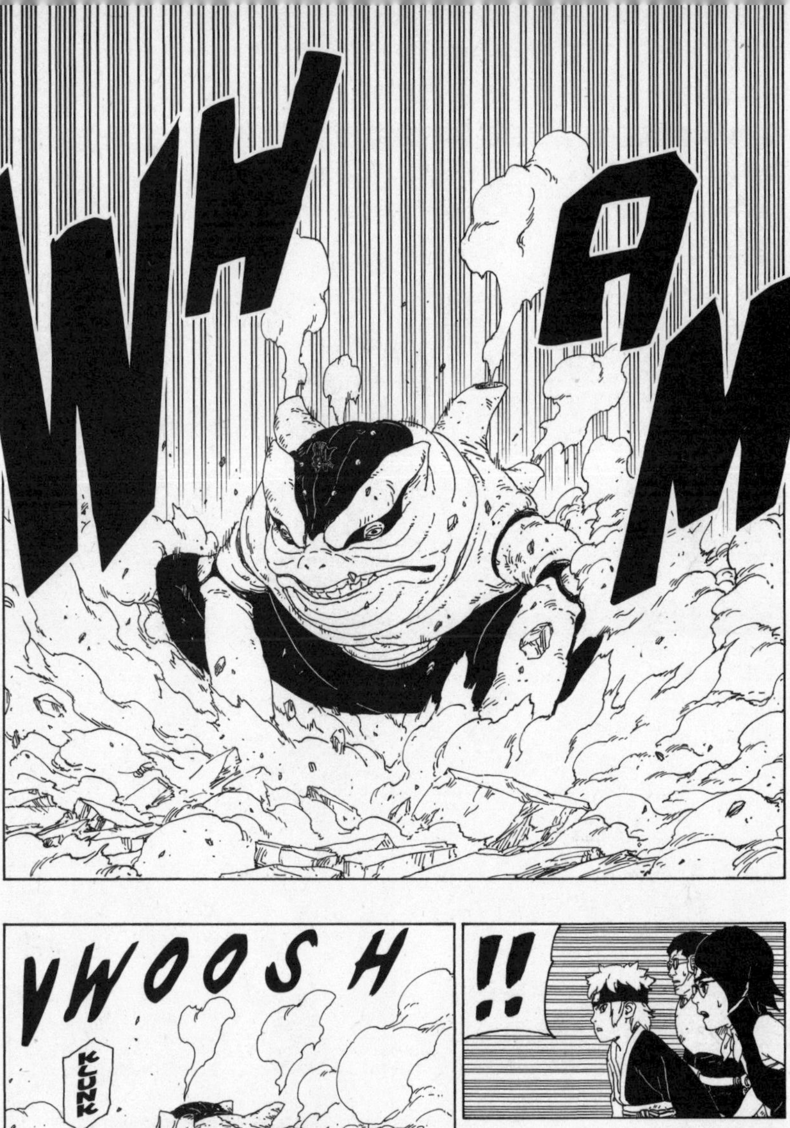
WHAM
!!
!
VWOOSH
KLUNK
KLATTER
KLATTER

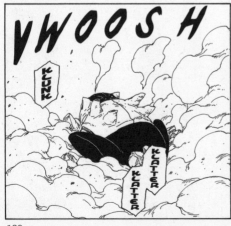

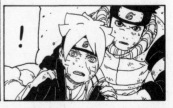

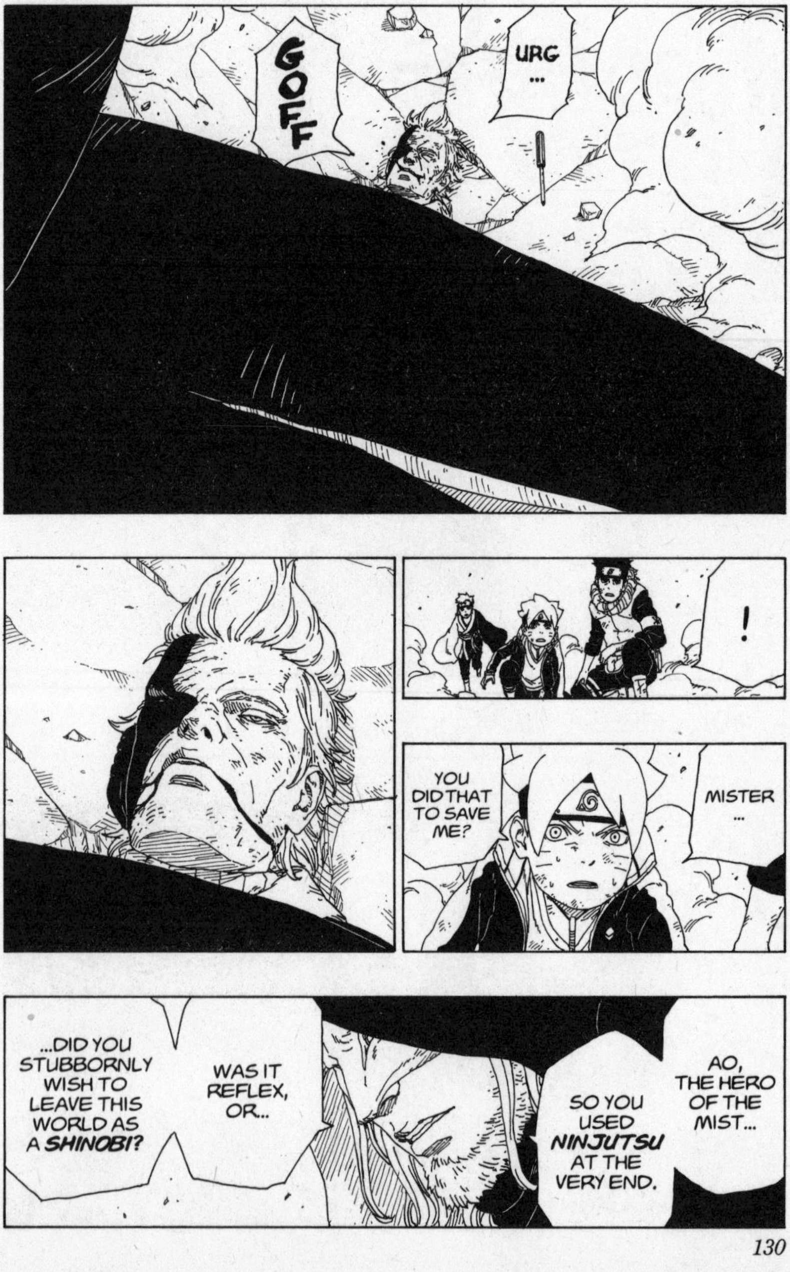
URG ...
GOFF
!
MISTER ...
YOU DID THAT TO SAVE ME?
AO, THE HERO OF THE MIST...
SO YOU USED *NINJUTSU* AT THE VERY END.
WAS IT REFLEX, OR...
...DID YOU STUBBORNLY WISH TO LEAVE THIS WORLD AS A *SHINOBI*?

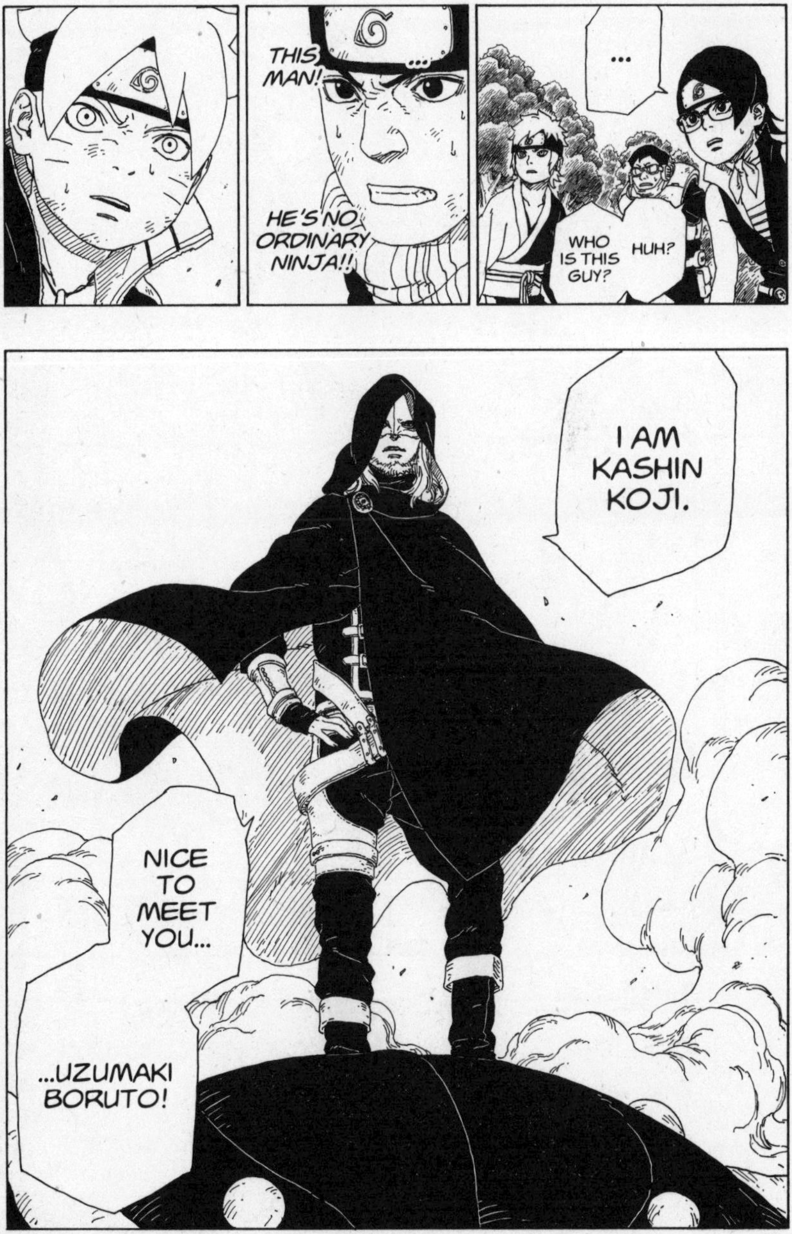
...
HUH?
WHO IS THIS GUY?
THIS MAN!
HE'S NO ORDINARY NINJA!!
I AM KASHIN KOJI.
NICE TO MEET YOU...
...UZUMAKI BORUTO!

NINJA ENCYCLOPEDIA • ENTRY 18

AO

"It all depends on how you use it..."

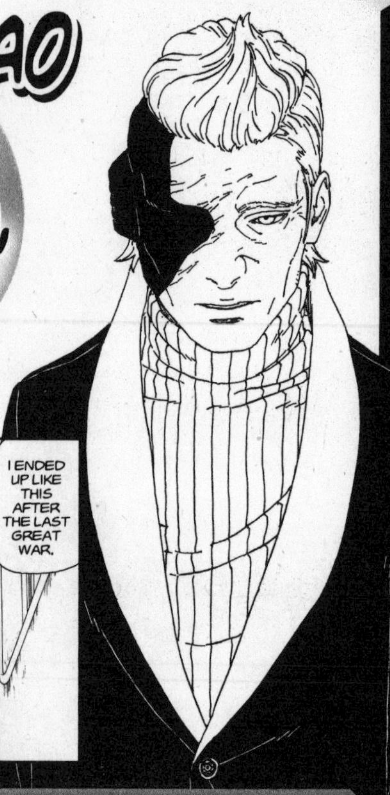

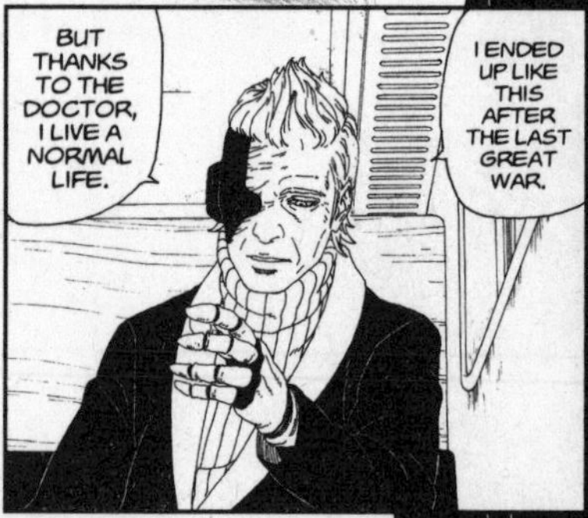

I ENDED UP LIKE THIS AFTER THE LAST GREAT WAR.
BUT THANKS TO THE DOCTOR, I LIVE A NORMAL LIFE.

Attributes

Strength	40 [140]	Dexterity	32 [132]
Intelligence	135	Chakra	77
Perception	55 [145]	Negotiation	96

Skills

Marksmanship ☆☆☆☆ Covert movement ☆☆☆☆

Shinobi-Ware

Mode 3 Shinobi Gauntlet, Chakra Absorber Mk II, etc.

*Average attribute value is 60 for ordinary people and 90 for genin. Skill values range from 1 to 5☆ with 5☆ signifying super top-notch.

Number 23: Karma

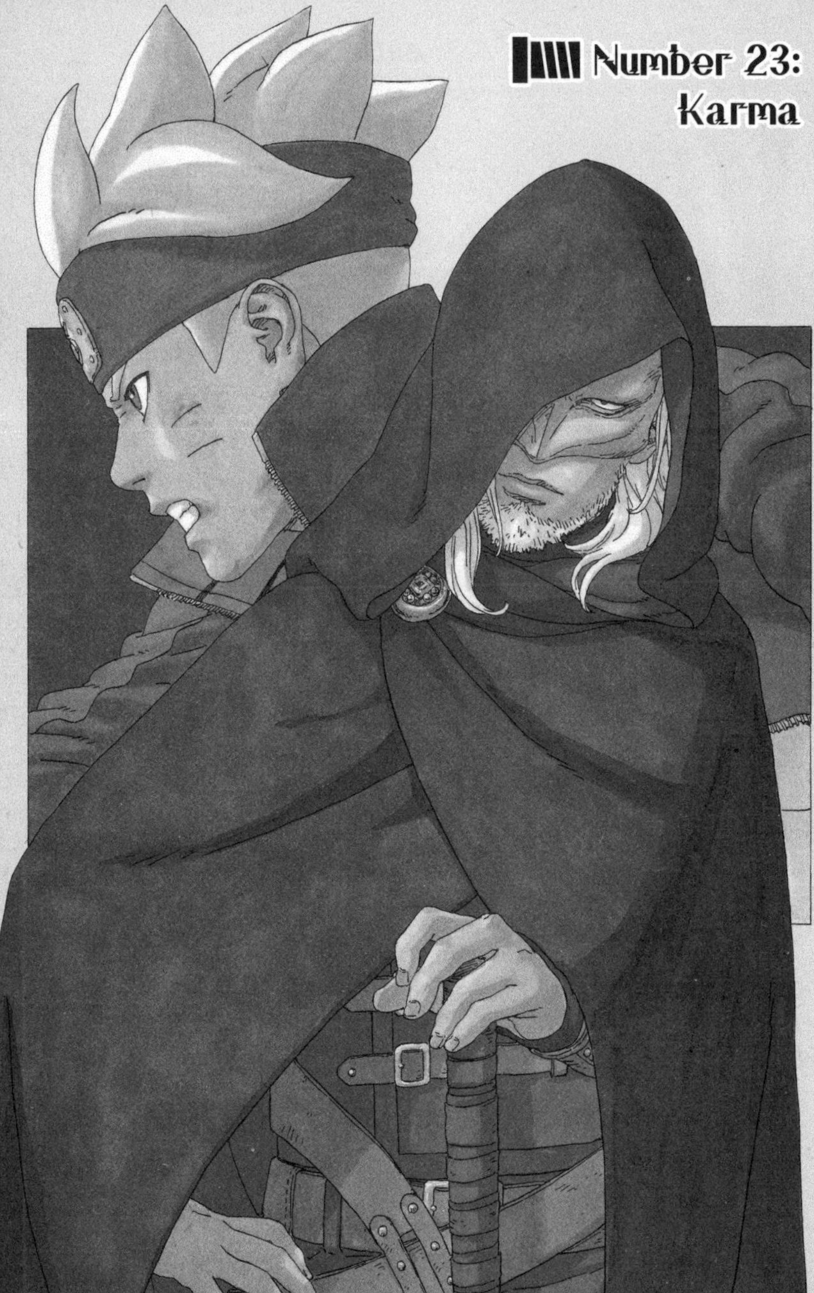

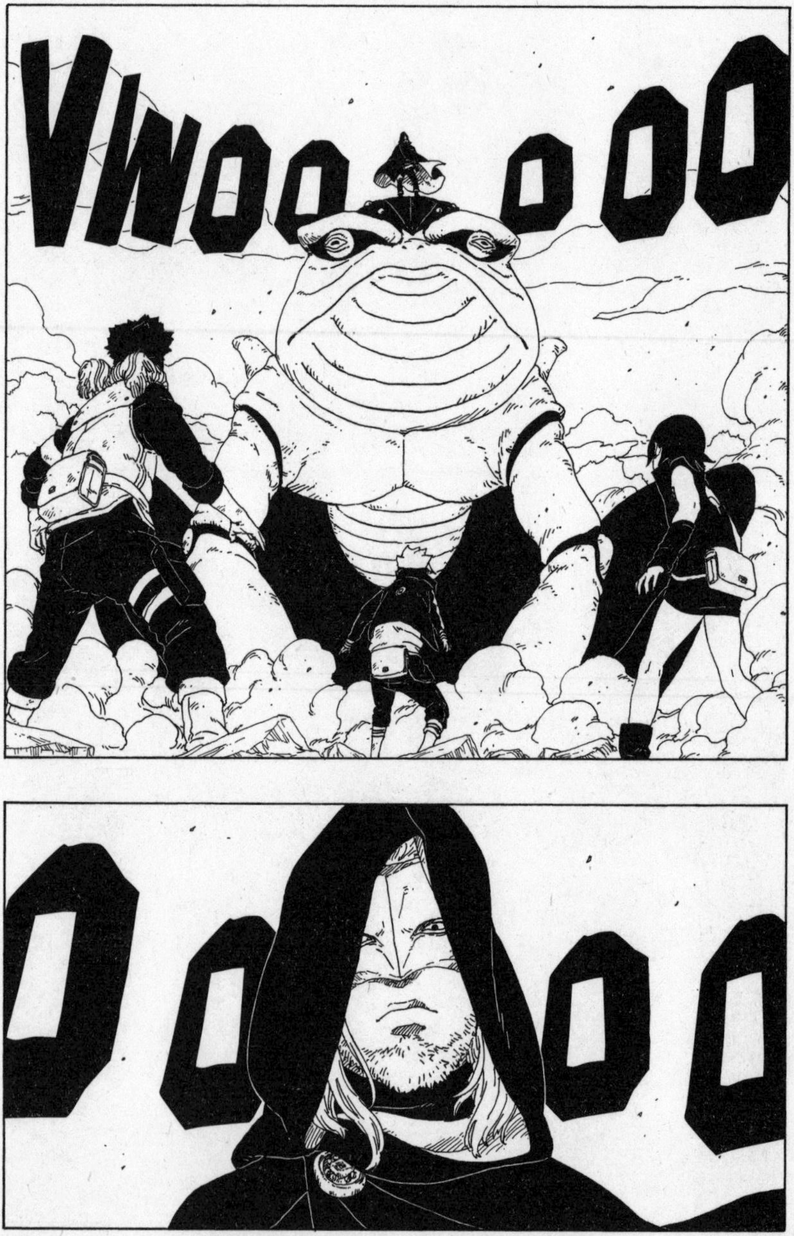
VWOOOOO
OOOOO

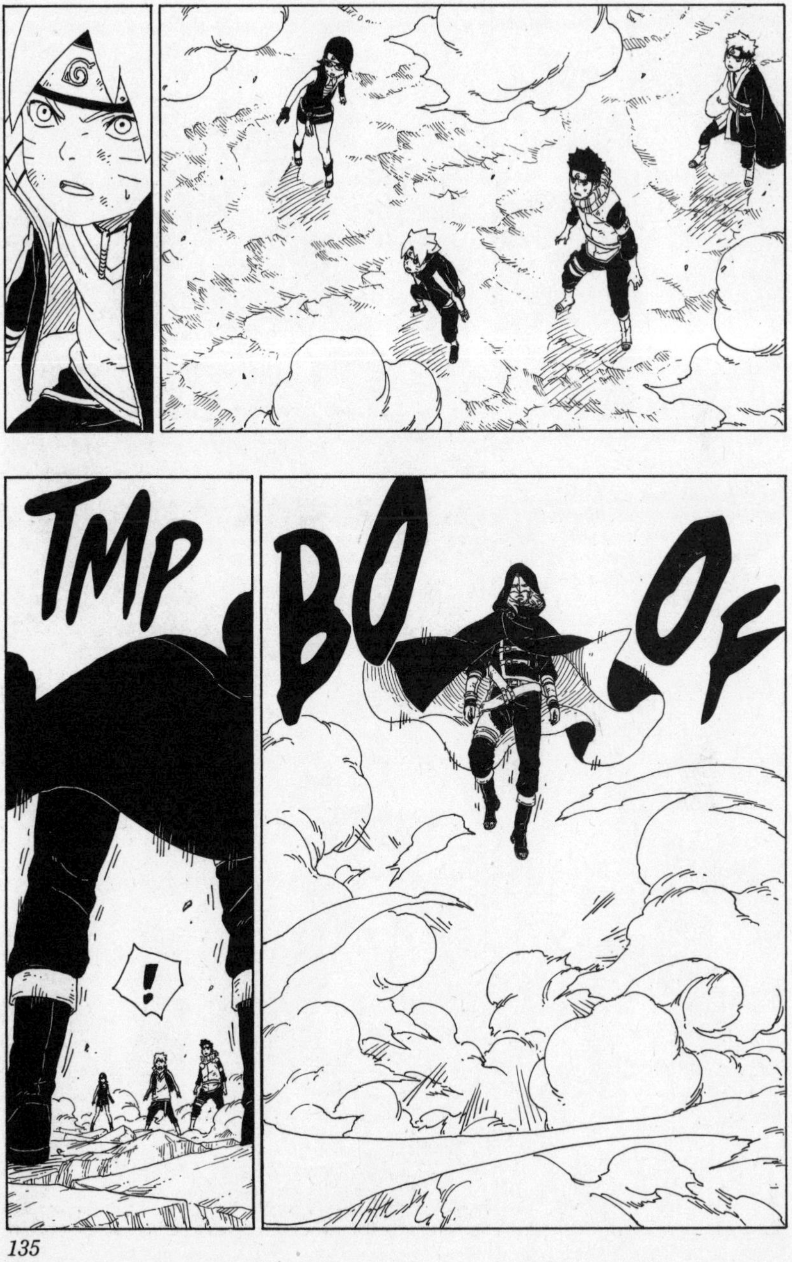
BOOF
TMP
!

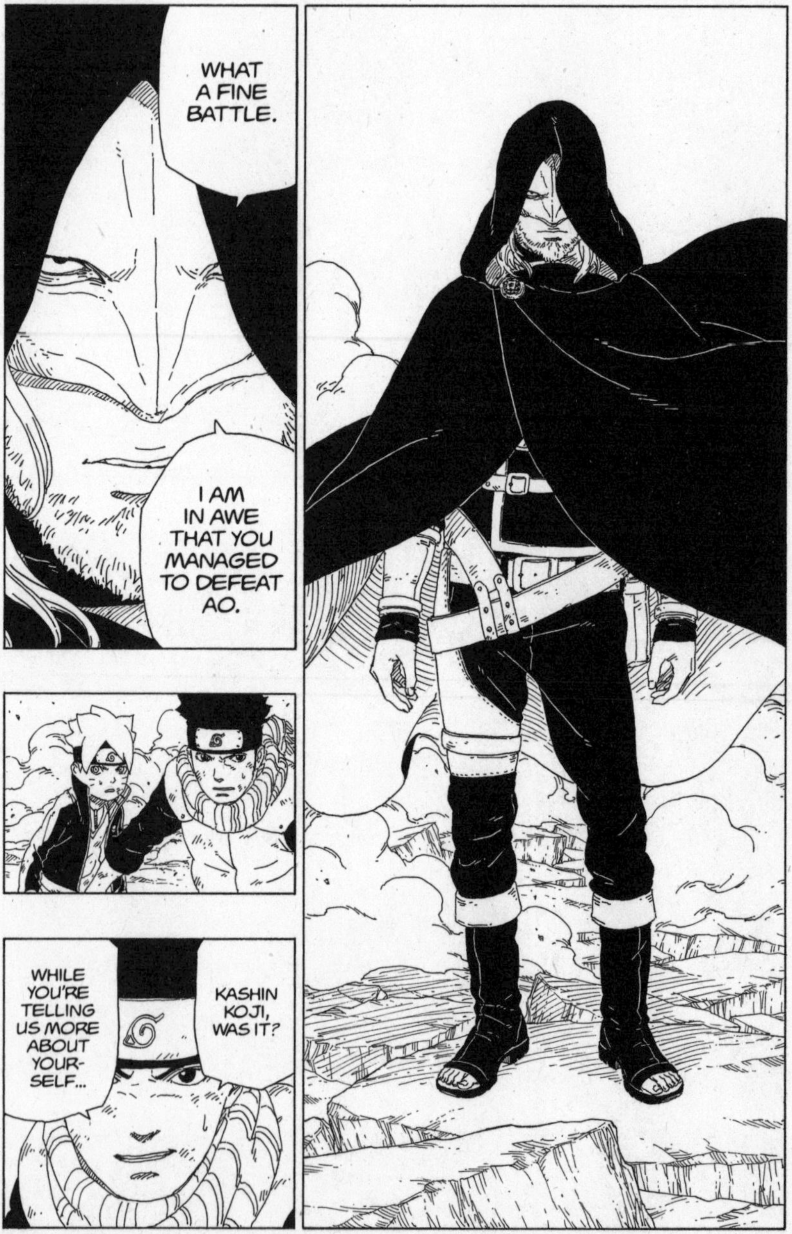
WHAT A FINE BATTLE.
I AM IN AWE THAT YOU MANAGED TO DEFEAT AO.
KASHIN KOJI, WAS IT?
WHILE YOU'RE TELLING US MORE ABOUT YOUR-SELF...

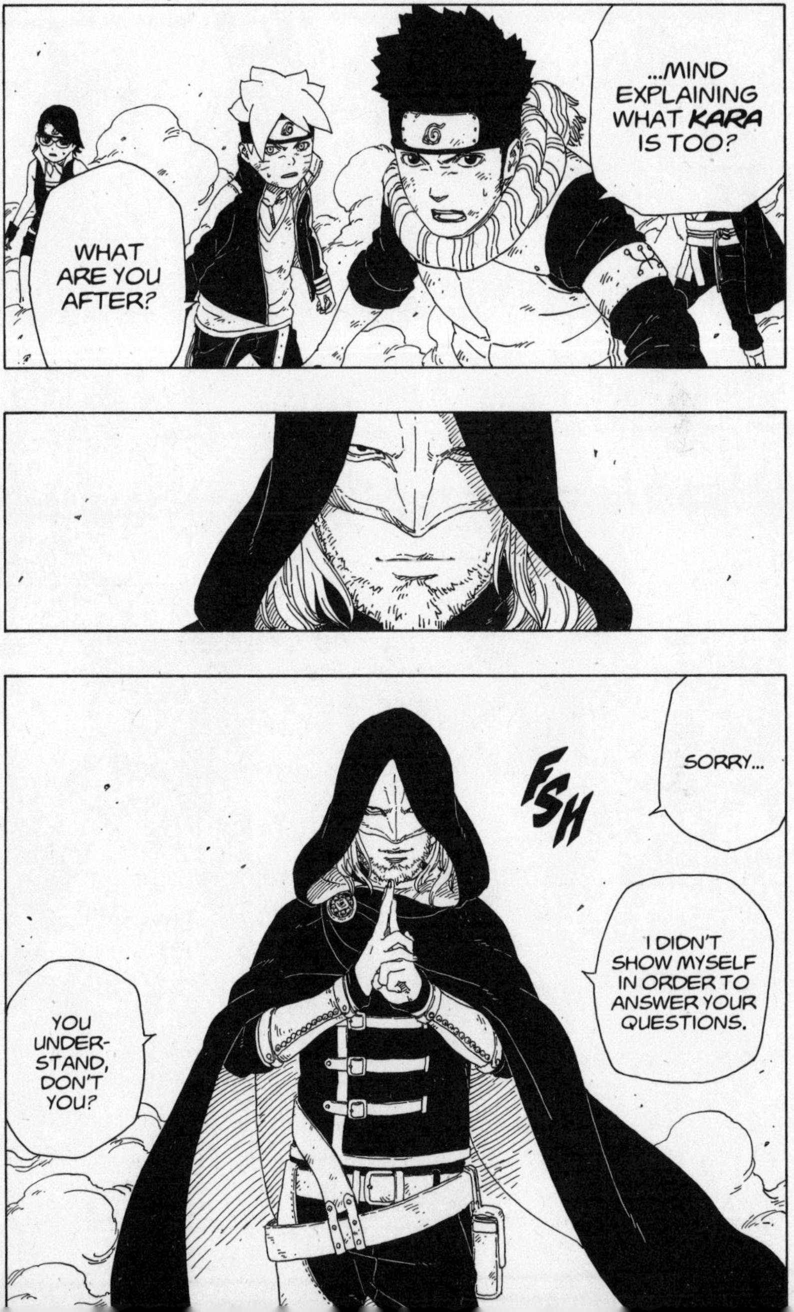
...MIND EXPLAINING WHAT KARA IS TOO?
WHAT ARE YOU AFTER?
SORRY...
FSH
I DIDN'T SHOW MYSELF IN ORDER TO ANSWER YOUR QUESTIONS.
YOU UNDER-STAND, DON'T YOU?

ZW
ZW
W
SEALING JUTSU!
FROG GULP!!
KR- KRACKLE
UGH!!!

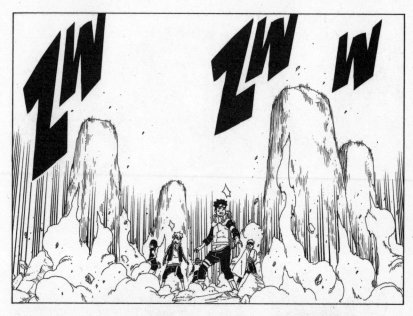

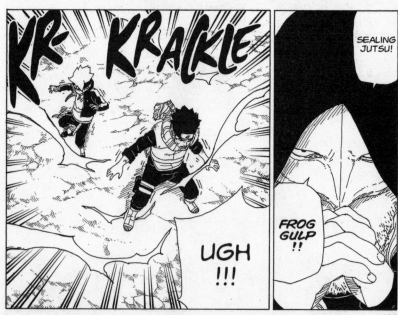

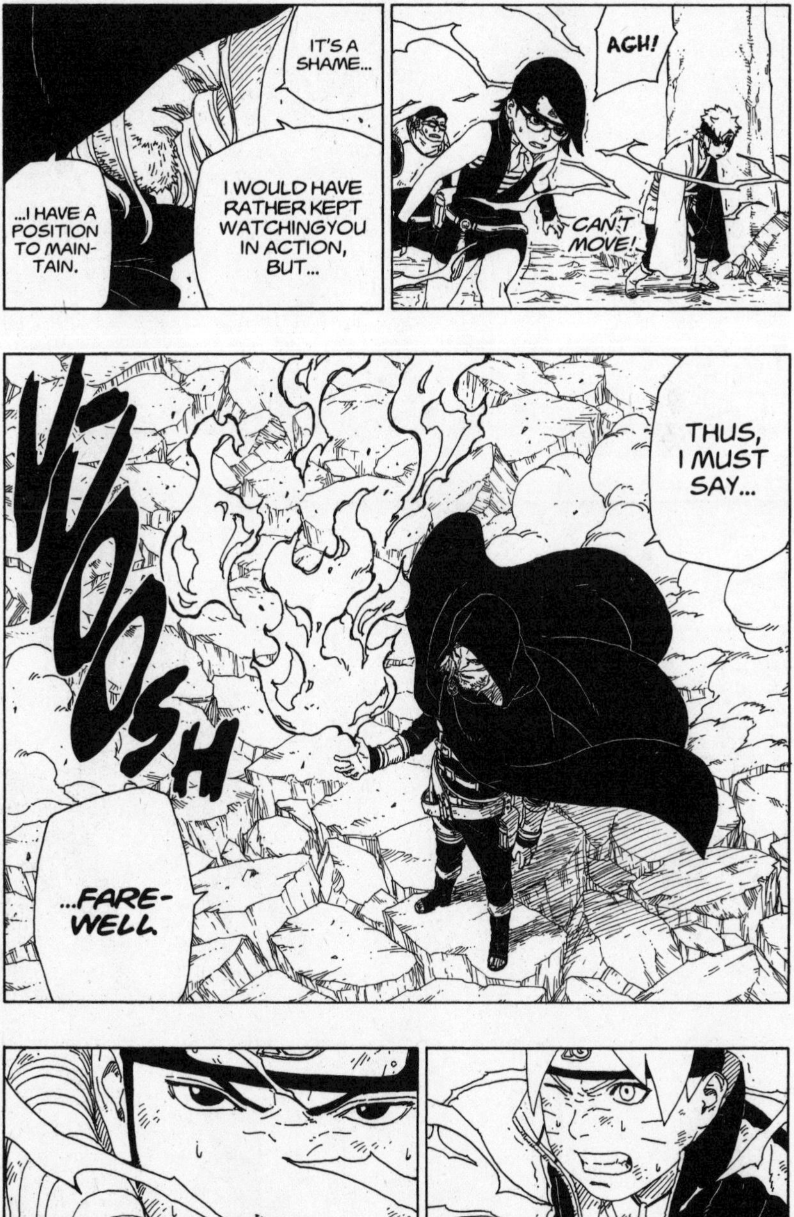
AGH!
CAN'T MOVE!
IT'S A SHAME...
I WOULD HAVE RATHER KEPT WATCHING YOU IN ACTION, BUT...
...I HAVE A POSITION TO MAIN-TAIN.
THUS, I MUST SAY...
VWOOSH
...FARE-WELL.

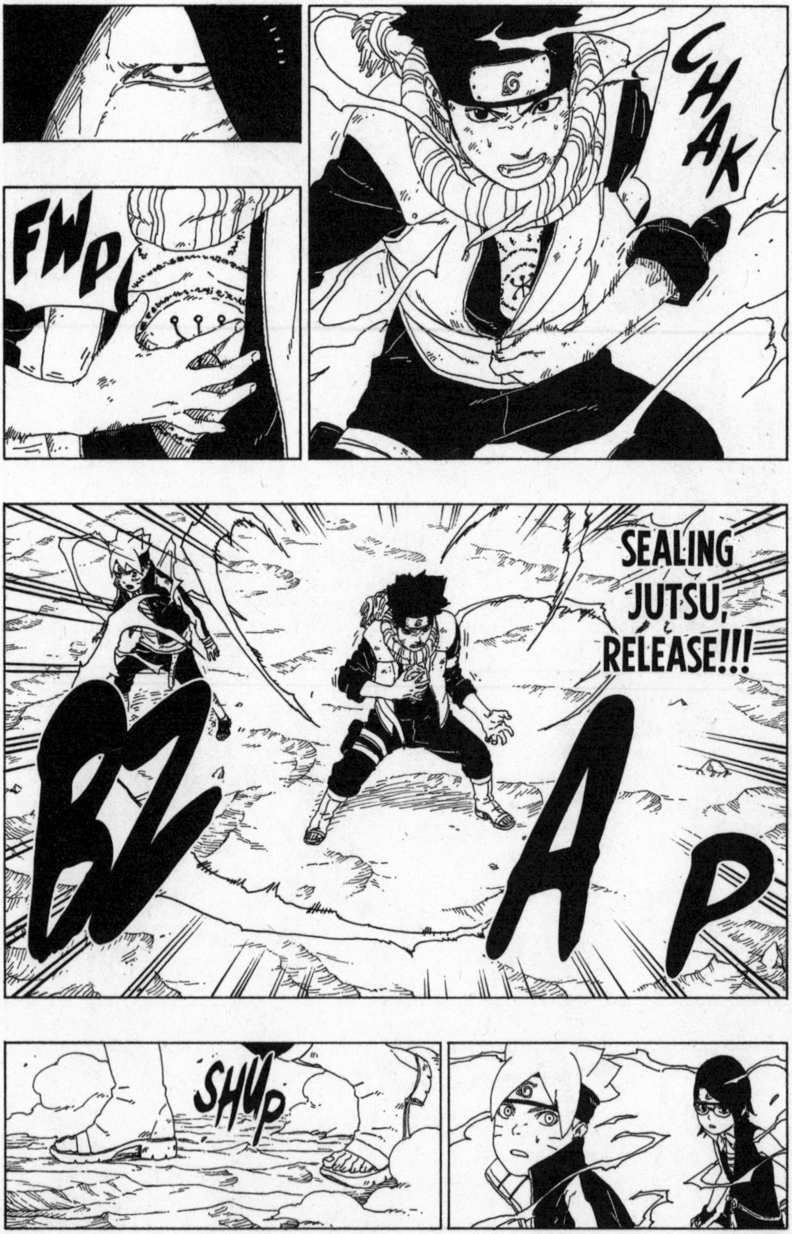
CHAK
FWP
SEALING JUTSU, RELEASE!!!
BZAP
SHUP

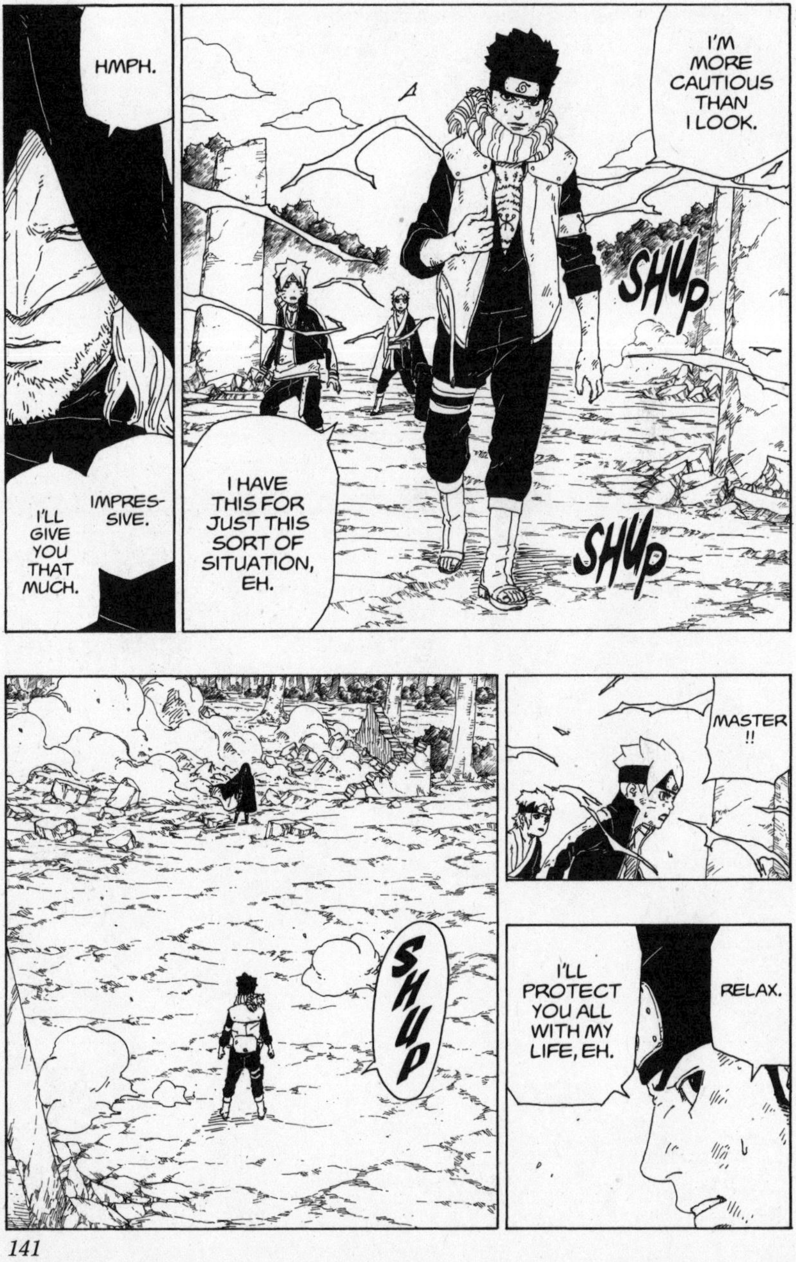
I'M MORE CAUTIOUS THAN I LOOK.
SHUP
SHUP
I HAVE THIS FOR JUST THIS SORT OF SITUATION, EH.
HMPH.
IMPRES-SIVE.
I'LL GIVE YOU THAT MUCH.
MASTER!!
RELAX.
I'LL PROTECT YOU ALL WITH MY LIFE, EH.
SHUP

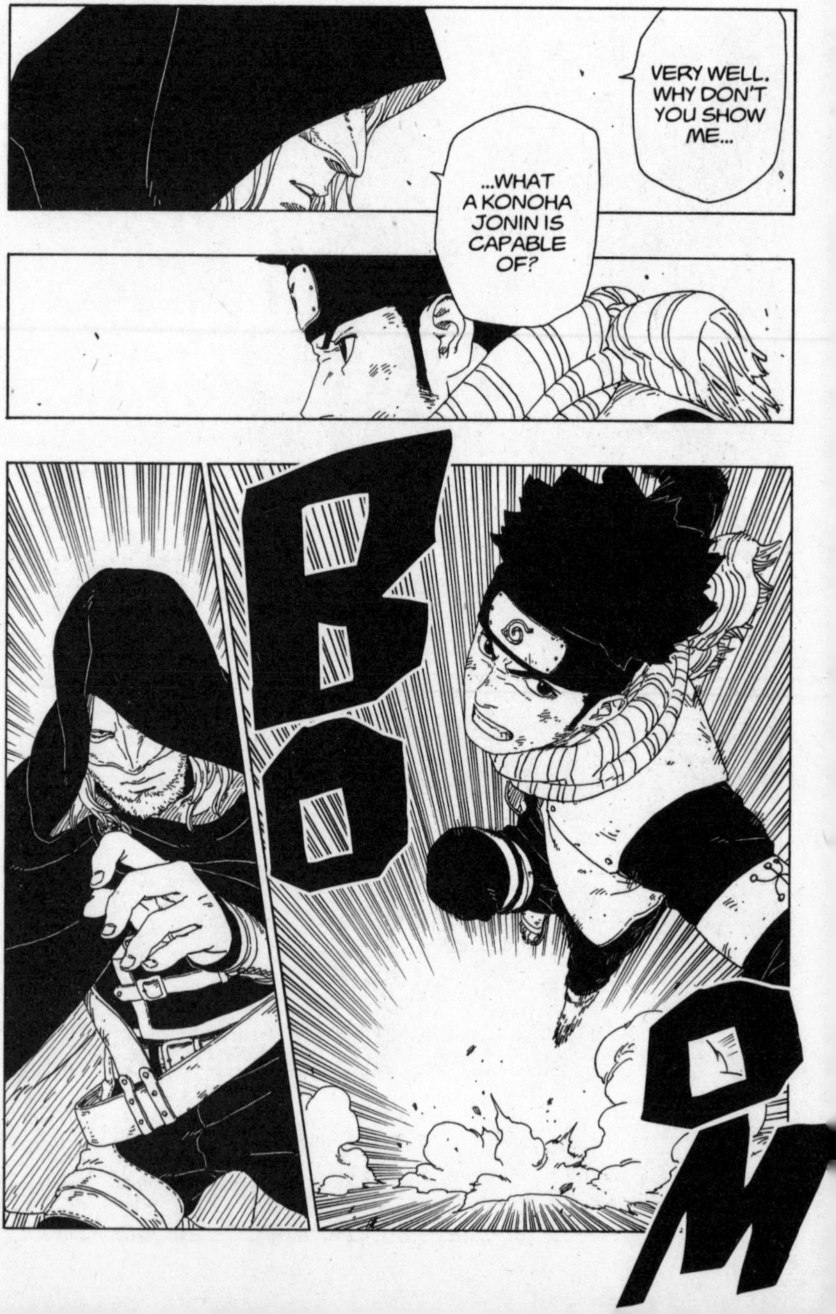
VERY WELL. WHY DON'T YOU SHOW ME...
...WHAT A KONOHA JONIN IS CAPABLE OF?
BOOM

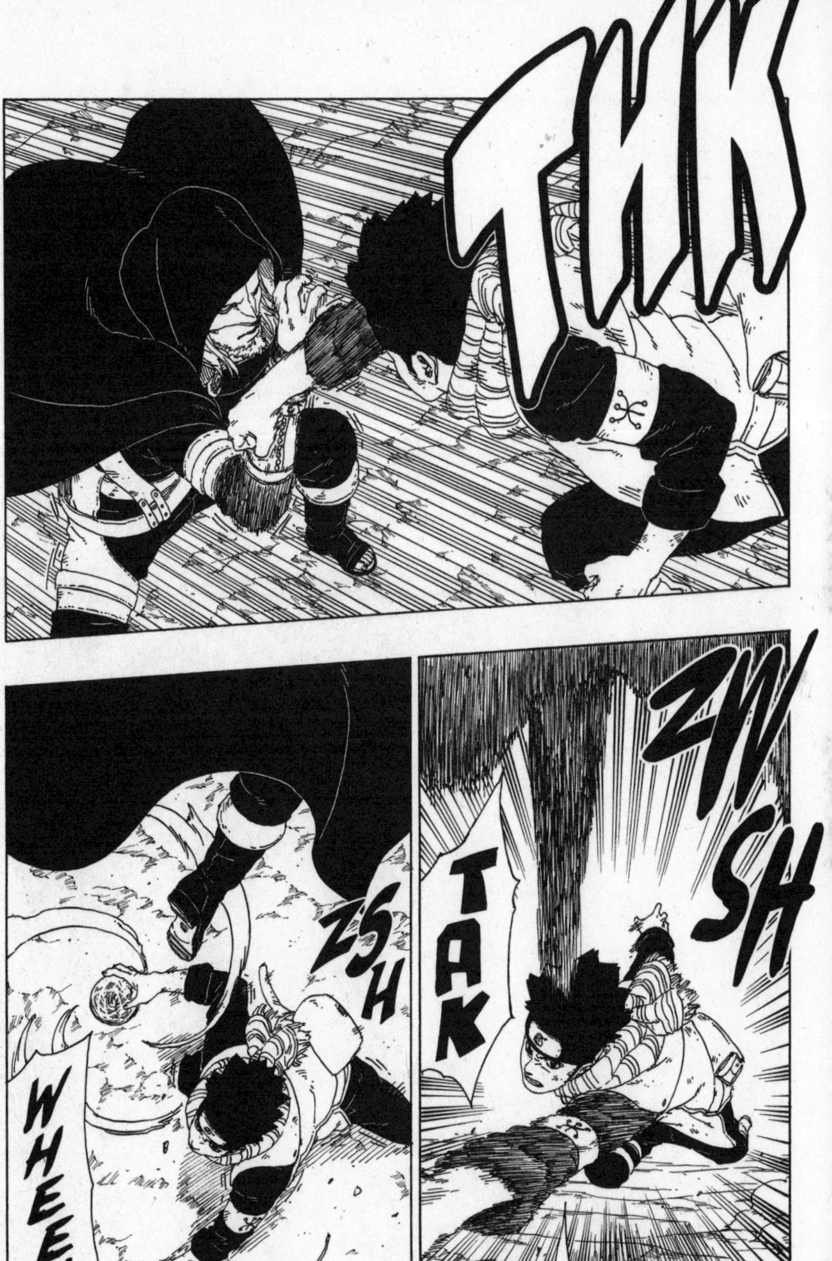
THK
ZWSH
TAK
ZSH
WHEEN

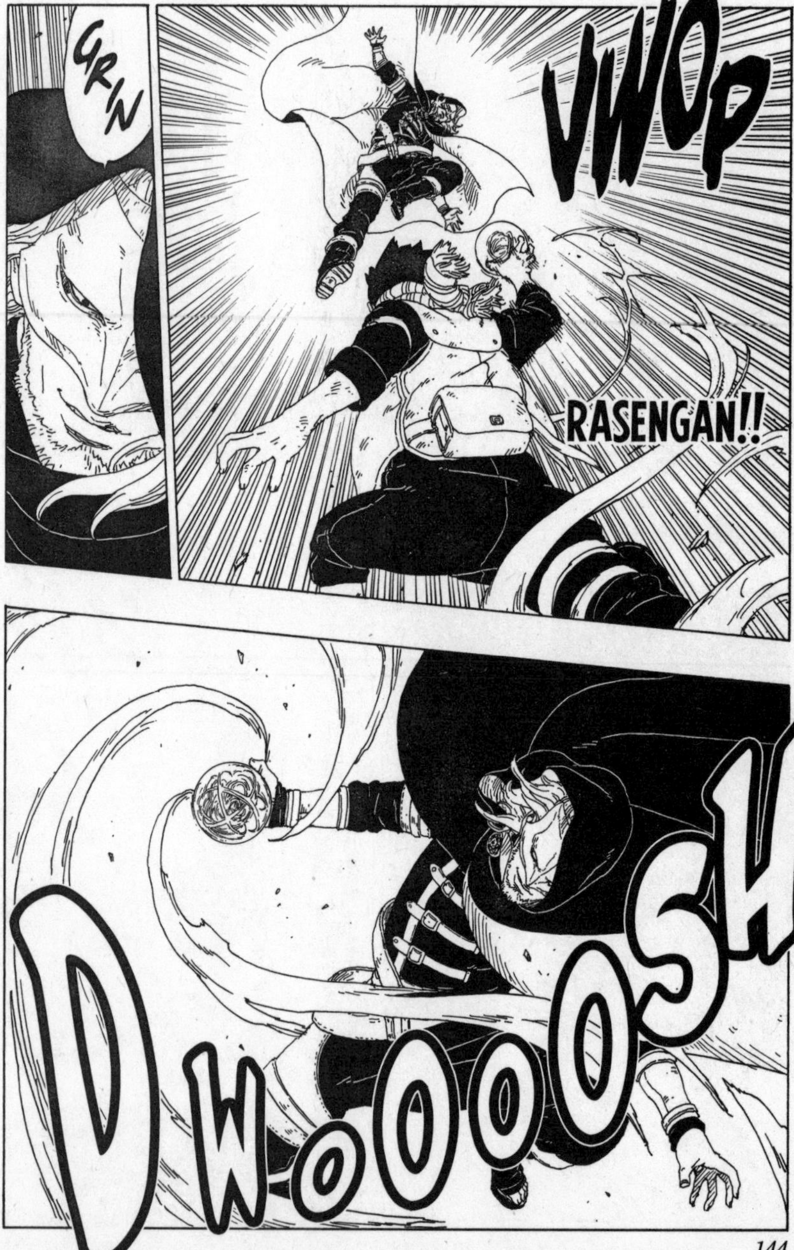
VWOP
RASENGAN!!
GRIN
DWOOOOSH

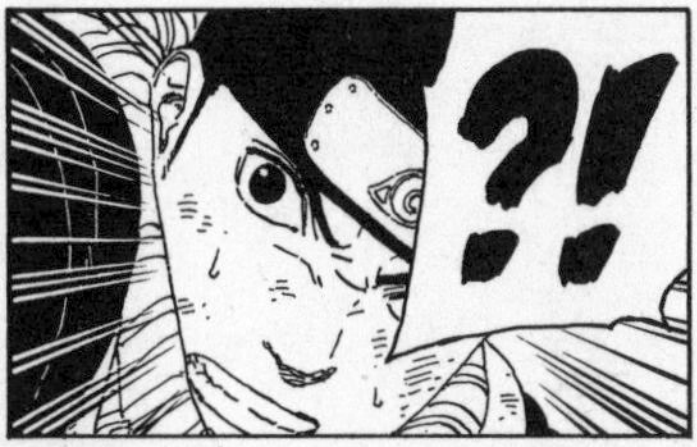
?!

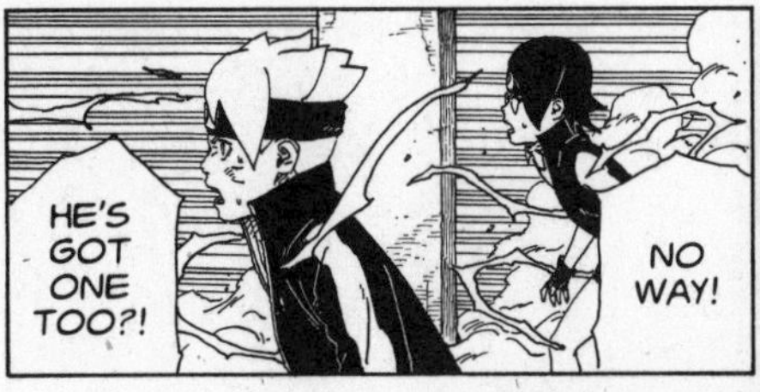
NO WAY!
HE'S GOT ONE TOO?!

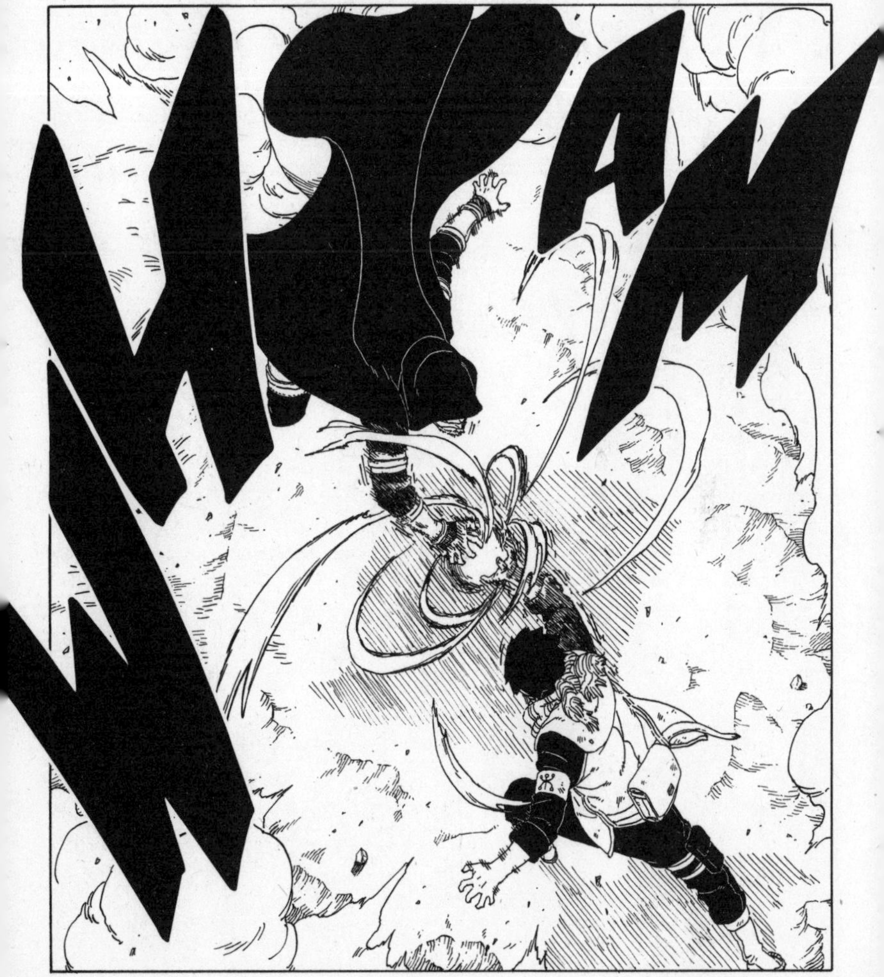
WHAM

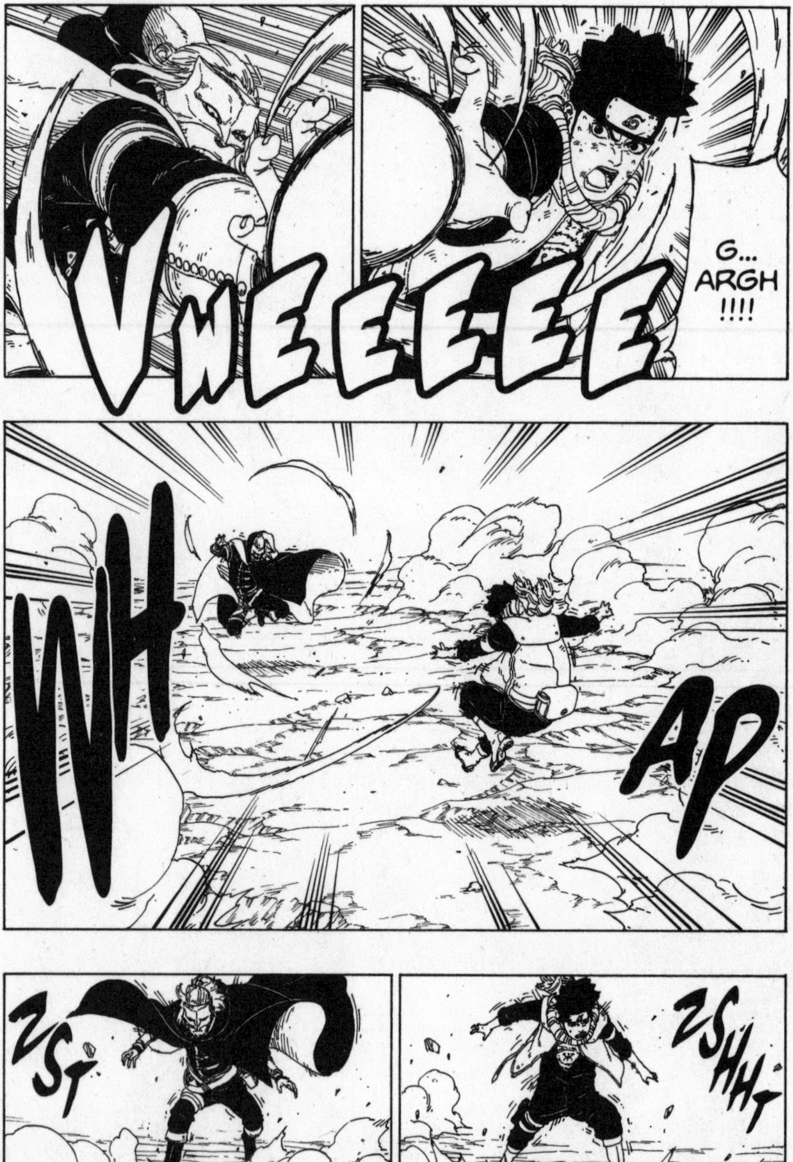
G... ARGH !!!!
VWEEEE
WHAP
ZSHHT
ZST

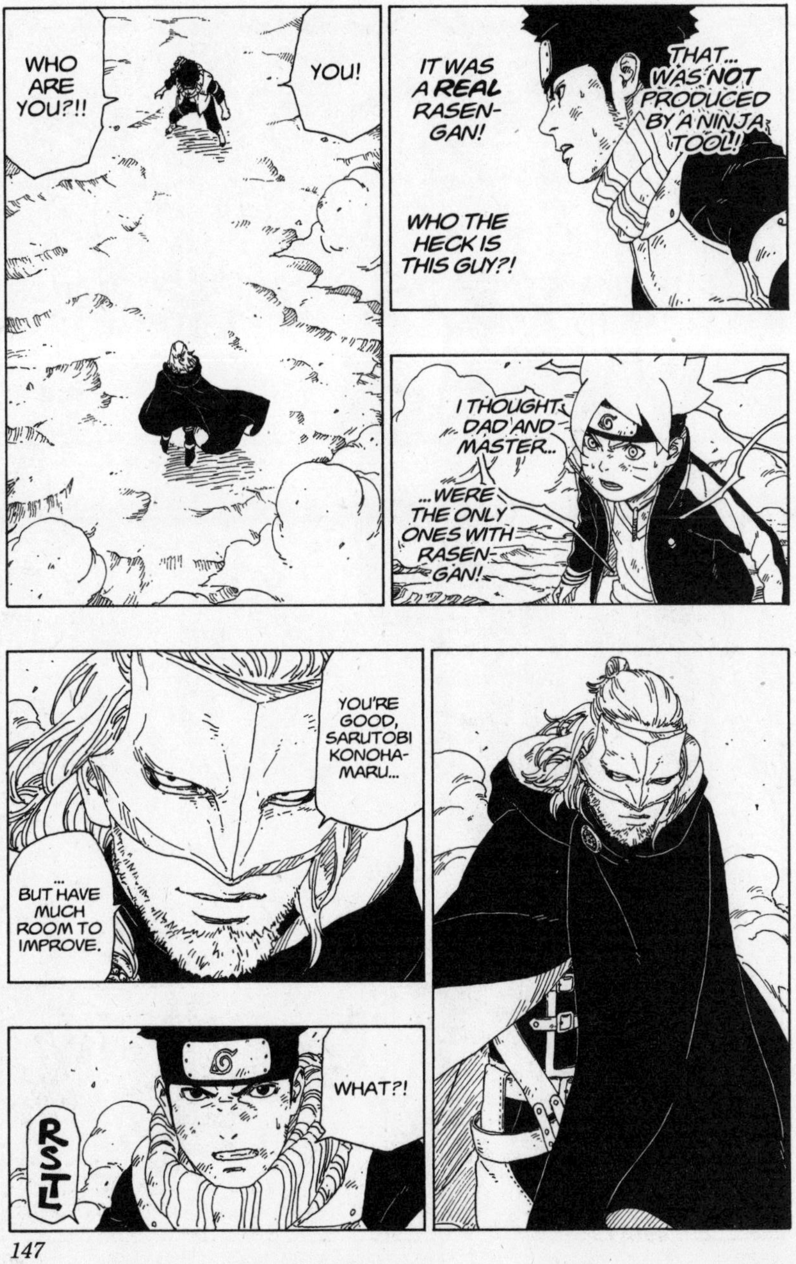
THAT... WAS NOT PRODUCED BY A NINJA TOOL!!
IT WAS A REAL RASEN-GAN!
WHO THE HECK IS THIS GUY?!
I THOUGHT DAD AND MASTER...
...WERE THE ONLY ONES WITH RASEN-GAN!
YOU!
WHO ARE YOU?!!
YOU'RE GOOD, SARUTOBI KONOHA-MARU...
...BUT HAVE MUCH ROOM TO IMPROVE.
WHAT?!
RSTL

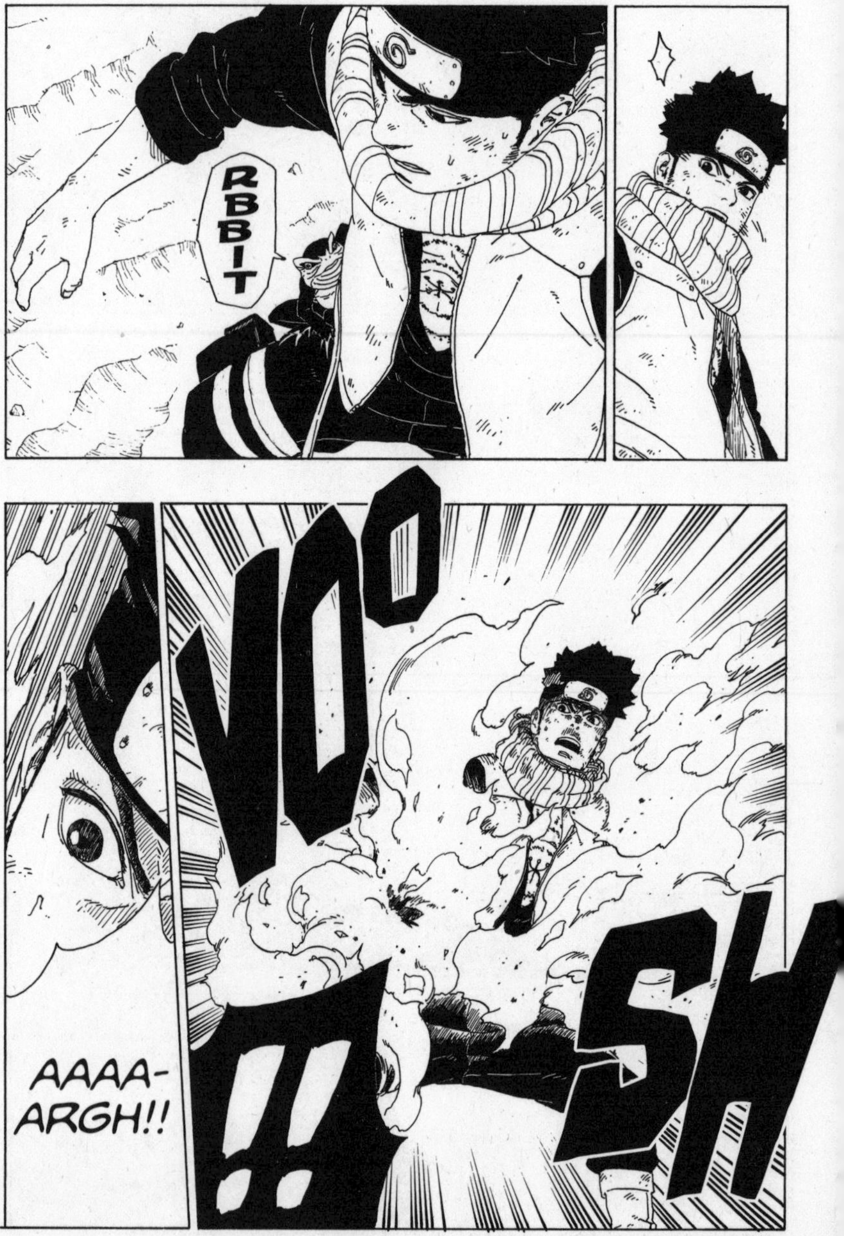
RBBIT
VOO
SH!!
AAAA-ARGH!!

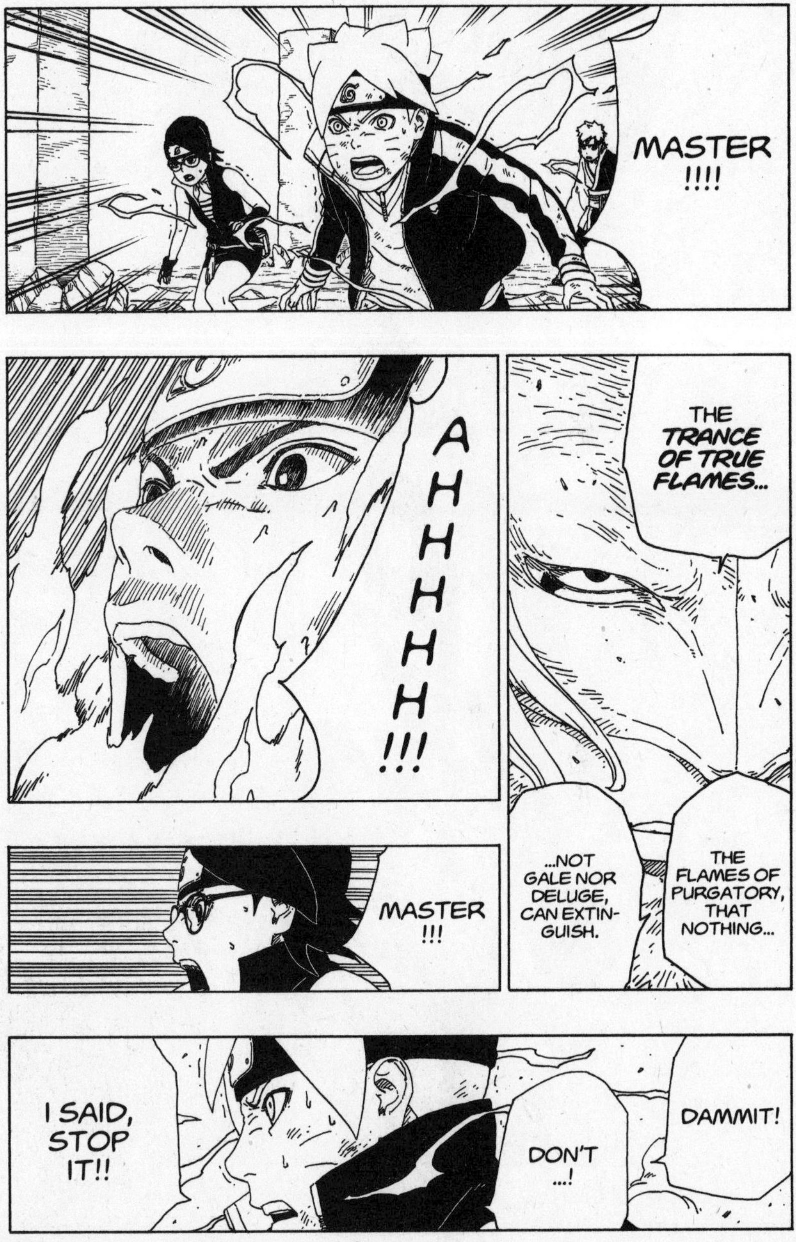
MASTER !!!!
THE TRANCE OF TRUE FLAMES...
THE FLAMES OF PURGATORY, THAT NOTHING...
...NOT GALE NOR DELUGE, CAN EXTINGUISH.
AHHHHH!!!
MASTER !!!
DAMMIT!
DON'T ...!
I SAID, STOP IT!!

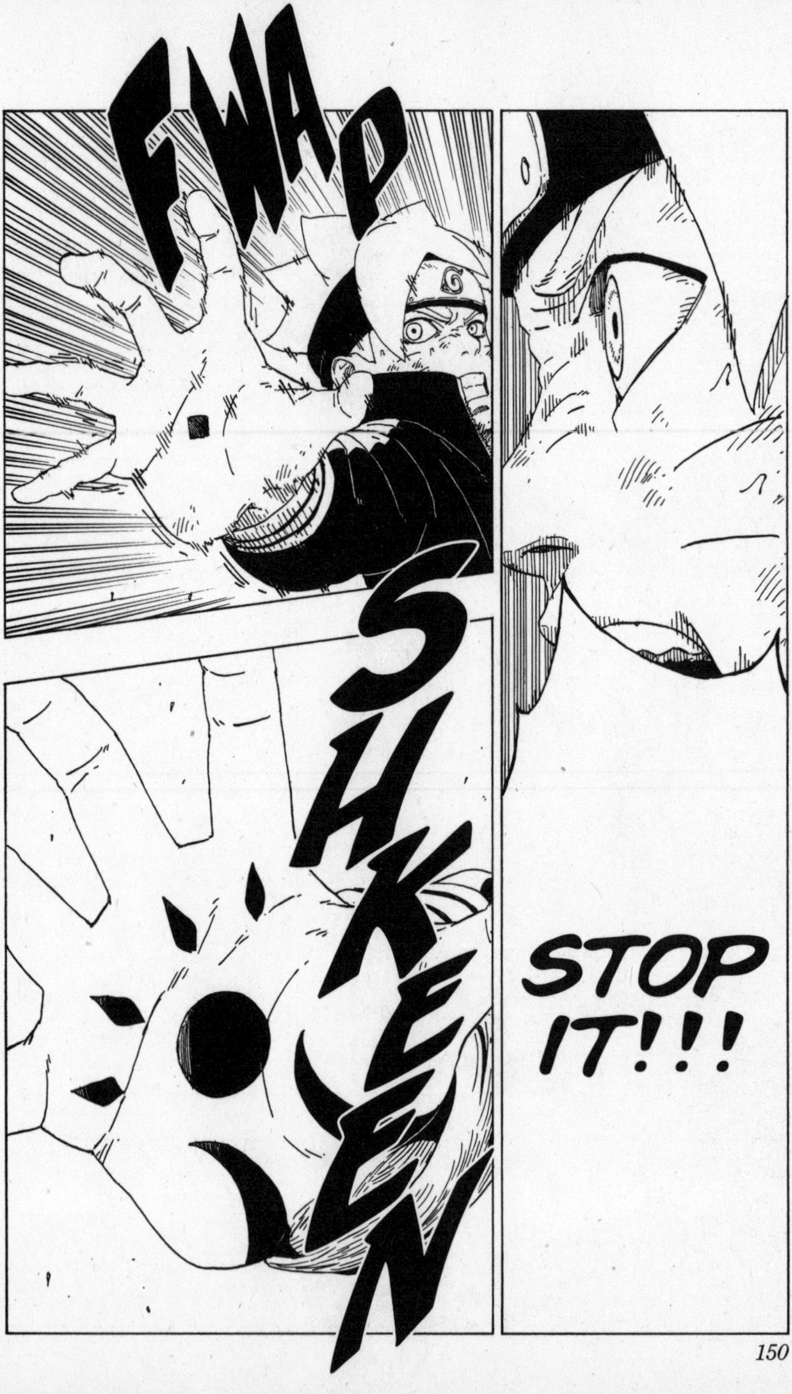
STOP IT!!!
FWAP
SHKEEEN

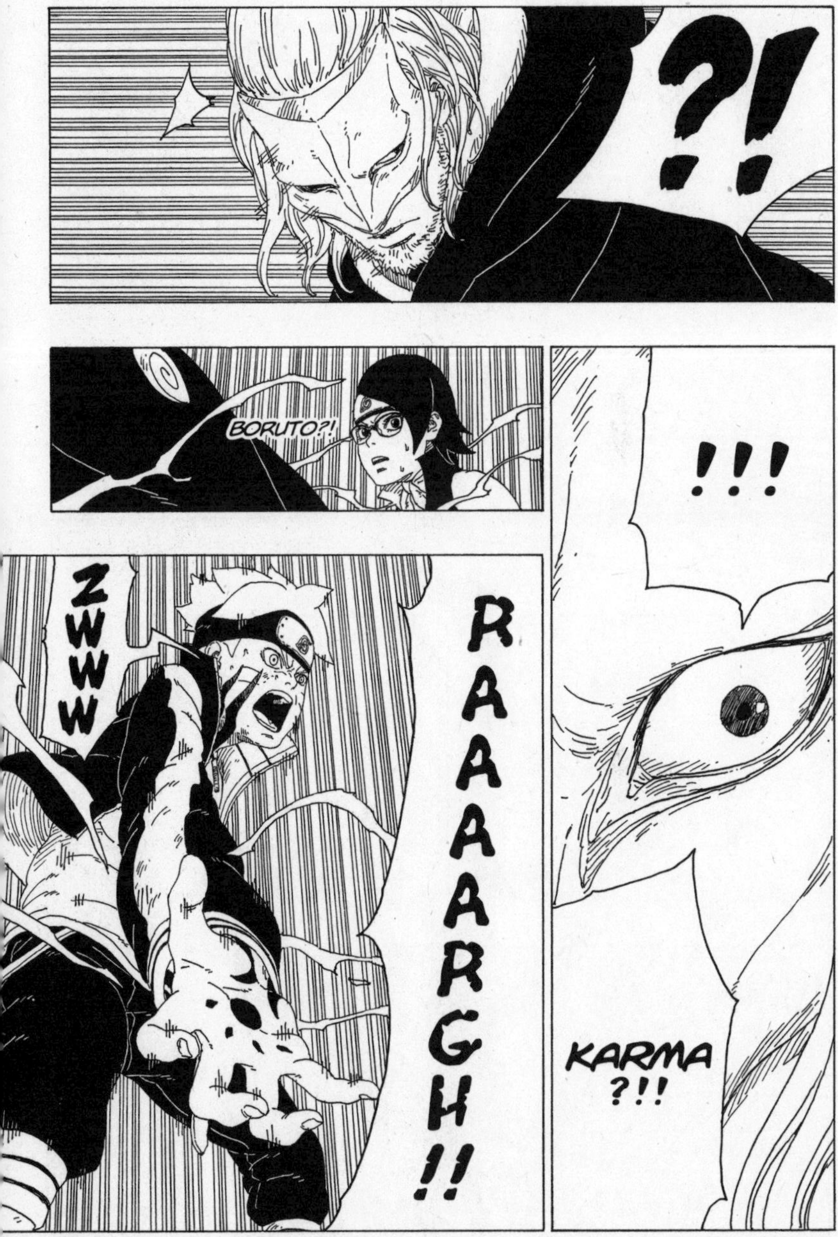
?!
!!!
KARMA ?!!
BORUTO?!
RAAAARGH!!
ZWWW

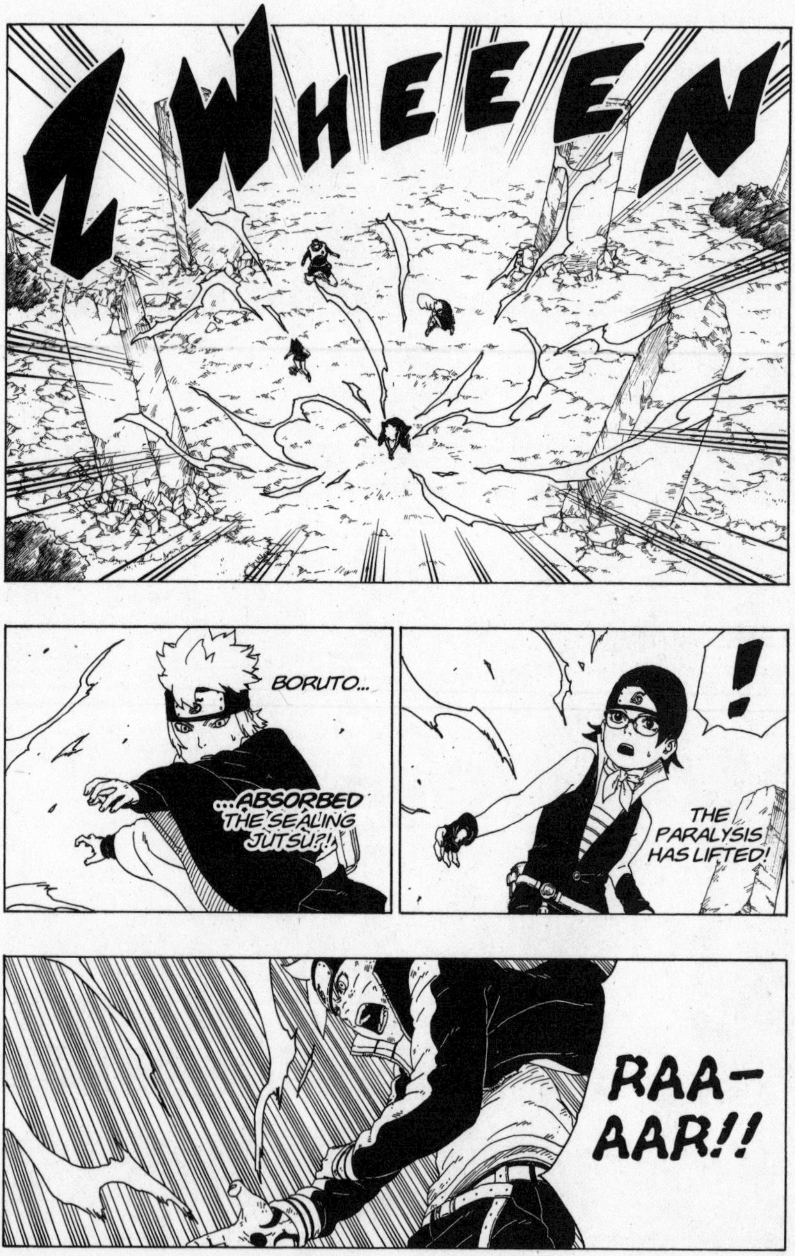
ZWHEEEN
!
THE PARALYSIS HAS LIFTED!
BORUTO...
...ABSORBED THE SEALING JUTSU?!
RAA-AAR!!

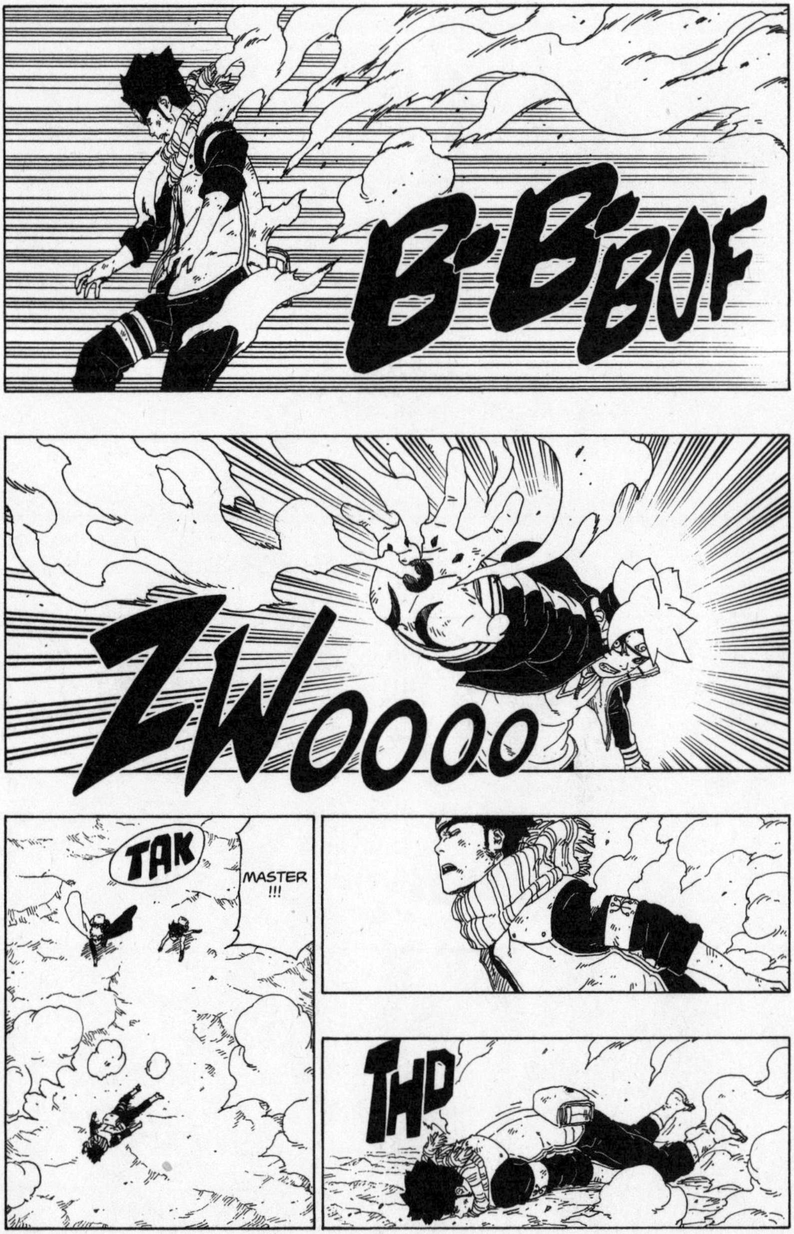
B-B-BOF
ZWOOOO
THD
TAK
MASTER!!!

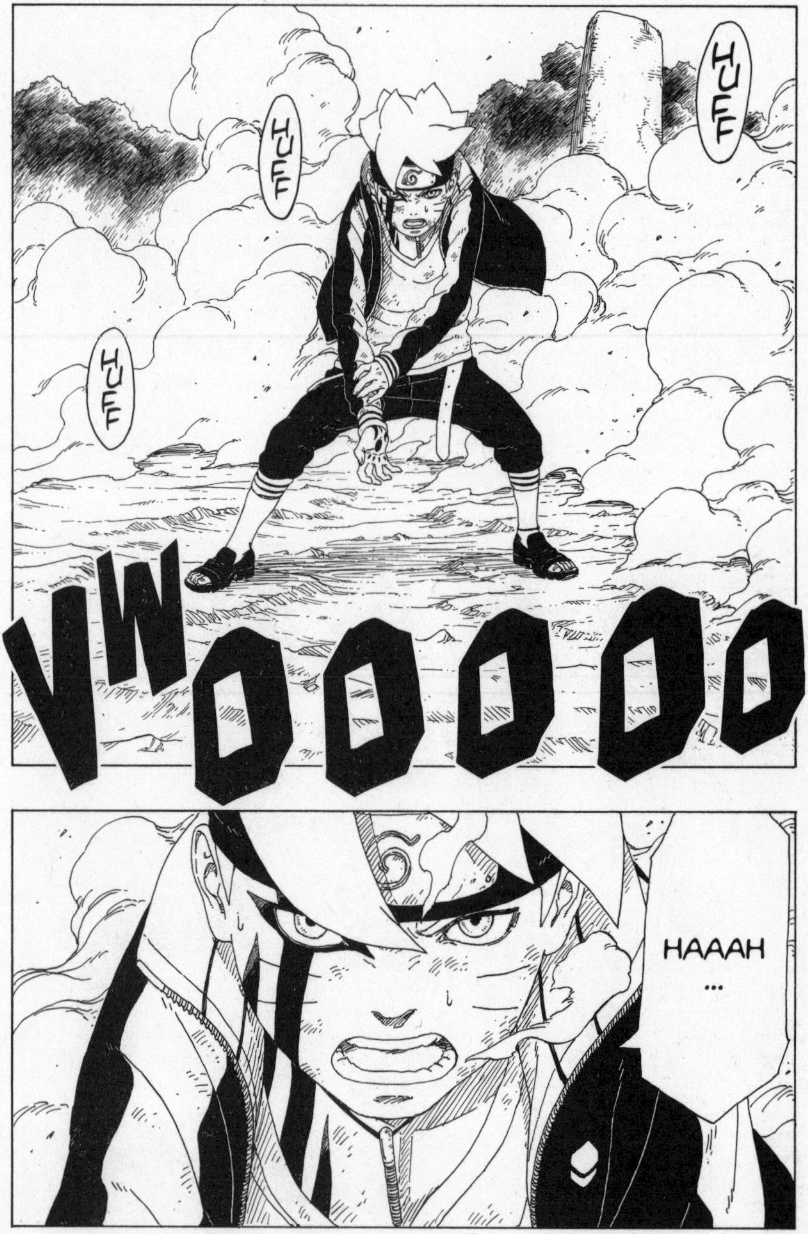
HUFF HUFF
HUFF HUFF
HUFF HUFF
VWOOOOO
HAAAH ...

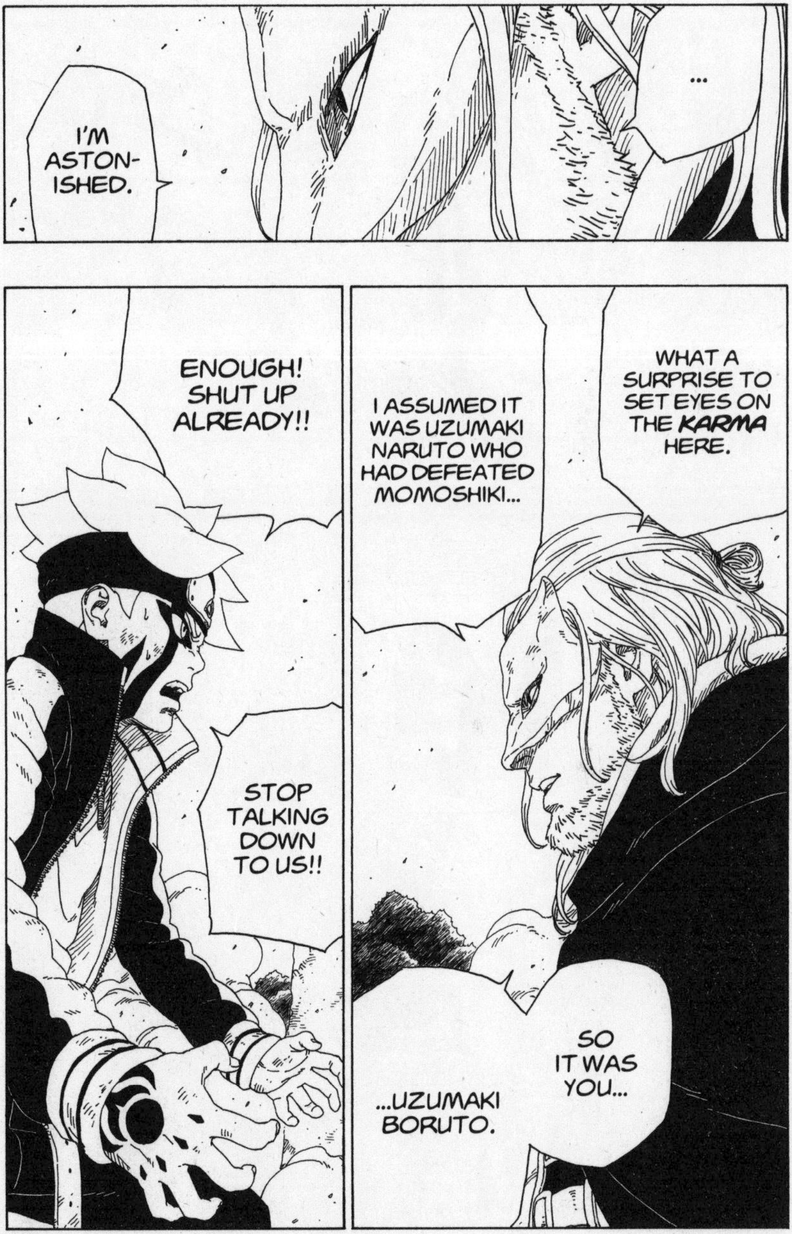
...
I'M ASTON-ISHED.
WHAT A SURPRISE TO SET EYES ON THE *KARMA* HERE.
I ASSUMED IT WAS UZUMAKI NARUTO WHO HAD DEFEATED MOMOSHIKI...
SO IT WAS YOU...
...UZUMAKI BORUTO.
ENOUGH! SHUT UP ALREADY!!
STOP TALKING DOWN TO US!!

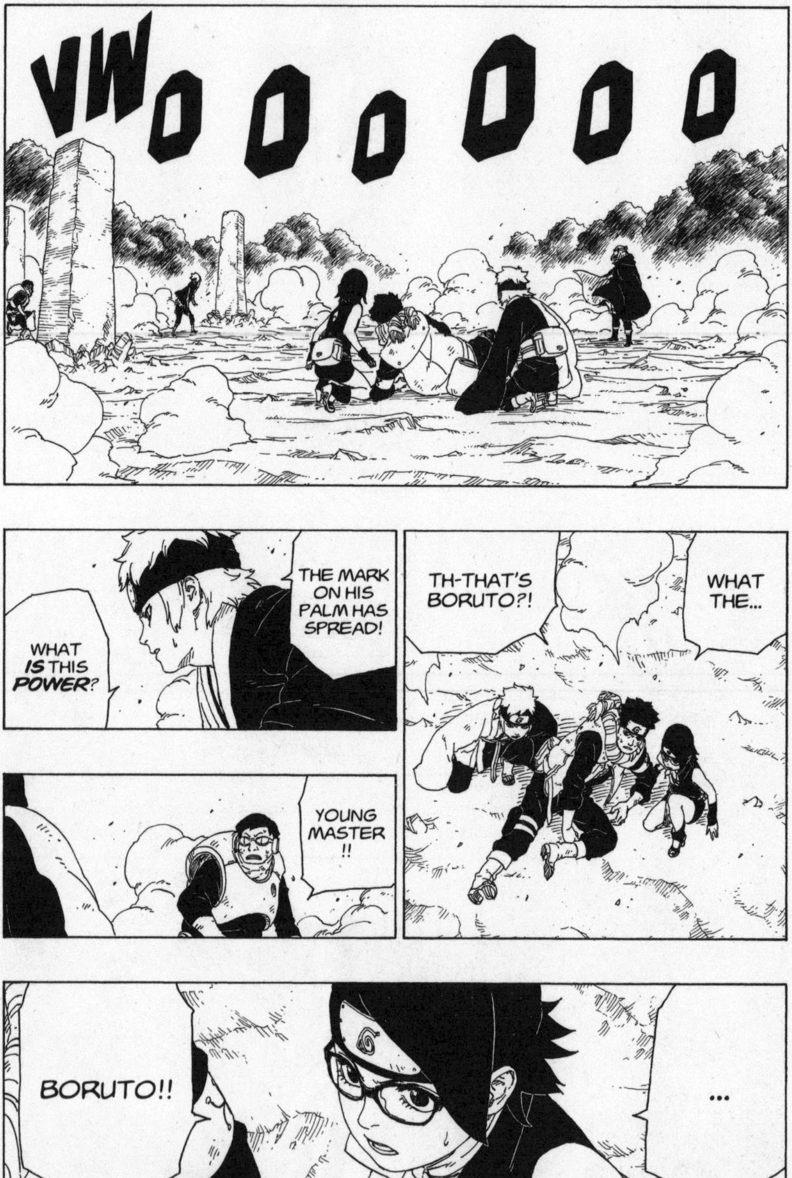
VWOOOOOO
WHAT THE...
TH-THAT'S BORUTO?!
THE MARK ON HIS PALM HAS SPREAD!
WHAT IS THIS POWER?
YOUNG MASTER!!
...
BORUTO!!

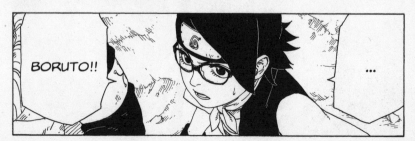

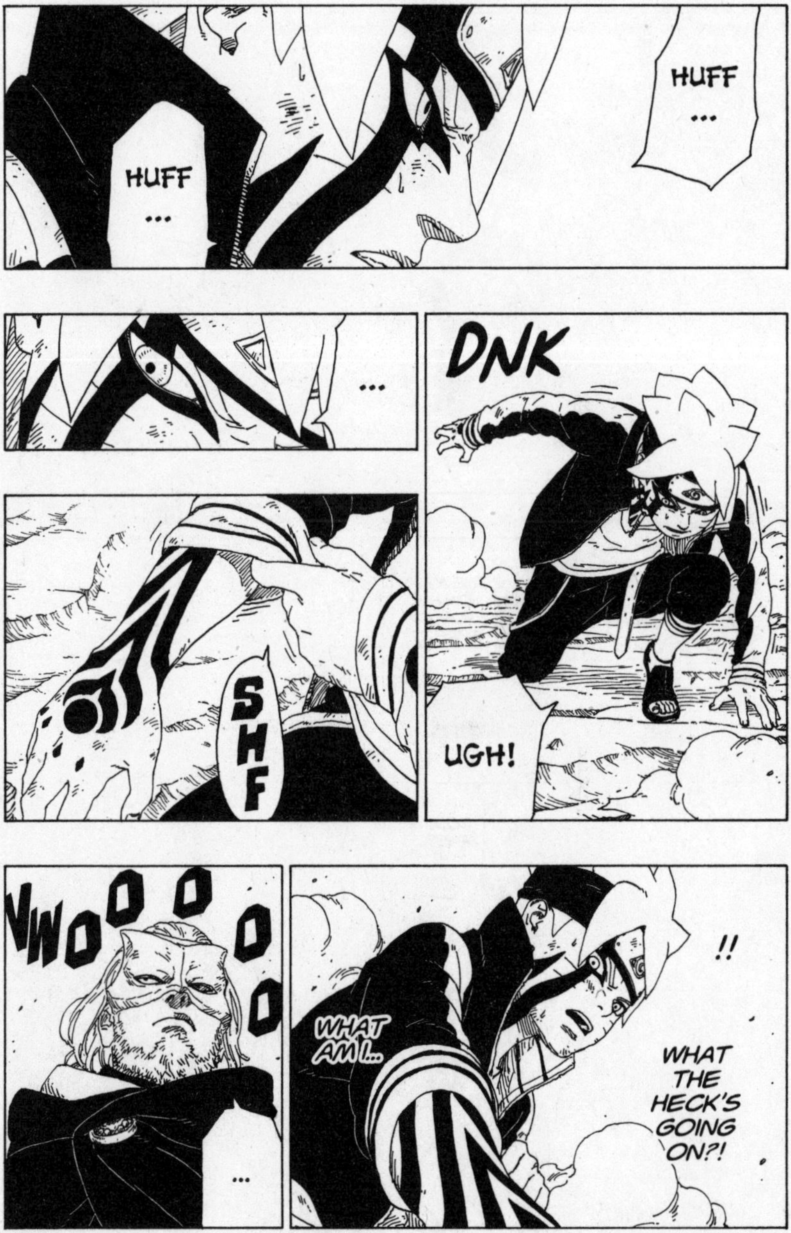
HUFF ...
HUFF ...
DNK
UGH!
...
SHF
!!
WHAT AM I...
WHAT THE HECK'S GOING ON?!
NWOOOOOOO
...

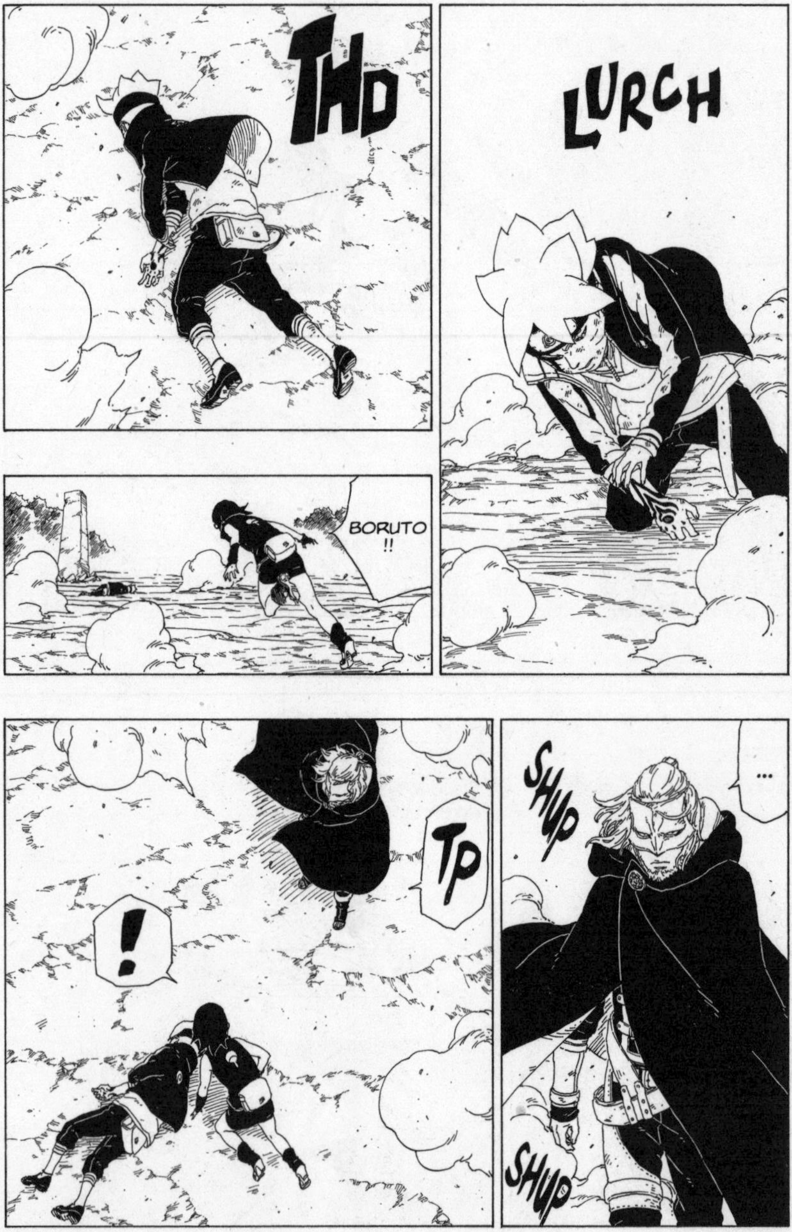
LURCH
THD
BORUTO !!
SHUP
...
SHUP
TP
!

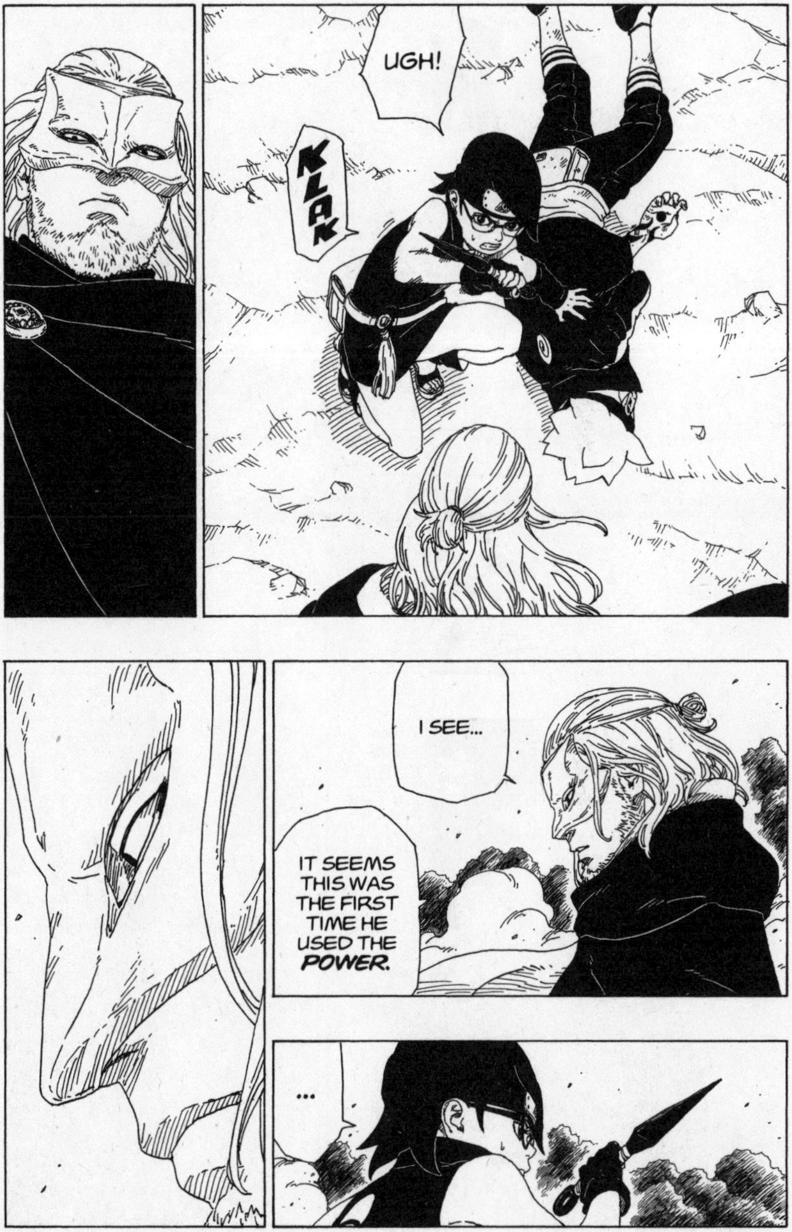
UGH!
KLAK
I SEE...
IT SEEMS THIS WAS THE FIRST TIME HE USED THE *POWER.*
...

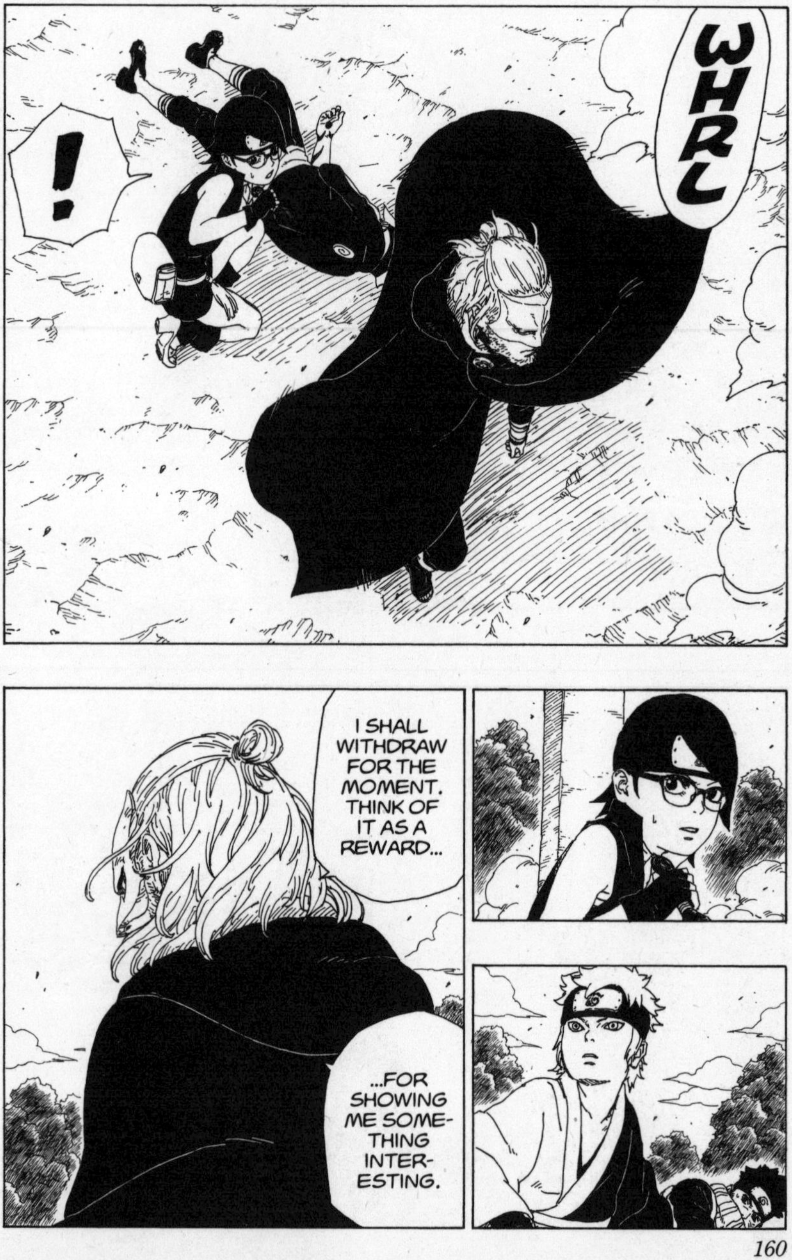
WHRL
!
I SHALL WITHDRAW FOR THE MOMENT. THINK OF IT AS A REWARD...
...FOR SHOWING ME SOME-THING INTER-ESTING.

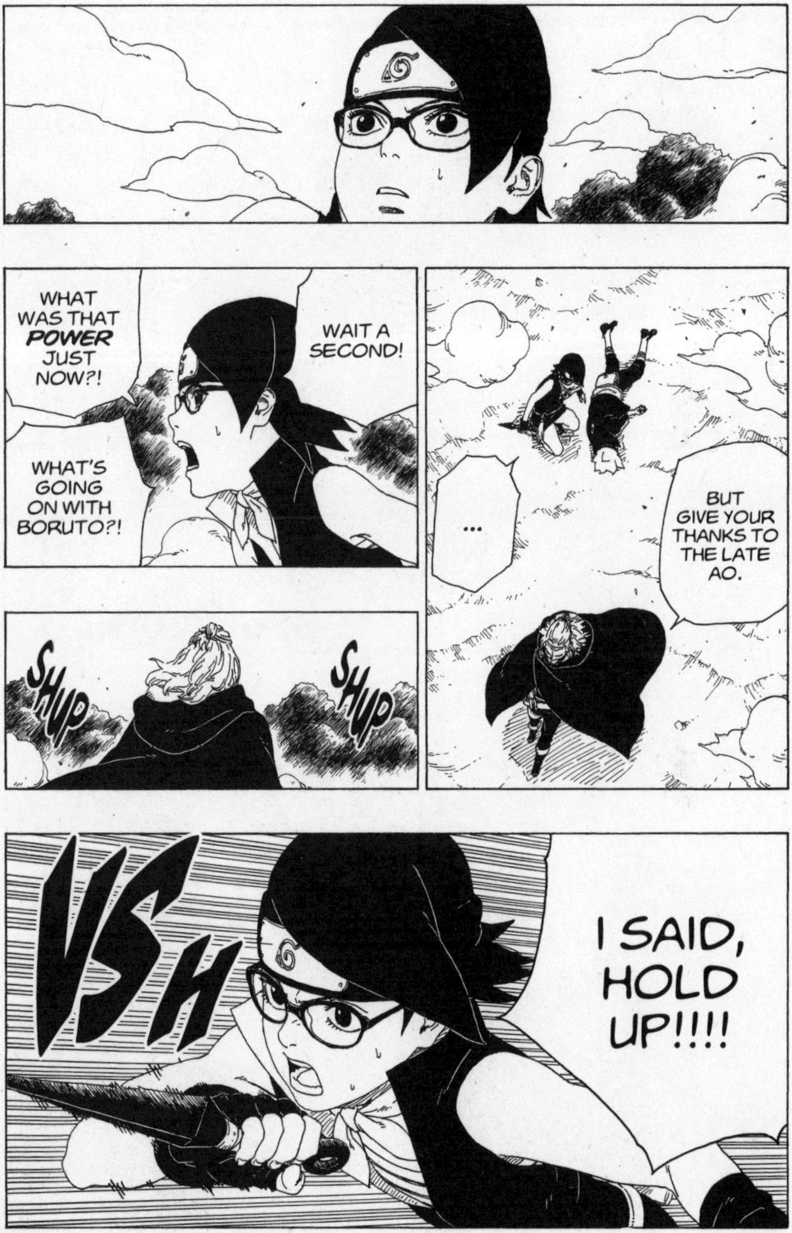
BUT GIVE YOUR THANKS TO THE LATE AO.
...
WAIT A SECOND!
WHAT WAS THAT POWER JUST NOW?!
WHAT'S GOING ON WITH BORUTO?!
SHUP
SHUP
I SAID, HOLD UP!!!!
VSH

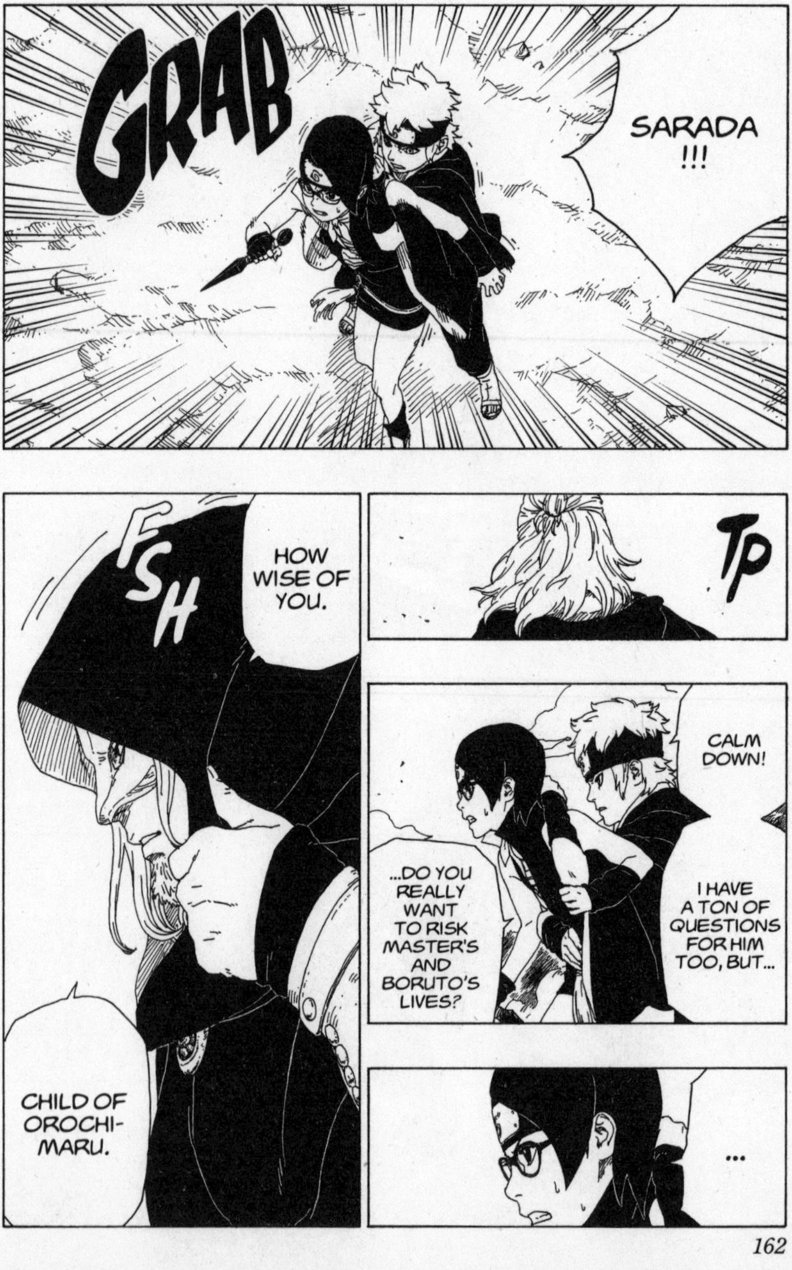
SARADA!!!
GRAB
TP
CALM DOWN!
I HAVE A TON OF QUESTIONS FOR HIM TOO, BUT...
...DO YOU REALLY WANT TO RISK MASTER'S AND BORUTO'S LIVES?
...
HOW WISE OF YOU.
FSH
CHILD OF OROCHI-MARU.

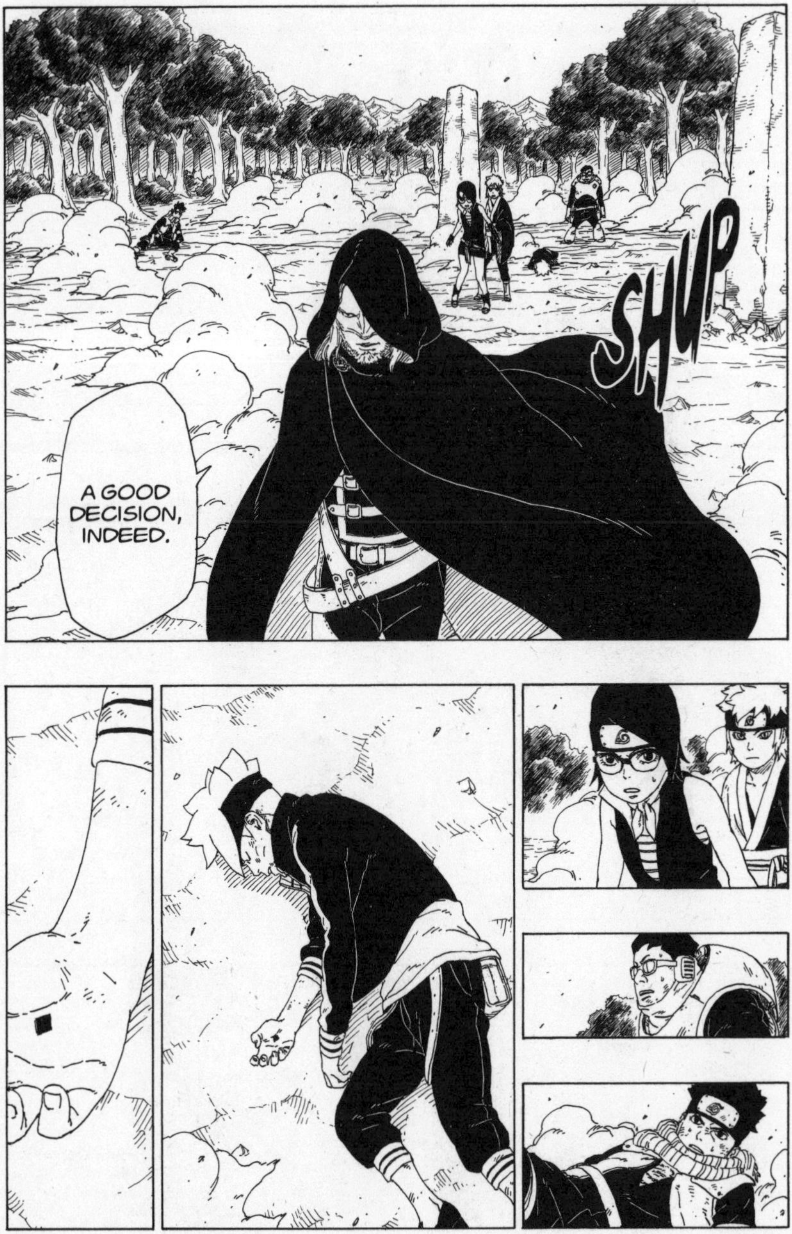
SHUP
A GOOD DECISION, INDEED.

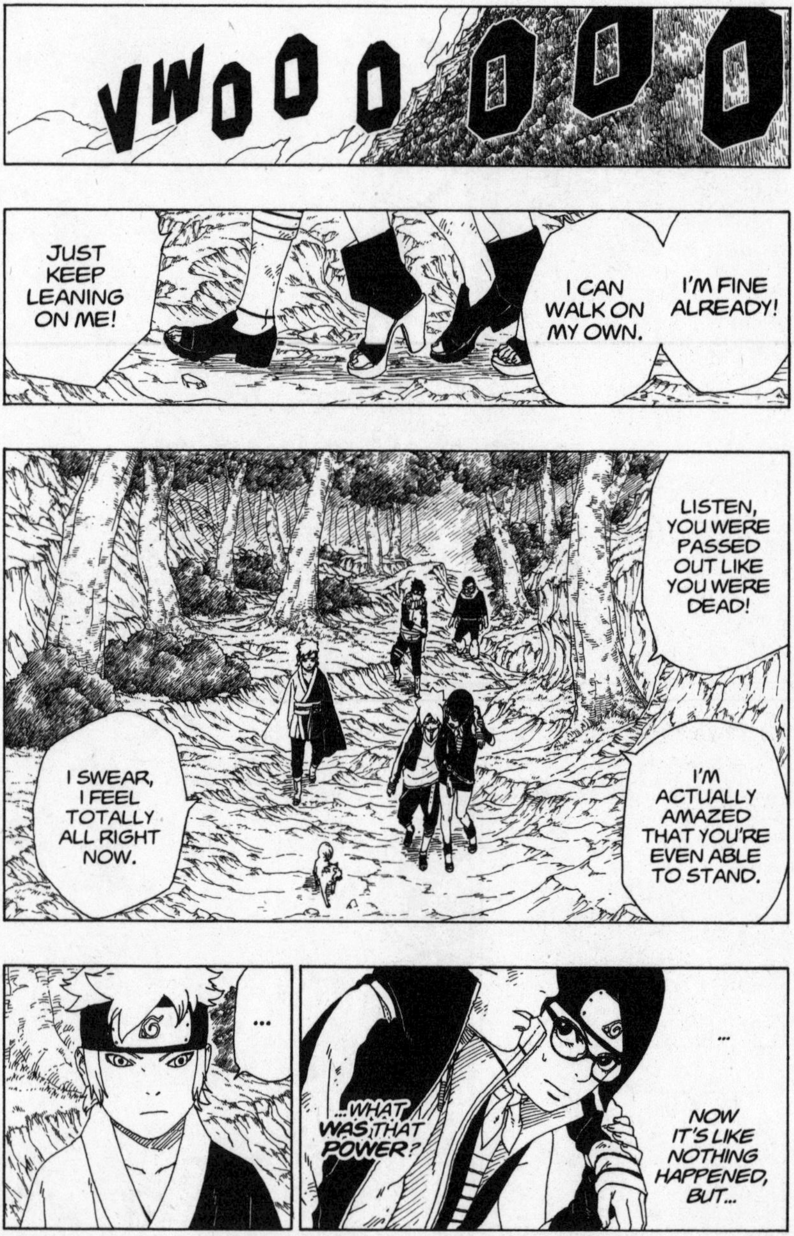
VWOOOOOO
I'M FINE ALREADY!
I CAN WALK ON MY OWN.
JUST KEEP LEANING ON ME!
LISTEN, YOU WERE PASSED OUT LIKE YOU WERE DEAD!
I'M ACTUALLY AMAZED THAT YOU'RE EVEN ABLE TO STAND.
I SWEAR, I FEEL TOTALLY ALL RIGHT NOW.
...
NOW IT'S LIKE NOTHING HAPPENED, BUT...
...WHAT WAS THAT POWER?
...

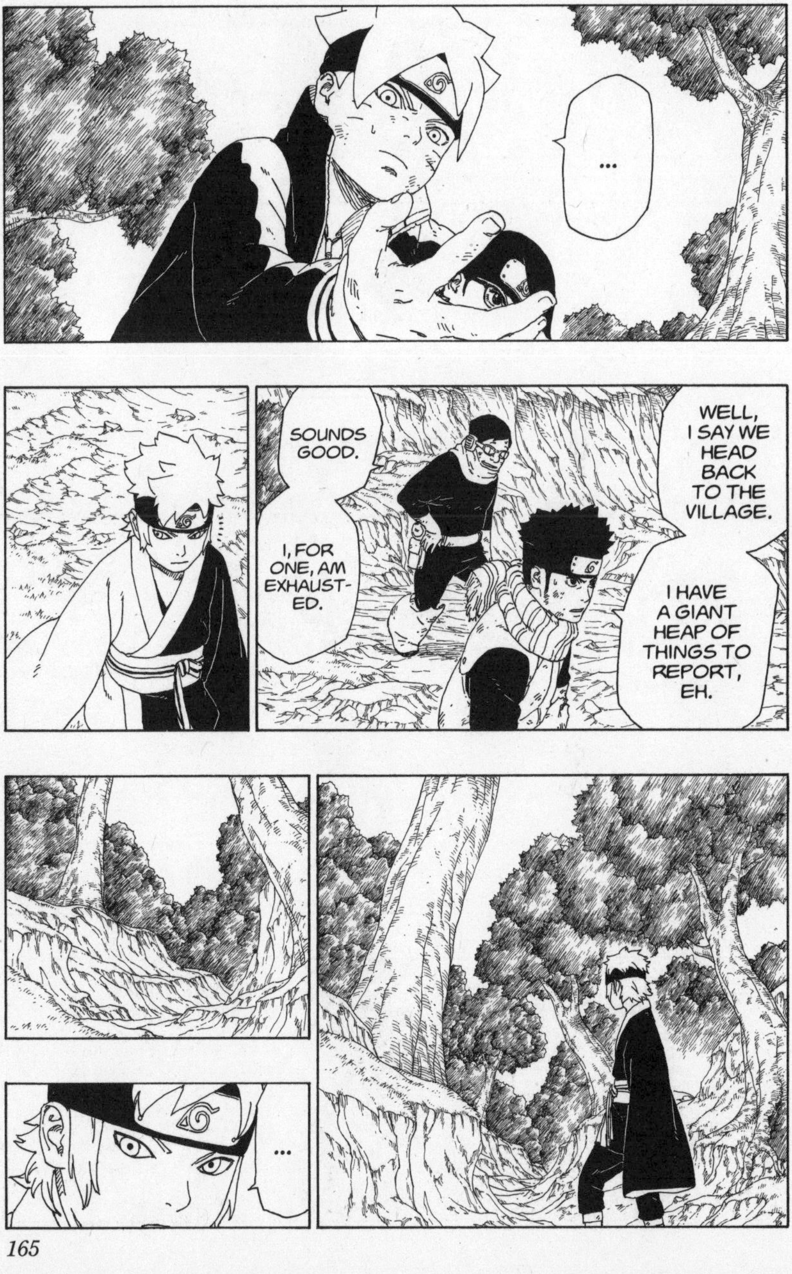
...
WELL, I SAY WE HEAD BACK TO THE VILLAGE.
I HAVE A GIANT HEAP OF THINGS TO REPORT, EH.
SOUNDS GOOD.
I, FOR ONE, AM EXHAUSTED.
...
...

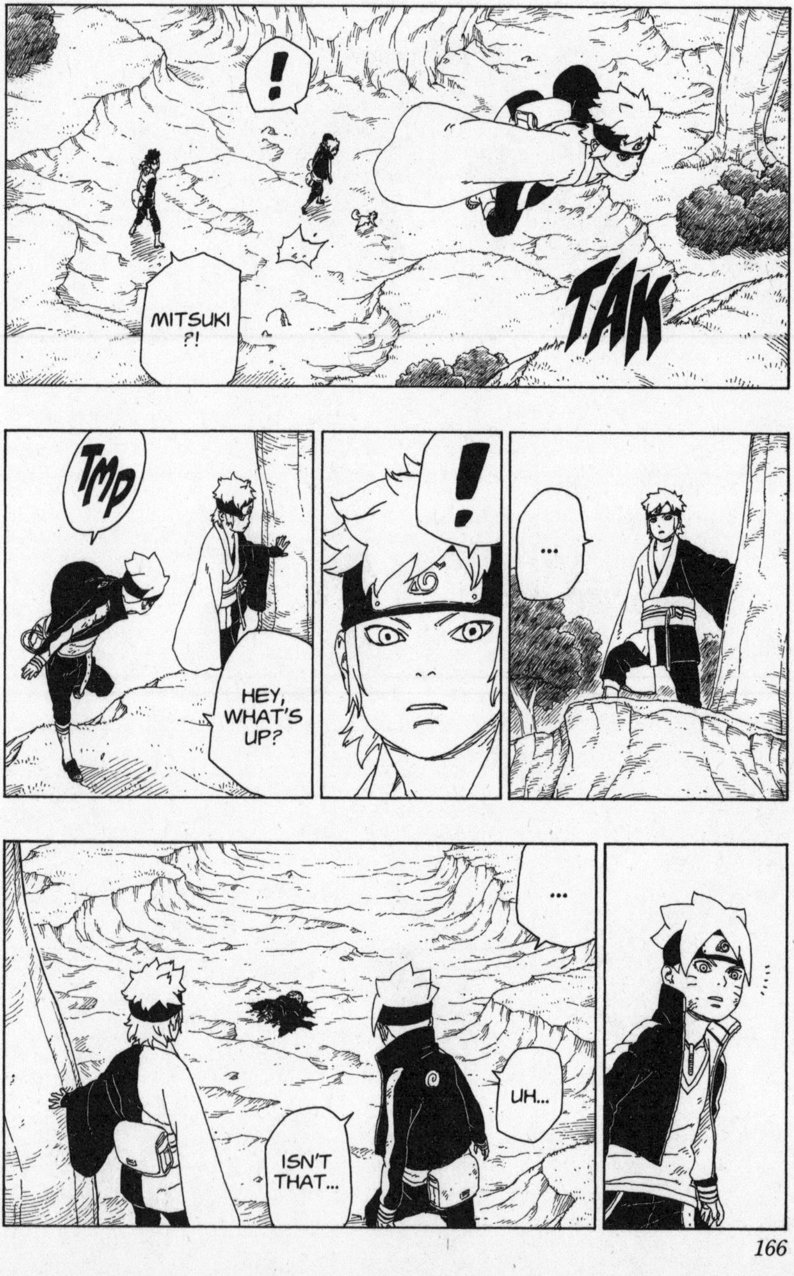
!
TAK
MITSUKI ?!
...
!
TMP
HEY, WHAT'S UP?
...
UH...
ISN'T THAT...

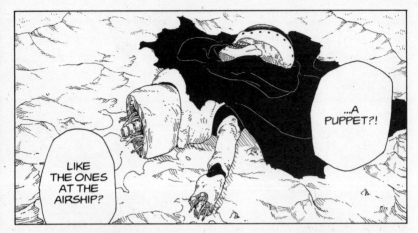

...A PUPPET?!

LIKE THE ONES AT THE AIRSHIP?

YOU'RE RIGHT... WHAT IS IT DOING HERE?!

THE CRASH SITE IS FARTHER OFF.

SO THIS LOOKS TO BE SEPARATE FROM THE ONES WE BATTLED.

WHAT DO YOU MEAN?

SOME-ONE ELSE ALSO FOUGHT HERE?

LET'S LOOK AROUND.

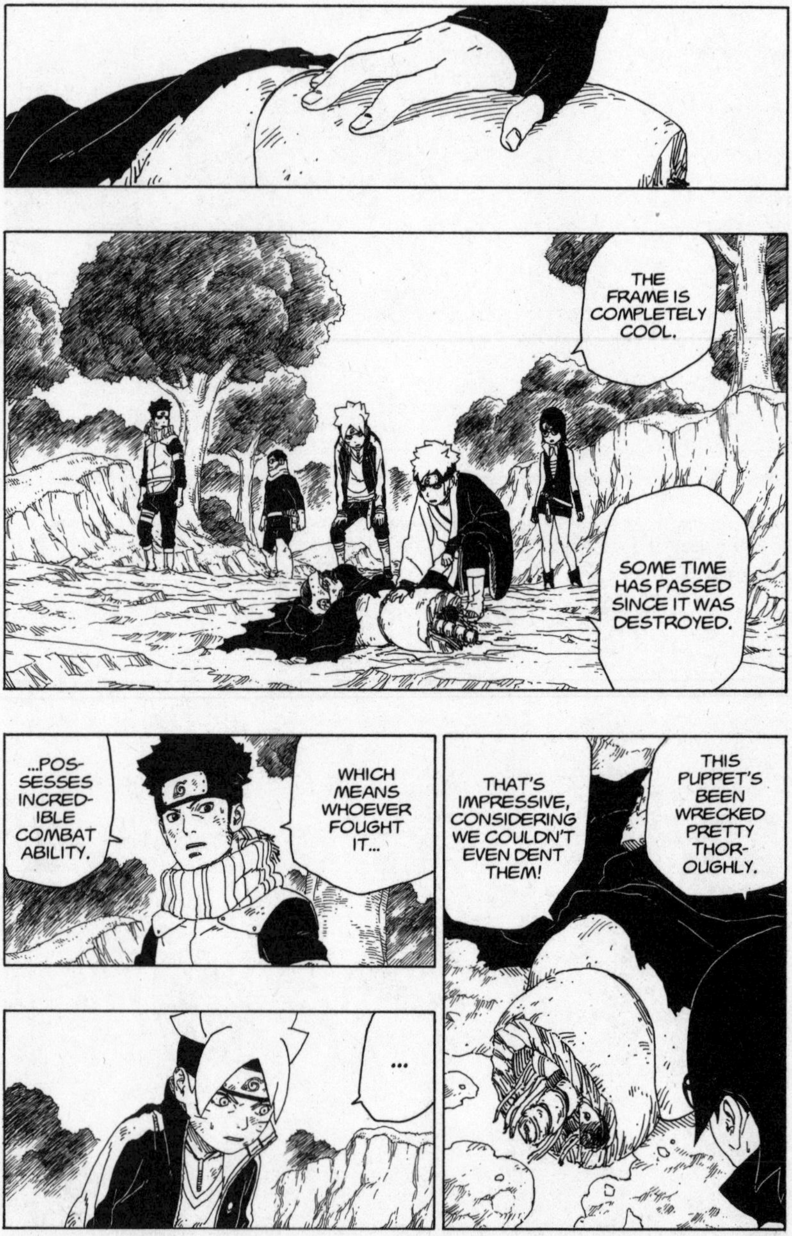
THE FRAME IS COMPLETELY COOL.
SOME TIME HAS PASSED SINCE IT WAS DESTROYED.
THIS PUPPET'S BEEN WRECKED PRETTY THOROUGHLY.
THAT'S IMPRESSIVE, CONSIDERING WE COULDN'T EVEN DENT THEM!
WHICH MEANS WHOEVER FOUGHT IT...
...POSSESSES INCREDIBLE COMBAT ABILITY.
...

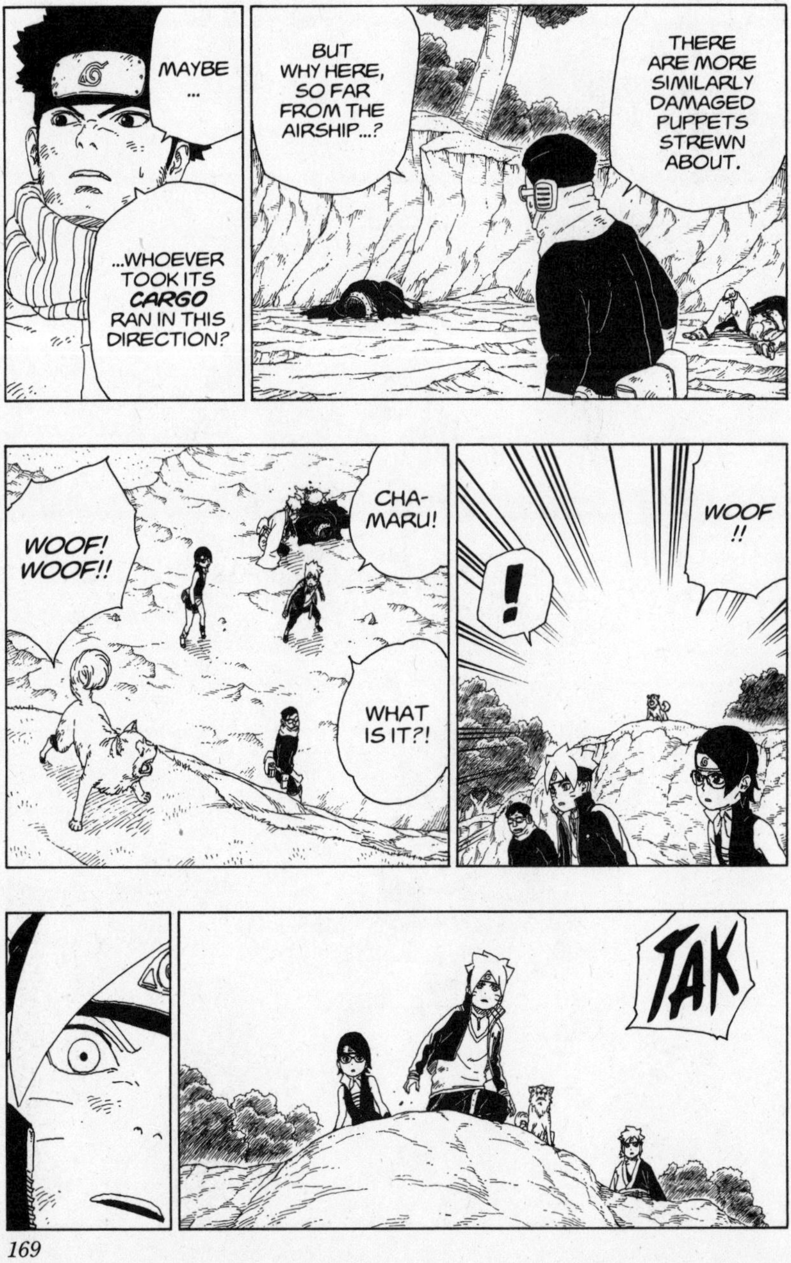
THERE ARE MORE SIMILARLY DAMAGED PUPPETS STREWN ABOUT.
BUT WHY HERE, SO FAR FROM THE AIRSHIP...?
MAYBE ...
...WHOEVER TOOK ITS *CARGO* RAN IN THIS DIRECTION?
WOOF !!
!
CHA-MARU!
WOOF! WOOF!!
WHAT IS IT?!
TAK

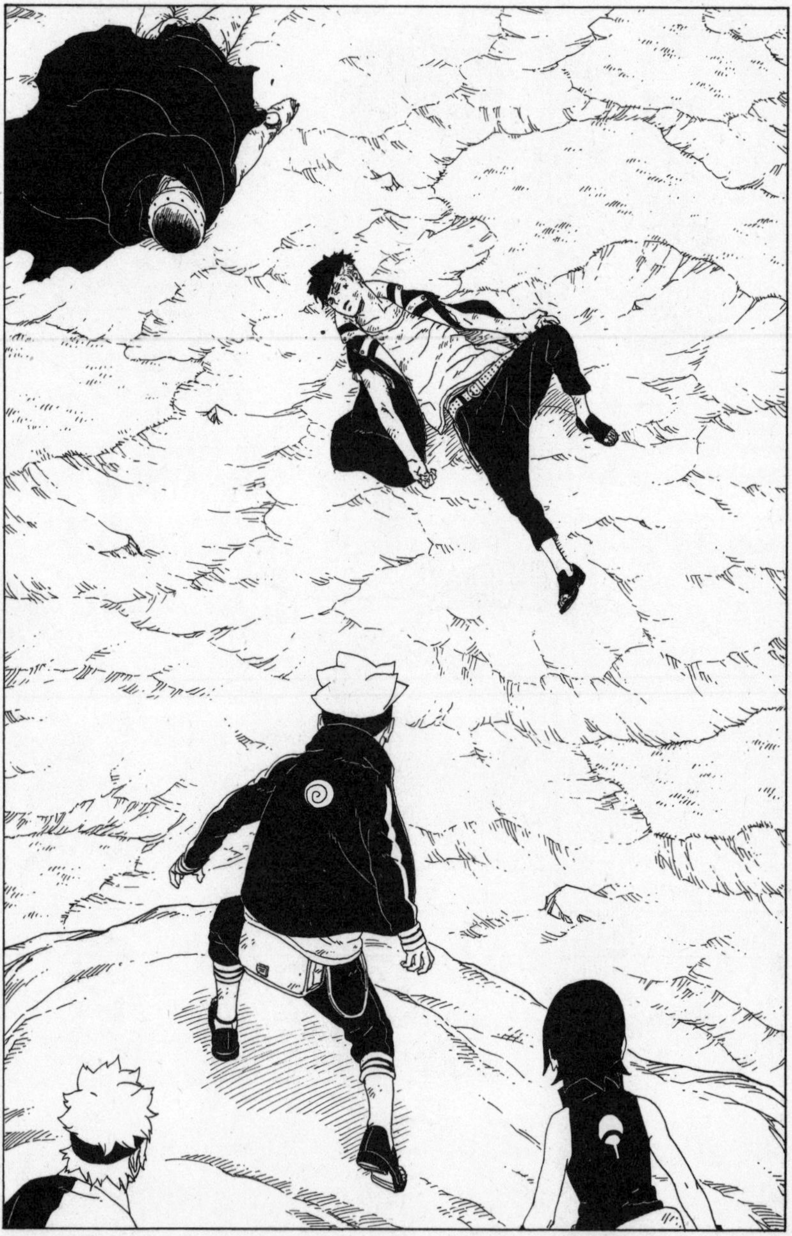

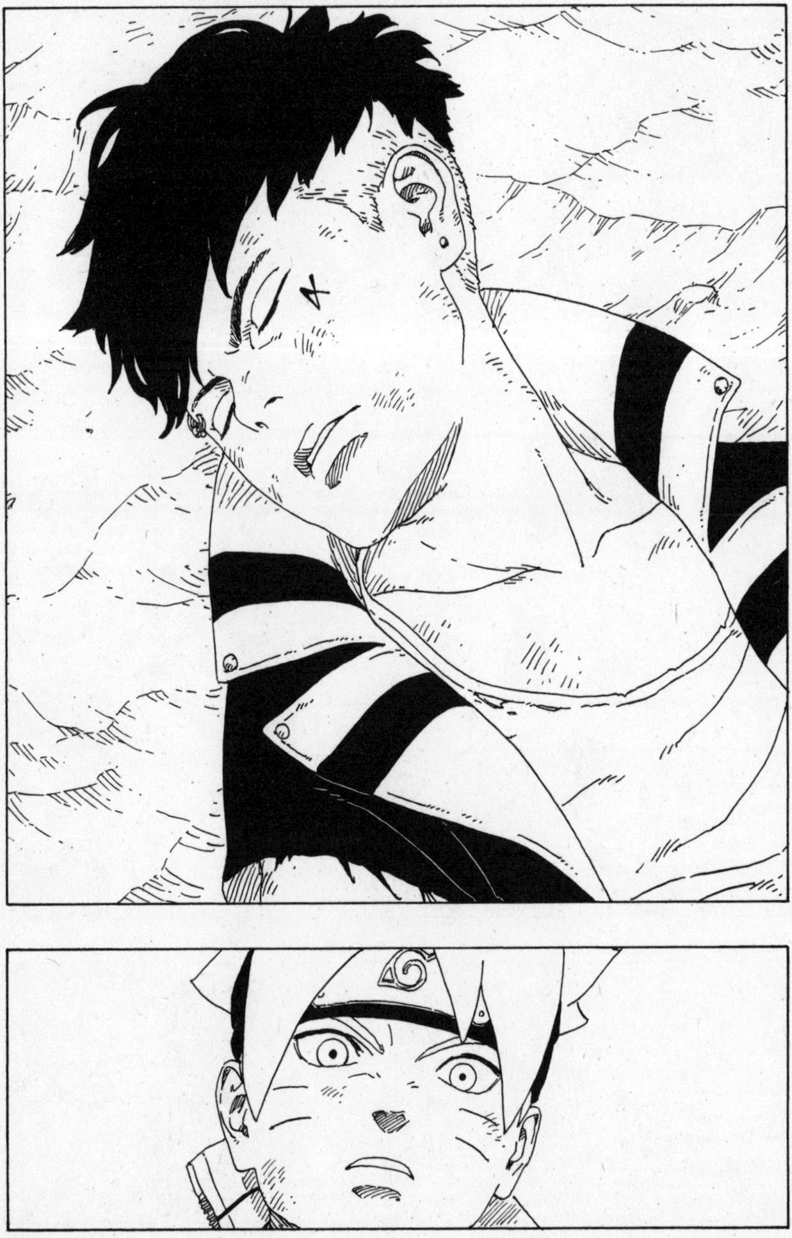

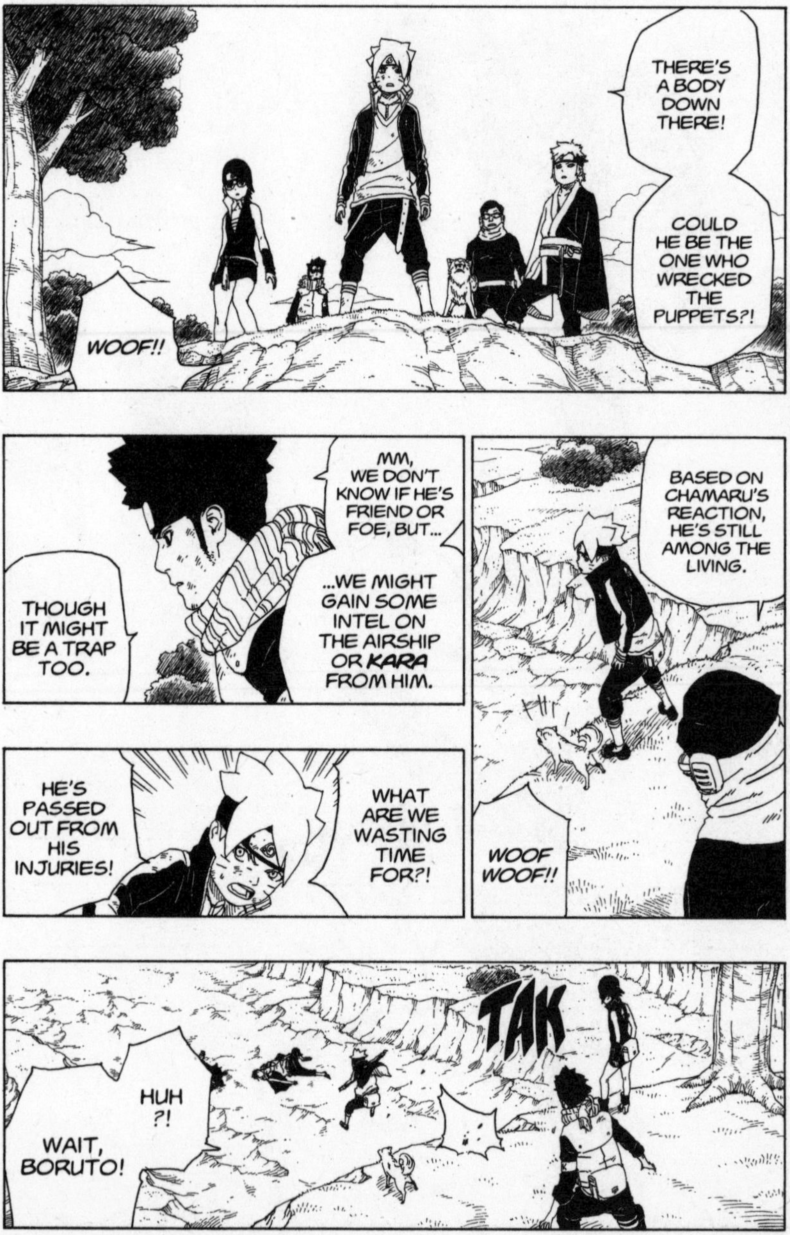
THERE'S A BODY DOWN THERE!
COULD HE BE THE ONE WHO WRECKED THE PUPPETS?!
WOOF!!
BASED ON CHAMARU'S REACTION, HE'S STILL AMONG THE LIVING.
WOOF WOOF!!
MM, WE DON'T KNOW IF HE'S FRIEND OR FOE, BUT...
...WE MIGHT GAIN SOME INTEL ON THE AIRSHIP OR KARA FROM HIM.
THOUGH IT MIGHT BE A TRAP TOO.
WHAT ARE WE WASTING TIME FOR?!
HE'S PASSED OUT FROM HIS INJURIES!
TAK
HUH ?!
WAIT, BORUTO!

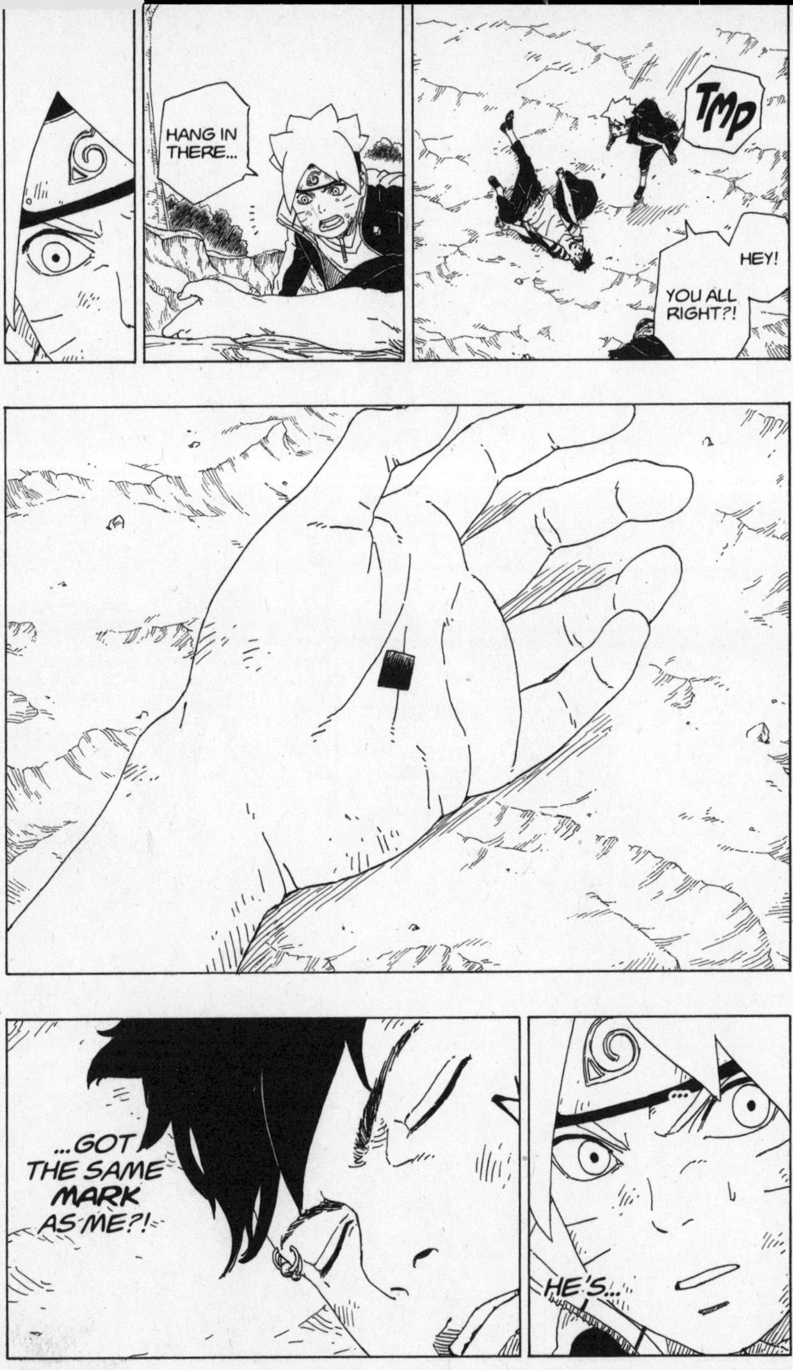
TMP
HEY!
YOU ALL RIGHT?!
HANG IN THERE...
HE'S...
...GOT THE SAME MARK AS ME?!

Black ✦ Clover

STORY & ART BY YŪKI TABATA

Asta is a young boy who dreams of becoming the greatest mage in the kingdom. Only one problem—he can't use any magic! Luckily for Asta, he receives the incredibly rare five-leaf clover grimoire that gives him the power of anti-magic. Can someone who can't use magic really become the Wizard King? One thing's for sure—Asta will never give up!

SHONEN JUMP   VIZ media
www.viz.com

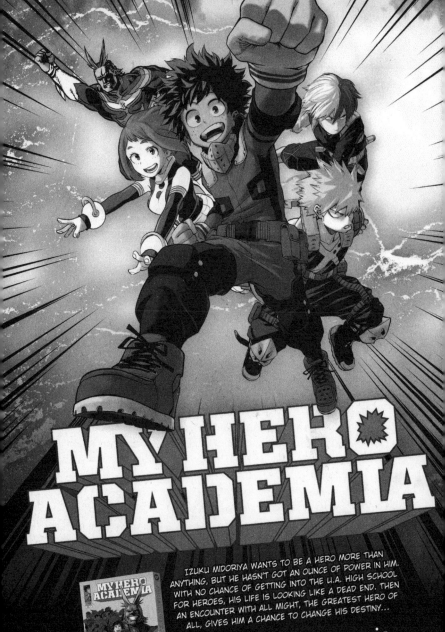

MY HERO ACADEMIA

IZUKU MIDORIYA WANTS TO BE A HERO MORE THAN ANYTHING, BUT HE HASN'T GOT AN OUNCE OF POWER IN HIM. WITH NO CHANCE OF GETTING INTO THE U.A. HIGH SCHOOL FOR HEROES, HIS LIFE IS LOOKING LIKE A DEAD END. THEN AN ENCOUNTER WITH ALL MIGHT, THE GREATEST HERO OF ALL, GIVES HIM A CHANCE TO CHANGE HIS DESTINY...

YOU'RE READING

IN THE

WRONG DIRECTION!!

WHOOPS! Guess what? You're starting at the wrong end of the comic!

...It's true! In keeping with the original Japanese format, **Boruto** is meant to be read from right to left, starting in the upper-right corner.

Unlike English, which is read from left to right, Japanese is read from right to left, meaning that action, sound effects and word-balloon order are completely reversed... something which can make readers unfamiliar with Japanese feel pretty backwards themselves. For this reason, manga or Japanese comics published in the U.S. in English have sometimes been published "flopped"—that is, printed in exact reverse order, as though seen from the other side of a mirror.

By flopping pages, U.S. publishers can avoid confusing readers, but the compromise is not without its downside. For one thing, a character in a flopped manga series who once wore in the original Japanese version a T-shirt emblazoned with "M A Y" (as in "the merry month of") now wears one which reads "Y A M"!

Additionally, many manga creators in Japan are themselves unhappy with the process, as some feel the mirror-imaging of their art alters their original intentions.

We are proud to bring you **Boruto** in the original unflopped format. Turn to the other side of the book and let the ninjutsu begin...!

—Editor

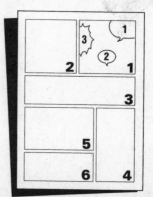